Bram Stoker's *Dracula* is the most famous vampire in literature and film. This new collection of sixteen essays brings together a range of internationally renowned scholars to provide a series of pathways through this celebrated Gothic novel and its innumerable adaptations and translations. The volume illuminates the novel's various pre-histories, critical contexts and subsequent cultural transformations. Chapters explore literary history, Gothic revival scholarship, folklore, anthropology, psychology, sexology, philosophy, occultism, cultural history, critical race theory, theatre and film history and the place of the vampire in Europe and beyond. These studies provide an accessible guide of cutting-edge scholarship to one of the most celebrated modern Gothic horror stories. This companion will serve as a key resource for scholars, teachers and students interested in the enduring force of *Dracula* and the seemingly inexhaustible range of the contexts it requires and readings it might generate.

ROGER LUCKHURST is Professor in Modern and Contemporary Literature at Birkbeck College, University of London. His previous publications include *The Mummy's Curse: The True Story of a Dark Fantasy* (2012) and critical studies of the films *The Shining* (2013) and *Alien* (2014). He has also co-edited books including *The Fin de Siècle: A Reader in Cultural History c. 1880–1900* (2000) and *Transactions and Encounters: Science and Culture in the Nineteenth Century* (2002). He has edited numerous Gothic classics, including Robert Louis Stevenson's *Strange Case of Jekyll and Hyde* (2006), Bram Stoker's *Dracula* (2011) and H. G. Wells's *The Time Machine* (2017).

A complete list of books in the series is at the back of the book.

THE CAMBRIDGE
COMPANION TO
DRACULA

EDITED BY
ROGER LUCKHURST
Birkbeck College, University of London

CAMBRIDGE
UNIVERSITY PRESS

University Printing House, Cambridge CB2 8BS, United Kingdom

One Liberty Plaza, 20th Floor, New York, NY 10006, USA

477 Williamstown Road, Port Melbourne, VIC 3207, Australia

314-321, 3rd Floor, Plot 3, Splendor Forum, Jasola District Centre, New Delhi - 110025, India

79 Anson Road, #06-04/06, Singapore 079906

Cambridge University Press is part of the University of Cambridge.

It furthers the University's mission by disseminating knowledge in the pursuit of
education, learning and research at the highest international levels of excellence.

www.cambridge.org
Information on this title: www.cambridge.org/9781316607084
DOI: 10.1017/9781316597217

© Cambridge University Press 2018

First published 2018

A catalogue record for this publication is available from the British Library

Library of Congress Cataloging in Publication data
NAMES: Luckhurst, Roger.
TITLE: The Cambridge companion to Dracula / edited by Roger Luckhurst.
DESCRIPTION: Cambridge, United Kingdom ; New York, NY :
Cambridge University Press, 2018. | Series: Cambridge companions to literature |
Includes bibliographical references and index.
IDENTIFIERS: LCCN 2017029496 | ISBN 9781107153172 (hardback) |
ISBN 9781316607084 (paperback)
SUBJECTS: LCSH: Stoker, Bram, 1847-1912. Dracula. | Dracula, Count (Fictitious character) |
Vampires in literature. | Vampires in mass media. | Vampire films—History and criticism. |
Gothic revival (Literature)—History and criticism.
CLASSIFICATION: LCC PR6037.T617 D782223 2018 | DDC 823/.8–dc23
LC record available at https://lccn.loc.gov/2017029496

ISBN 978-1-107-15317-2 Hardback
ISBN 978-1-316-60708-4 Paperback

In memory of Diane Long Hoeveler

CONTENTS

CONTENTS

NOTES ON CONTRIBUTORS

STACEY ABBOTT is a reader in Film and Television Studies at the University of Roehampton in London. She is the author of *Celluloid Vampires* (2007), *Angel: TV Milestone* (2009) and *Undead Apocalypse: Vampires and Zombies in the 21st Century* (2016) and co-author of *TV Horror: The Dark Side of the Small Screen* (2013, with Lorna Jowett).

ANTHONY BALE is Professor of Medieval Studies at Birkbeck College, University of London. He has published widely on medieval religion and culture and was an academic adviser for the exhibition *Blood: Uniting and Dividing* at the Jewish Museum London (2015–2016).

HEIKE BAUER is Senior Lecturer in English and Gender Studies at Birkbeck College, University of London. She has published widely on the history of sexuality, nineteenth and twentieth-century literary culture and graphic memoirs. She is author of *The Hirschfeld Archives: Violence, Death and Modern Queer Culture* (2017) and *English Literary Sexology 1860–1930* (2009) and editor of *Women and Cross-Dressing, 1800–1939*, 3 vols. (2006), *Queer 1950s: Rethinking Sexuality in the Postwar Years* (2012, with Matt Cook) and *Sexology and Translation: Cultural and Scientific Encounters across the Modern World* (2015).

MARK BLACKLOCK is Lecturer in Modern and Contemporary Literature at Birkbeck College, University of London. He is the author of *The Emergence of the Fourth Dimension* (2017), and his first novel, *I'm Jack*, was published in 2015.

CHRISTINE FERGUSON is Professor in English Literature at the University of Stirling in Scotland, where her research focuses on the entwined histories of the literary gothic and the British occult revival in the late nineteenth and early twentieth century. She is the author of *Determined Spirits: Eugenics, Heredity, and Racial Regeneration in Anglo-American Spiritualist Writing 1848–1930* (2012) and *Language, Science, and Popular Fiction in the Victorian Fin de Siècle* (2006).

KEN GELDER is Professor of English at the University of Melbourne, Australia. His books include *Reading the Vampire* (1994), *Uncanny Australia: Sacredness and Identity in a Postcolonial Nation* (1998, with Jane M. Jacobs), *Subcultures: Social Histories and Cultural Practice* (2007), *New Vampire Cinema* (2012) and *Colonial Australian Fiction: Character Types, Social Formations and the Colonial Economy* (2017, with Rachel Weaver).

MATTHEW GIBSON is Associate Professor of English Literature at the University of Macau in China. He is the author of several books, including *Dracula and the Eastern Question: British and French Vampire Narratives of the Nineteenth-Century Near East* (2006). With William Hughes, he is currently collecting the correspondence of Bram Stoker.

DAVID GLOVER is Emeritus Professor of English at the University of Southampton in England. His publications include *Vampires, Mummies, and Liberals: Bram Stoker and the Politics of Popular Fiction* (1996) and *Literature, Immigration and Diaspora in Fin-de-Siècle England: A Cultural History of the 1905 Aliens Act* (2012). He co-edited *The Cambridge Companion to Popular Fiction* (2012, with Scott McCracken).

NICK GROOM is Professor in English at the University of Exeter in England. His books include *The Gothic: A Very Short Introduction* (2012) and editions of *The Castle of Otranto* (2014), *The Monk* (2016), *The Italian* (2017) and *Frankenstein* (2018), in addition to essays on topics ranging from the culture of ruins to the songs of Nick Cave. He also works on cultural environmentalism, national identity and intangible heritage.

WILLIAM HUGHES is Professor of Medical Humanities and Gothic Literature at Bath Spa University in England. He is the author, editor or co-editor of seventeen books, including *Beyond Dracula: Bram Stoker's Fiction and Its Cultural Context* (2000), two student guides to the criticism of *Dracula* and critical editions of both *Dracula* and Stoker's Edwardian faux-vampire novel *The Lady of the Shroud*. His most recent book is *That Devil's Trick: Mesmerism and the Victorian Popular Imagination* (2015).

ROGER LUCKHURST is Professor of Modern Literature at Birkbeck College, University of London. He is the author of *The Invention of Telepathy* (2002), *The Mummy's Curse* (2012), *The Shining* (2013) and *Zombies: A Cultural History* (2015). He is the editor of the Oxford World's Classics edition of Stoker's *Dracula*.

ALISON PEIRSE is Lecturer in Writing for Screen and Stage at the University of Leeds in England. She is the author of *After Dracula: The 1930s Horror Film* (2013), co-editor of *Korean Horror Cinema* (2013) and is currently writing *The Talking Dead: British Horror Cinema and Spiritualism* (2017). She is also a scriptwriter and a script consultant to the British film industry.

XAVIER ALDANA REYES is Senior Lecturer in English Literature and Film at Manchester Metropolitan University and a founding member of the Manchester Centre for Gothic Studies in England. His books include *Spanish Gothic* (2017), *Horror: A Literary History* (2016), *Horror Film and Affect* (2016), *Digital Horror* (2015, co-edited with I. B. Tauris) and *Body Gothic* (2014). He is chief editor of Horror Studies book series for the University of Wales Press.

CAROL SENF is Professor in the School of Literature and Communication at Georgia Tech in the United States and has been publishing on *Dracula* for forty-five years. She is the author of *The Vampire in Nineteenth Century Literature* (1988) and *Dracula: Between Tradition and Modernism* (1998). She also works on the Brontes, Thomas Hardy, George Eliot and popular culture.

ALEX WARWICK is Professor of English and Head of the Department of English, Linguistics and Cultural Studies at the University of Westminster in London. Her work is mainly in nineteenth-century studies, and she has published work on Oscar Wilde, on Gothic, on the Whitechapel Murders and on Andrew Lang.

CATHERINE WYNNE teaches at the University of Hull in England. She is the author of *The Colonial Conan Doyle: British Imperialism, Irish Nationalism, and the Gothic* (2002) and *Bram Stoker, Dracula and the Victorian Gothic Stage* (2012). She has edited *Bram Stoker and the Stage: Reviews, Reminiscences, Essays and Fiction*, 2 vols. (2012) and *Bram Stoker and the Gothic: Formations to Transformations* (2016).

NOTE ON THE TEXT

The contributors refer to the Oxford World's Classics edition of *Dracula*, edited by Roger Luckhurst (2009), using the shorthand *D* in the main text.

CHRONOLOGY

1847   Abraham Stoker, born 8 November, Dublin. Part of Protestant middle-class group in midst of Catholic majority, although parents not wealthy. In Dublin, moved in close circle of Sir William and Lady Wilde (parents of Oscar Wilde) and Gothic writer Joseph Sheridan Le Fanu.

1863–67 Attends Trinity College Dublin, where active in the Philosophical Society.

1865   First sees the actor Henry Irving perform.

1868   Enters Civil Service, following his father Abraham. Begins reading Walt Whitman.

1870   Finally graduates from Trinity, with science degree.

1871   Begins writing play reviews and criticism for *Dublin Evening Mail*, part owned by Sheridan Le Fanu, the writer of Gothic stories and novels.

1872   Writes letter to Walt Whitman in passionate admiration of *Leaves of Grass* but decides not to send it. Publishes his first story in *London Society*. Sheridan Le Fanu publishes story 'Carmilla', about a female aristocratic vampire from Styria, on the southern edge of the Austrian Empire; key influence on *Dracula*, initially set in Styria.

1873   Sees the actor Geneviève Ward on stage for first time; becomes lifelong friend.

1875   First Gothic story, 'The Chain of Destiny', published.

1876   Gives vote of thanks to actor Henry Irving on one of his visits to Dublin, praising Irving's 'historic genius' in his performance and becomes ardent admirer.

1877   Irving in Dublin performs both *Othello* and *Hamlet*.

1878   Publishes *The Duties of Clerks of Petty Sessions in Ireland*. In October leaves his Civil Service job to become manager of Lyceum Theatre in London for Henry Irving, at three times his annual civil service salary. Marries Florence Balcombe days before leaving Dublin; she had relatively recently turned down a proposal from Oscar Wilde. At Lyceum, begins a lifelong friendship with actor Ellen Terry.

Only son born. Christened Irving Noel Thornley Stoker.

George Stoker, his brother, publishes *With 'the Unspeakables'*, an account of his time as a doctor in the Russo-Turkish war in Bulgaria. George lodges with Bram for several months, full of stories of the Eastern fringes of Europe.

1879–84 Lives at 27 Cheyne Walk, Chelsea, a fashionable address near the homes of Dante Gabriel Rossetti, Algernon Swinburne and James Whistler. Meets Rossetti's assistant, Hall Caine, who becomes close friend and later best-selling author (*Dracula* is dedicated to him). Through the Lyceum, becomes friends with William Gladstone, Baroness Burdett-Coutts, Richard Burton and many other celebrated figures. Florence Stoker considered a great beauty of the time and gathers admirers including the librettist and writer, W. S. Gilbert.

1882 First collection of stories, *Under the Sunset*. Acquires some fame for jumping into Thames in attempt to rescue a suicide, for which he is awarded a Humanitarian medal.

1883 First visit to America, touring with Irving (between 1883–1905, Stoker estimated he spent four years in America on the eight tours he took with Irving). Meets Walt Whitman.

1885 Irving plays *Faust* at Lyceum. Emily Gerard publishes 'Transylvanian Superstitions'. Essay used for folkloric touches in *Dracula*.

1886 Publishes lecture, 'A Glimpse of America'.

1887 Wife and son shipwrecked in the Channel, but both survive. Publishes sadistic tale, 'The Dualitists'.

1890 Publishes first novel, *The Snake's Pass*. Qualifies as a barrister, called to bar at the Inner Temple. Makes first notes on new Gothic novel to be called *The Undead*. Finds Wilkinson's *An Account of the Principalities of Wallachia and Moldavia* whilst on holiday in Whitby.

1891 Becomes investor in new publishing venture by William Heinemann.

1894 Novel, *The Watter's Mou'*. Stoker encourages staging of Arthur Conan Doyle's play *Waterloo* at the Lyceum. Doyle publishes 'The Parasite', a psychic vampire tale. Edvard Munch completes four versions of the painting 'Love and Pain', also known as 'The Vampire' for his *Frieze of Life* series. Count Stenbock, 'The Sad Story of a Vampire', in *Studies of Death: Romantic Tales*.

1895   Novel, *The Shoulder of Shasta*. Brother, Thornley, knighted for services to medicine. Henry Irving knighted, the first actor to gain the honour. Oscar Wilde imprisoned. On American tour meets Theodore Roosevelt.

1896   Suffers financial difficulties when investment in Heinemann fails. Requests loan from friend Hall Caine, on hope that his new book will allow him to return the money. Mary E. Braddon's story, 'The Good Lady Ducayne', about an ancient aristocrat extending life with blood transfusions from healthy young girls. George Stetson, 'The Animistic Vampire in New England'. An anthropological discussion of belief that tuberculosis is a form of vampirism in isolated Rhode Island community. George Méliès, *The Haunted Castle*, the first vampire film in the first year of cinema: a bat flies into a castle and transforms into a man.

1897   Stoker submits novel *The Undead* to Constable; appears on 26 May as *Dracula*. Stage version read at Lyceum on 18 May to establish copyright, but Irving refuses to stage it. Florence Marryat publishes *The Blood of the Vampire*. Exhibition in London of Philip Burne-Jones's painting, 'The Vampire', prompting Rudyard Kipling's poem 'The Vampire'.

1898   Novel, *Miss Betty*.

1899   Novel, *Snowbound*.

1900   Irving loses control of the Lyceum, and the theatre is sold on. Stoker continues as Irving's personal manager.
        Cheap edition of *Dracula*, abridged by Stoker.

1902   Novel, *Mystery of the Sea*.

1903   Novel, *The Jewel of the Seven Stars*.

1905   Novel, *The Man*. Death of Henry Irving. Stoker suffers stroke, affecting his sight.

1906   *Personal Reminiscences of Henry Irving*, a two-volume biography of his boss. Considered by *The Times* as likely to be Stoker's lasting work.

1908   Novel, *Lady Athlyne*. Publishes the essay 'The Censorship of Fiction'. Interviews William Churchill for *Daily Chronicle*.

1909   Novel, *The Lady of the Shroud*.

1910   *Famous Impostors*, which includes portrait of Franz Anton Mesmer. First (now lost) film of *Dracula* made in Hungary.

1911   Last novel, *The Lair of the White Worm*. Stoker's illness and financial difficulty result in appeal to Royal Literary Fund for pension.

1912	Stoker dies 20 April, aged 64. Controversy still attends cause of death; in the 1970s biographer Daniel Farson first claimed Stoker died from the sexually transmitted infection syphilis.
1914	His widow, Florence, publishes 'Dracula's Guest' in collection of short stories.
1922	Florence first becomes aware of the German film *Nosferatu* and sues the producers for breach of copyright of *Dracula*, initially through the Society of Authors. She succeeds in getting copies of the film destroyed, chasing prints for over a decade.
1924	Florence agrees to authorised stage version of *Dracula* adapted by Hamilton Deane. It opens in the provinces, then transfers to London in 1927 where it is critically panned yet plays to packed houses for over a year.
1927	Deane's script is streamlined by John Balderston, and the play opens on Broadway with Hungarian-born actor Bela Lugosi in the role of Dracula. Another great success.
1931	After much negotiation, Lugosi stars in the famous Universal Studio version of *Dracula*, the film that helped to establish the 'horror' genre in the cinema. Deane, Balderston and Florence Stoker are paid for the rights.
1937	Death of Florence Stoker.

ROGER LUCKHURST

Introduction

Cuadecuc, Vampir is probably the most provoking adaptation of *Dracula* you have never seen, for it is vanishingly rare. The film was directed in 1971 by Pere Portabella, the legendary Spanish producer of scandalous films by Luis Bunuel, a documentarist in his own right and later a leading Catalan politician. It is a strange collection of scratchy, black-and-white footage taken on the set of Jess Franco's *Count Dracula* (1970), an Italian-Spanish-German production that – like many Hammer House of Horror films – starred Christopher Lee as the aristocratic vampire. In *Cuadecuc*, however, instead of lurid Technicolor melodrama, Portabella's camera keeps drifting beyond the staged action to reveal stage-hands tinkering with smoke machines, spraying cob-webs on cardboard tombs, tensing the guide wires for very unconvincing rubber bats, or catching Lee in make-up, out of character, laughing and joking as he slips on his wig. The soundtrack is a dissonant avant-garde composition by Carles Santos, full of industrial noise, gratings and grindings, which further alienates the viewer from the action. The film ends with Lee reading out the last page of Stoker's novel, the scene of Dracula's death (his own character's death), yet even here the camera stays rolling slightly too long, and an awkward silence stretches out before the director eventually shouts 'Cut!'

Cuadecuc, Vampir was shown at the Cannes film festival to acclaim but was immediately banned in Spain. Although there is nothing explicitly stated, the Fascist authorities that tightly controlled cultural expression in Spain under the dictatorship of General Franco got the message loud and clear. Count Dracula is meant to represent the undead dictator Franco, but Portabella's strategy is to show *Count Dracula* as a flimsy Gothic concoction, his camera revealing the simple devices that create the illusion of power, fear and Mesmeric control. He is pulling away the curtain, just like the end of *The Wizard of Oz*.

Why start here? Because Bram Stoker's *Dracula* is rarely approached except through the myriad adaptations, transpositions and revisions of the novel since it was first published in 1897. Portabella's meta-film, a film of images appropriated from another, amplifies this filtering effect. We come at *Dracula* as if it were always already 'found footage'. We somehow already know the arbitrary rules of vampirism and how to protect ourselves against it, we come decked out with crucifixes and garlic flowers, and we know the narrative arc of this story, from margin to centre and back again. Florence Stoker, Bram's widow, attempted to use the courts to stop the circulation of F. W. Murnau's masterpiece, *Nosferatu* (1922) for breach of her husband's copyright, but by 1932 she accepted a deal with Universal Studios when they hired Bela Lugosi to repeat his stage success in *Dracula*. The text, already a success in popular editions and on stage, has since been in unceasing circulation. It wandered so wide and far, that Francis Ford Coppola's hugely successful adaptation in the 1990s was called *Bram Stoker's Dracula*, as if it was a novelty to plan a return to the originating text itself.

Dracula is what Chris Baldick has called a modern myth, like Mary Shelley's *Frankenstein* (1818) or Robert Louis Stevenson's *Strange Case of Jekyll and Hyde* (1886), a text that is open to all kinds of adaptation but that carries a basic set of narrative structures and meanings, even through the worst translation.[1] *Dracula* speaks very specifically to the heady world of fin-de-siècle London in the year of Queen Victoria's diamond jubilee, but it also offers allegorical potential to a sclerotic Spain in the last years of Franco's dictatorship. The myth-structure of the arrival of an insidious, alluring vampire carrying a deadly contagion that threatens modernity itself but is fought off – just about – by an improvised Praetorian guard, has since found vectors around the world and embedded itself in all kinds of surprising local contexts (some of which Ken Gelder explores in his chapter below).

Yet rather than merely saying that Stoker taps into the mythopoeic – primitive or archetypal stubs of storytelling that prove easy to repeat and transmute – *Cuadecuc, Vampir* reinforces the lesson that *Dracula* is always thoroughly political and context-specific. Indeed, as Nick Groom details in the opening chapter here, the word 'vampire' enters the English language in the 1730s as a satirical political metaphor long before it appears in fiction. Never mind the strange peasant stories of buried bodies that refuse to die and come back to feast on their neighbours, stories that were being reported from the very edges of civilised Europe in confused accounts hailing from the bloody Balkans. The 'Riflers of the Kingdom' in London or Paris were the merchants, bankers and politicians who were regularly termed blood-suckers or vampires in the vibrant pages of the disputatious newspaper press of the emergent bourgeois public sphere. The vampire was a mobile metaphor long before Stoker picked up and transformed William Polidori's portrait of the demonic aristocrat Lord Ruthven in his short Gothic tale, 'The Vampyre' (1819).

To study Bram Stoker's *Dracula*, then, requires a number of long perspectives, from before and after its publication in 1897. A reader needs a sense of the mobility of the vampire as folkloric term and agile metaphor in the 150 years before publication, in literature, folklore, anthropology and the geopolitics of Europe. But we also need a grasp of the renewed narrative energy and concentrated form Stoker gave the vampire that meant it could leap so effortlessly from text to stage to many different kinds of screen (film, TV, computer game) in the 120 years since its publication. This *Companion* aims to provide that long view in its opening and closing sections, which offer various pre-histories and subsequent cultural trans-formations of Stoker's text. These longer perspectives are intrinsic to understanding what Stoker's melodrama consolidated in its exuberant narrative form.

But we also have to address the specific puzzle of what Stoker did in *Dracula* that secured its astounding success as a modern myth. On publica-tion, the book was regarded a cynical pot-boiler that was seeking slightly too hard to join what some newspapers denounced as the Culture of the Hor-rible, written by a hack writer better known for his management of the Lyceum Theatre under famous actor Henry Irving. Stoker's *Times* obituary recognised that 'he was the master of a particularly lurid and creepy kind of fiction, represented by "Dracula" and other novels', but confidently pre-dicted that 'his chief literary memorial will be his Reminiscences of Irving'.[2] This was the bid to secure a respectable place for Stoker in posterity, and was completely wrong.

In 1897, readers of contemporary fiction seemed to have been more willing to countenance Richard Marsh's *The Beetle*, a thematically similar tale of London menaced by a supernaturally powerful foreign agent, or Florence Marryat's tale of the psychological attenuation of her mixed-race protagonist in *The Blood of the Vampire*.

It is impossible to over-emphasise how culturally invisible popular fiction such as *Dracula* was to the formation of literary canons and the training of literary taste for much of the twentieth century. When David Punter wrote about *Dracula* in his pioneering survey *The Literature of Terror* in 1980, it was presented as an act of recovery of a novel he modestly suggests has been under-rated and largely forgotten under the welter of horror films that shared its name. There was a slight kerfuffle about literary value when it was announced *Dracula* would be included in the Oxford World's Classics series for the first time in 1983. *Dracula* was not helped along by any intrinsic literary merit, the critical consensus seemed to say, but this actually allowed the Dracula myth to escape the confines of its routine, entirely adequate text.

Yet the form of *Dracula* has something to do with its posthumous revival, an ingenious construction of different kinds of textual fragments, diaries, newspaper reports, phonographic transcriptions, log books and other data. Within the text, that modern girl Mina Harker (who sometimes calls herself a New Woman) emerges as the organising secretary who creates, shuffles and organises this 'mass of typewriting' (*D*, 351), reducing diverse details into equivalent informational bits that can be sorted by the hapless men around her. Mina is a kind of embodied search-engine herself, with sailing times and train timetables at her fingertips. She even becomes a kind of occult communication device herself, a new-fangled two-legged telephone, able to dial up the Count from afar once she is in mesmeric rapport. She sends in weather updates, travel reports, and neatly summarises scientific findings on the 'criminal mind'. It is having more efficient information systems than the Count that in the end defeats the vampire threat. In contrast, Dracula relies on blue books and civil lists in his mouldering library to learn the institutional contours of the British state he sets out to infiltrate. 'Vampirism is a chain reaction, and can therefore only be fought with the techniques of mechanical text reproduction', Friedrich Kittler observes. The novel is therefore, in his reading, 'the written account of our bureaucratisation'.[3]

This device of constructing narrative through fictitious assemblage was borrowed from Wilkie Collins's sensation fictions of the 1860s, but it is greatly amplified by Stoker, and turns *Dracula* into a breathless rendition of modernity itself, racing on with the whizz of trains and omnibuses, of letters and telegrams speeding through wires or voices caught in real time on wax cylinders. It might have felt crude and vulgar to cultivated aesthetic taste in the 1890s, but it makes *Dracula* part of the new century, not the old.

This narrative structure of informational bits also makes the novel seem – to switch analogy – like an open grid, built from tiles of a mosaic that can be shuffled and re-shuffled into new pictures over and over again. Judith Halberstam, in resisting the temptation to produce a single key or code to unlock the novel, instead called it 'technology of monstrosity', a machine that works to 'produce the monster as a remarkably mobile, permeable and infinitely interpretable body'.[4] This is a reflection of the whole libraries of critical work that has now grown up around *Dracula*. If it sometimes feels like a generative machine for criticism, that is because the novel is so informationally dense, taking on the rich colourings of many artistic, cultural, political, social and scientific discourses that swirled anxiously through the public sphere in the 1890s.

Dracula was published in London at a period of intense contradictions in 1897. Queen Victoria headed an empire that finally had belligerent ideological spokesmen advocating greater expansion (the 'Jingos'), but was also riven with fears of attack, over-extension and the massing of rival power in Germany, Russia and America. The economic engine of the British industrial revolution that had powered Britain to world leadership was seriously stalling. The uneasy truce between Capital and Labour seemed to be fraying, with the unemployed sleeping in numbers in London squares, unions gaining power in the coal industry and calling workers out on strike, the formation of Socialist political parties, and demonstrations bursting into riots in Trafalgar Square. Women demanded increasing political representation and legal rights, with any advances always accompanied by a conservative counter-discourse of imminent sexual anarchy and race suicide. The great liberal tradition of England as a sanctuary of tolerance from religious persecution was still upheld, yet the influx of Jews to the East End escaping from the Russian pogroms caused much anxiety and new controls over the entry of immigrants. A pseudo-scientific discourse of the hierarchy of the races hardened. Some from the more bestial races, Russian Nihilists and Irish revolutionaries demanding home rule for Ireland, haunted the city streets as bomb-throwing monsters threatening the domestic security of the heart of the Empire. Invasion narratives, just like *Dracula*, were written in their hundreds.

Scientific and technological discoveries related to the second great industrial revolution – the electrical one – seemed to reinvent the possibilities of everyday life. There were new communication technologies, wireless telegraphy and mysterious Hertzian waves, a new psychology revealing the depths of the 'subliminal mind', a new physics of 'dark matter' and invisible radiation, a new biology of nerves and synapses. The co-discoverer of evolutionary theory, Alfred Russell Wallace, declared it *The Wonderful Century* in 1898. Yet men of science also seemed overcome with pessimistic accounts of decline and collapse. At the end of his life, T. H. Huxley's lecture, 'Evolution and Ethics' (1893), seemed to indicate that the advances of civilisation were now in conflict with basic biological imperatives. An upstart young journalist, H. G. Wells, used his brand new type of education in science under Huxley to repeatedly imagine the end of the world in *The Time Machine* (1895) or *The War of the Worlds* (1898).

Cultural frontiers of freedom of expression had been pushed back by aesthetes and Decadents and by a new popular press, yet the conservative establishment viciously countered with the arrest and imprisonment of campaigning journalist W. T. Stead for publishing about child prostitution in London in 1885 and Oscar Wilde in 1895. The leading light of the Decadents was sentenced to two-years hard labour for acts of gross indecency with young men in London hotels. Stoker knew Stead in London, and had been Wilde's neighbour in Dublin, a long-time visitor as a young man to the salons held by Sir William and Lady Wilde. The Dublin beauty Florence Balcombe turned down Wilde's proposal and married Stoker instead. Some speculate on the shadow Wilde cast over *Dracula*, a text largely composed while Wilde's health was being determinedly broken on the treadmills of Reading Gaol. Stoker was a social and political conservative, an Irishman in the colonial centre, but who lived in very liberal journalistic and bohemian circles of London's literary and theatrical culture. He was perfectly positioned to experience the full torque of these many over-lapping contradictory forces of advance and counter-reaction. Stoker is not necessarily in control of these forces, even as they surface through his headlong prose.

The core work of this *Companion* is to provide a series of routes through the text. *Dracula* is such an open matrix of a novel that the reader can take many different kinds of pathway through it, taking routes that sometimes reinforce each other, but at others appear never quite to intersect and indeed even contradict each other. That is the product of its feverish over-determination, its openness to history. Hence in this *Companion*, once Nick Groom, William Hughes and Alex Warwick have set *Dracula* in relation to the capacious tradition of the Gothic romance, a sequence of essays focus narrowly on the novel's relationships to specific discourses. Christine Ferguson explores *Dracula*'s relationship with the late Victorian occult revival, which wanted to reshape the relationship of modernity to the 'supernatural', just as the novel does. Roger Luckhurst examines how the novel lies on the cusp of shifting paradigms of self and subjectivity in psychology, just as Heike Bauer relates how closely interwoven the vision of the polymorphous vampire is with a new language of sexuality and sexual perversion. Popular genres were intrinsically part of the scientific and cultural work of defining the boundaries of the normal and the pathological.

It is crucial to be aware of the investments *Dracula* has in discourses about race in the late Victorian period, and so David Glover explains the anxious discourse about the effect of mass migration to the imperial metropolis, while Matthew Gibson teases out the complex meanings Western Europe assigned to the Balkans and Transylvania in particular at this time. As the Count explains his origins in the whirlpool of races in his passionate speeches to Jonathan Harker at the start of the novel, this region existed on the very edge of Christian Europe, a blurred border zone where European civilisation met the Ottoman Empire, a rival power and a rival religion centred in Constantinople (now Istanbul). Anthony Bale details how *Dracula* is underpinned by what the symbolics of blood, the bearer of sacred meanings in the Christian tradition but also the focus for centuries of fantasies of contamination and desecration by that race of perennial outsiders/insiders, the Jews. The monstrosity of Dracula, the contagion of vampirism, is in uncomfortable proximity to these ancient and modern discourses of race.

In this section of contexts, Carol Senf also makes us aware of how the novel embodies contradictory notions of gender and sexuality in the pairing of Lucy Westenra and Mina Harker, at once liberated New Women and the antipathy of that liberation in the course of the plot.

It was in the millennial angst of the 1980s and 1990s that there was a revival of interest in the last century's fin de siècle, a revival that buoyed up the interest in Stoker's novel. There have been many readings of *Dracula* in relation to Karl Marx's famous metaphor of capital sucking the life-blood from dead labour: Franco Moretti's remains the most often read, although there are many others.[5] But in the 1990s, identity politics dominated critical accounts of *Dracula*, the sense that the novel had to be explored through the identity categories of class, race and gender. An emergent critical language in this period was Queer Theory, which found a rich seam to explore dissident sexualities in the late Victorian era, because this was exactly the era when (as Heike Bauer details) the notion of homosexuality and heterosexuality were formulated. The Gothic was an exemplary genre for expressing ambivalence about sexualities that were just on the threshold of being enunciated. *Dracula* staunchly defends the northern Protestant Christian family and the sacred duties of motherhood, blasting the monstrous alternative represented by the Count. Yet it also indulges in precisely these fantasies of alternative vampire sexuality and non-reproductive pleasures, imagining them into existence in impressively hallucinated scenes. All the men in *Dracula*, somewhat campily, faint away at some point or other, like Gothic maidens overwhelmed by feelings that they cannot master.

This is why Queer Theory introduces the 'New Directions' section, since *Dracula* has only very belatedly come to be read in this context. Nor is this a stable, singular body of work: Xavier Aldana Reyes might be considered a second-generation Queer theorist, striving to keep the dynamic matrix of the text open to multiple possibilities, rather than trying to uncover a 'homosexual' secret buried or encoded in the text.

Dracula keeps on opening new pathways and directions. Part of the task of the new Horror Theory associated with object-oriented ontology is to displace familiar theoretical frameworks that have so often worked through 'depth reading', the phenomenology of literary interpretation that dominated the twentieth century. Mark Blacklock explores how much *Dracula* can be read as part of the revenge of the object world on the deluded subjects who thought they were in command, the vampire a figure of radical non-subjectivity, morphing as mist, or fog or rats. If this is a new approach, so is

Ken Gelder's attention to transnational and transmedial translations of the *Dracula* narrative across the 'Southern Gothic' in America, in Japan and in Sweden. Like a hybrid plant, *Dracula* flowers with strange new blooms when transplanted to different cultural ecologies.

The enduring force of *Dracula* is the seeming inexhaustibility of the contexts it requires and the readings it might generate. Lack of space has squeezed out a particular focus on Stoker's place in the Anglo-Irish Gothic, although there is lots of work available elsewhere on this.[6] Emergent paradigms like medical humanities inevitably re-imagines *Dracula* as a contagion narrative, perfectly fitting the paradigm of the lone 'typhoid Mary' that arrives as an advent of an epidemic.[7] The *Companion* might have stretched its already detailed accounts of adaptations of stage, film and TV to include comics or computer games. The further reading at the end of this *Companion* will help consolidate established paradigms, but also indicate emergent readings too. The tiles of this mosaic will keep being re-arranged. This is only testament to *Dracula*'s place in the pantheon of modern myths.

Notes

1 Chris Baldick, *In Frankenstein's Shadow: Myth, Monstrosity, and Nineteenth-Century Writing* (Oxford: Clarendon, 1987).
2 'Mr. Bram Stoker', *The Times* (22 April 1912), 15.
3 Friedrich Kittler, 'Dracula's Legacy', *Stanford Humanities Review* 1 (1989), 162, 164.
4 Judith Halberstam, *Skin Shows: Gothic Horror and the Technology of Monsters* (Durham: Duke University Press, 1995), 21.
5 Franco Moretti, 'The Dialectic of Fear' in *Signs Taken for Wonders: Essays on the Sociology of Literary Forms* (London: Verso, 1983). For a detailed reading of the Marx's use of the vampire metaphor, see Mark Neocleous, 'The Political Economy of the Dead: Marx's Vampires', *History of Political Thought* 34, no. 4 (2003), 668–84.
6 See Raymond T. McNally, 'Bram Stoker and the Irish Gothic', in J. Holte, ed., *The Fantastic Vampire: Studies in the Children of the Night* (Westport, CT: Greenwood, 1997), pp. 11–21; Alison Millbank, '"Powers Old and New": Stoker's Alliances with Anglo-Irish Gothic', in A. Smith and W. Hughes, ed., *Bram Stoker: History, Psychoanalysis, and the Gothic* (London: Macmillan, 1998), pp. 12–28.
7 See Priscilla Wald, *Contagious: Cultures, Carriers, and the Outbreak Narrative*, (Durham: Duke University Press, 2008).

PART I

Dracula in the Gothic Tradition

I

NICK GROOM

Dracula's Pre-History

The Advent of the Vampire

Blood-sucking demons have haunted civilised society since biblical times. Lilith was a female demon, the first rebellious wife of Adam; her name has been translated as 'vampire'. Lamia was a bisexual female monster of ancient Greece who drank the blood of children, sometimes treated as synonymous with the Judaeo-Christian Lilith. The Romans were familiar with ghosts that sucked blood and brought nightmares, and they attributed such characteristics to the marauding Goths (also known as Scythians) who sacked Rome in the fifth century: 'they thought that Thessalian witches, accompanying the barbarian armies, were darkening her rays with their country's magic spells'.[1] The invading Huns too were steeped in blood and ruin: 'Behold the wolves, not of Arabia, but of the North, were let loose upon us last year from the far-off rocks of the Caucasus, and in a little while overran great provinces', bemoaned Saint Jerome. 'How many monasteries were captured, how many streams were reddened with human blood!'[2] Their leader Attila (who choked on his own blood) was lamented 'not by effeminate wailings and tears but by the blood of men'.[3]

In Norse myth, which drew on Hunnish and Gothic legends, the *draugrs* were corporeal undead revenants, sometimes simply guarding hoards but often raiding the living – for example in the pagan corpus the *Eyrbyggja Saga*. The twelfth-century chronicler William of Malmesbury described the Devil re-animating his servants to continue his work from beyond the grave, and William of Newburgh and the Monk of Byland likewise recorded several stories of the dead returning – either to revisit their kin, terrorise their enemies or simply through restlessness of spirit. One of Newburgh's revenants is only dispatched when, discovered in the grave engorged with blood, it is summarily exhumed, has its heart torn out and is cremated. The later Hungarian countess Elizabeth Bathory was reputed to bathe in the blood of young girls in order to retain her youthful beauty, and the fifteenth-century Wallachian warlord Vlad Țepeș allegedly executed tens of thousands by torture and impalement: roasting children and feeding them to their mothers, forcing husbands to devour wives, and ultimately impaling all of his victims. Stoker would have been familiar with this material through Victorian surveys such as Sabine Baring-Gould's *Book of Werewolves* (1865). Closer to home, the English and Scottish ballad tradition is haunted by demon lovers, ghosts and wraiths in verses such as 'The Unquiet Grave'.

There were other demons too that literally stirred the blood. Incubi and sucubi were sexual predators that defiled the innocent. They are described in witchcraft manuals such as the *Malleus Maleficarum* (1486) and appear in Thomas Middleton's Jacobean drama *The Witch* (written between 1609 and 1616, first published in 1778), in which the central character declares:

> 'Tis Almachildes: fresh blood stirs in me –
> The man that I have lusted to enjoy,
> I've had him thrice in Incubus already.[4]

Elizabethan and Jacobean revenge tragedy is drenched in blood and bloody symbolism, and littered with corpses, as well as haunted by avenging ghosts and other supernatural beings, from hobgoblins to werewolves. Murdered bodies were believed to bleed in the presence of their killer, as noted by Shakespeare in *Richard III* (c. 1592–93):

> O gentlemen! See, see dead Henry's wounds
> Open their congeal'd mouths and bleed afresh.   (I. ii. 55–56)

King James's *Demonologie* (1597), which also recorded incubi possessing dead cadavers in order to rape their earthly lovers, gave the phenomenon of 'cruentation' legal force:

> as in a secret murder, if the dead carcass be at any time thereafter handled by the murderer it will gush out of blood, as if the blood were crying to the heaven for revenge of the murderer, God having appointed that secret supernatural sign for trial of that secret unnatural crime.[5]

This demonic tradition – bloody, vengeful, nightmarish and supernatural – that led to Stoker's *Dracula* evidently has deep roots, reaching back into antiquity and folklore and superstition. For instance, Stoker took the name Dracula from Vlad Țepeș, son of Vlad Dracul (the Dragon) who had the lupine lineage of the both Scythian witches and the fearsome Huns (D, 30). Vlad had a predilection for impalement, although not through the heart, but in ways that kept the victim alive for days. But there were other, much more recent and direct sources too. The vampire is in fact a relatively modern phenomenon, emerging predominantly from Enlightenment medicine, theology and social science.

Rumours of vampire activity as it would be recognised today emerged at the end of the seventeenth century. A vampire was reported in Ljubljana in 1689, the French gazette the *Mercure Galant* described vampires in Poland and Russia in 1693 and 1694 and there were notices in journals such as the *Glaneur Hollandois*. These creatures appeared between the hours of noon and midnight to suck the blood of humans and animals; once sated, blood would flow from their orifices and pores and their coffins were often found to be swimming in gore. They were known to feast on grave clothes, and, continuing this fascination with grisly nutrition, a prophylactic bread could be made from their blood affording protection against contracting vampirism.

There had, in fact, already been an empirical study of 'grave eating' or manducation: Phillip Rohr's *Dissertatio De Masticatione Mortuorum* (1679). This featured grisly details of graves being opened to reveal that the undead had been consuming their own shrouds and winding cloths, and had even devoured their own limbs and bowels. But what is most striking about these occurrences is perhaps the sounds that accompany infernal mastication. Like the 'churning' sound of the tongue as the female vampire in *Dracula* licks her teeth and lips (*D*, 39), the Devil makes 'curious noises' in manducation: 'he may lap like some thirsty animal, he may chaw, grunt and groan'.[6]

Rohr also includes remedies to prevent the dead from rising: clasping the hands of a corpse or placing earth on the lips, as well as decapitation or exhumation followed by staking through the heart to pin the corpse to the ground. Such activities were certainly still current in the eighteenth-century 'Age of Reason'. In *A Voyage into the Levant* (1718, reprinted 1741), Joseph Pitton de Tournefort gives an account dated 1 January 1701 of a Greek 'Vroucolacas' (*vrykolakas*) on the island of Mykonos: 'Corpses, which they [the locals] fancy come to life again after their Interment'.[7] The vroucolacas in question is aggressively physical, and attempts to destroy it by removing the heart from the original corpse and burning the organ prove unsuccessful. The vroucolacas continues to roam Mykonos until it is doused with Holy Water and the whole body is cremated. Tournefort's account is presented as a comic episode, mocking the islanders' credulity and asserting modern rationality over peasant superstition. Tournefort accordingly offers a scientific explanation: the inhabitants of Mykonos must be suffering from a disease of the brain, similar to the bite of mad dog.

Within a few years, however, ridicule had, for many, turned into reluctant conviction. The history of the vampire really begins at the frontiers of the Habsburg Empire in 1718 as a bizarre side-effect of Austria's annexation of the territories of Lesser Wallachia, parts of Serbia and northern parts of

Bosnia from the Ottoman Empire. These areas were effectively a buffer zone between the Austrian and Ottoman empires; they had highly mixed populations and pluralistic cultures and now became pawns in the manoeuvrings of international politics. The imposition of a military border enforced an authoritarian and foreign imperial regime that inevitably compromised local freedoms and rights; the result was that a weird epidemic took hold in these newly-seized edgelands.

Symptoms were both manifold and disturbing:

> Shivering, enduring nausea, pain in the stomach and intestines, in the kidney region and in the back and shoulderblades as well as the back of the head, further, a clouding of the eyes, deafness and speech problems. The tongue has a whitish-yellow to brownish-red coating, and dries out to the accompaniment of unquenchable thirst. The pulse is erratic and weak; on the throat and in the hypochondria, that is to say, in the area of the belly beneath the chest cartilage, livid or reddish spots are to be seen, though in part only after death. The paroxysm exhibits itself in extreme night terrors, associated with a loud cry, strong trembling, a spasmodic contraction of the muscles of the upper body, a constriction of the airway and hot flushes; with the additional symptom of constriction of the heart, that is, a sensation of anxiety in the hollow of the breast, associated with pain in the mouth of the stomach; lastly nightmares, which frequently evoke the image of the returning dead.[8]

That final, hallucinatory symptom is unnerving: 'nightmares [*incubus*], which frequently evoke the image of the returning dead'. Fearing these dreams to be reliable testimony rather than delusional fantasy, locals straightaway attributed the contagion to the undead, who apparently smothered and strangled their victims. Corpses were accordingly exhumed, staked, decapitated, and/or cremated (a practice of the Goths). The outbreak, meanwhile, showed no signs of abating, and on 21 July 1725, the Austrian newspaper *Wiener Diarium* carried a report of one Peter Plogojowitz, who was allegedly responsible for the murders of nine people over eight days in the village of Kisolova. Plogojowitz had sucked his victims dry: he was one of the *vampiri* or 'bloodsuckers' (the word 'vampire' remains obscure in its origins, possibly deriving from Old Slav).

The case simmered in the public imagination until 1732 when two more outbreaks were reported in the Serbian village of Medwegya, near Belgrade. In 1727 a former soldier, Arnod Paole (or Arnold Paul or Paule), had returned and settled to farm in Medwegya, his native village, where he was betrothed to his neighbour's daughter Nina. Paole died before they could wed when a hay cart he was driving overturned, but it transpired that the reason he had left the army and fled home was that he had contracted vampirism, possibly from a Greek *vrykolakas*. He had been tormented by the creature and had tried to dispell it by eating earth from the vampire's grave and rubbing himself with its blood, but twenty or thirty days after his death he rose and killed four people. Although Paole appeared only at night, he could pass through locked doors and barred windows. A military commission oversaw the exhumation of his corpse, which 'had all the marks of an arch-vampire. His body was fresh and ruddy, his hair, beard, and nails were grown, and his veins were full of fluid blood'.[9] The corpse was accordingly staked and cremated, along with its victims.

A second wave of attacks followed in 1731, again attributed by locals to *vambyres*. Graves were once more exhumed and the corpses there were found to be fresh. The authorities sent a medical team to investigate: it was led by an epidemiologist, one Glaser and also present was Johann Flücklinger, a military surgeon and two apothecaries. They found that corpses feared to be vampires were being summarily decapitated and cremated. Glaser sent his report to Vienna, whereupon the case ignited European interest. Flücklinger, meanwhile, investigated the earlier incidents involving Arnod Paole and described them in detail in 1732.

At the same time Glaser's father, also a physician, wrote to the recently established weekly medical journal *Commercium Litterarium ad Rei Medicae et Scientiae* with the news that in Serbia

> a magical plague has been rampant there for some time. Perfectly normal buried dead are arising from their undisturbed graves to kill the living. These too, dead and buried in their turn, arise in the same way to kill yet more people. This occurs by the following means: the dead attack people by night, while they are asleep, and suck blood out of them, so that on the third day they all die. No cure has yet been found for this evil.[10]

Vampirism made the reputation of the *Commercium Litterarium*, which published seventeen articles on the subject in 1732 alone. Moreover, twenty-two learned treatises on vampirism were published across Europe over the next three years in cultural and intellectual centres such as Amsterdam, Halle, Jena, Leipzig, London and Vienna. Attention increasingly focused on the pathology of vampirism. John Heinrich Zopfius, Director of the Gymnasium of Essen, observed for example in his *Dissertatio de Uampiris Seruiensibus* (1733) that

> Vampires issue forth from their graves in the night, attack people sleeping quietly in their beds, suck out all their blood from their bodies and destroy them. They beset men, women and children alike, sparing neither age nor sex. Those who are under the fatal malignity of their influence complain of suffocation and a total deficiency of spirits, after which they soon expire. Some who, when at the point of death, have been asked if they can tell what is causing their

decease, reply that such and such persons, lately dead, have risen from the tomb to torment and torture them.[11]

In Britain, the news was reported in the *London Journal* for 11 March 1732 as a prodigy from Heyducken, Hungary: 'namely, of *dead Bodies* sucking, as it were, the Blood of the *Living*; for the *latter* visibly dry up, while the *former* are fill'd with Blood'.[12] Zopfius' account was reported in a travelogue, thus: '*Vampyres* are supposed to be the Bodies of deceased Persons, animated by evil Spirits, which come out of the Graves, in the Night-time, suck the Blood of many of the Living, and thereby destroy them'.[13] In 1739, the Marquis d'Argens returned to the Plogojowitz case with the details that that vampire had reappeared three days after his death, upon which villagers recounted that they had dreamt that he was sucking their blood from their throats; they subsequently fell ill and died. D'Argens described how, when staked, Plogojowitz's coffin had filled with blood, and that other corpses had then been protected with garlic and whitethorn – details that would be enthusiastically taken up by later writers. Plogojowitz may also have been ithyphallic, indicating a predatory sexual threat as well as the paranormal menace of the vampire. Such details fuelled printed reports, making vampires a runaway press sensation. Neither was this a backwoods phenomenon: in Vienna, it was rumoured that the Princess Eleonore von Schwarzenberg (1682–1741) had risen as a vampire following her death.

Further incidents followed in Banat, Moravia and Wallachia in the years 1754–56. Established physicians passed judgement, including Gerard van Swieten (personal physician to the emperor and head surgeon of the military), whose treatise was published in 1755, and Georg Tallar (a regimental surgeon), whose report appeared in 1756. Van Swieten made a concerted attempt to medicalise vampirism as a mass delusion rather than a physical condition. He proposed a colonialist social model of the enlightened centre taming and civilising the irrational and barbaric periphery. Tallar, meanwhile, described symptoms and then analysed the possible causes. He noted that, critically, the condition of vampirism did not affect German settlers or the military, but was confined to Greek Orthodox Wallachians, so it was evidently not an epidemic disease. He then examined the customary diet of the Wallachians – their winter fast, their subsistence on a broth of cabbage and pumpkin, and their proclivity to drink brandy – and concluded that their meagre diet and habits of fasting made them prone to anaemia. Interestingly, the Dutch paper *The Gleaner* had in 1733 already put vampire delusions down to diet: if people 'eat nothing but bread made of oats, roots, or the bark of trees' it will raise 'gloomy and disagreeable ideas in the imagination', and John Bond in his *Essay on the Incubus* (1753) similarly put nightmares down to 'a stagnation of the Blood' caused by diet and lifestyle.[14] Tallar prescribed letting blood, an end to fasting, and emetics: he was another missionary for enlightenment science. As Peter Bräunlein suggests: 'The politics of the body was conducted with scientific materials ... the order to ward off the vampire epidemic as a moral and physical plague came from the top [i.e. the government]'; this in turn led to 'a medicalisation of colonial policy or a militarisation of medicine'.[15] Vampires were then the focus for power struggles between competing conceptualisations of the body, citizenship and human identity, which is one reason why they appeared at imperial borders as an expression of resistance by local subjugated communities.

The advent of vampires in the European and ultimately the British imagination was first driven by cutting-edge medical research – and elements of this remain in *Dracula*, such as the use of blood transfusions. In these early accounts, vampirism was first treated as a genuine disease, then as a mass delusion of peripheral and backward communities – a pattern of response that Stoker actually reverses in his novel in order to reinforce its threat. Vampirism and undead literature cannot be understood without this context of bioscience and medical geopolitics, but there was a related spiritual dimension too, in which the vampire governed over a strange no-man's land between traditional Christianity and empirical science. The question was not whether vampires were supernatural (somehow beyond or independent of natural laws) – that was irrational reasoning. Rather, vampires offered a 'naturalisation of the preternatural': a direct opportunity to bring religion and reason together, which made them subjects for state-of-the-art theology.[16] Medical science and theology were both concerned with whether 'the relationship between the dead body and an illness of mind and body should be understood as a sympathetic, astral or diabolical effect'.[17] Consequently both physicians and divines adopted a plurality of deductive methods.

Among the first of the theologians to adopt the methods and arguments of rational scientific enquiry was Henry More. In *An Antidote against Atheism* (1655), More takes up two cases presented by Martinus Weinrichius, a Silesian physician and philosopher; retrospectively, these can be seen as forerunners of the vampire debate. The first case is of a shoemaker of Silesia, who committed suicide in 1591. The crime was hushed up and he was buried, but a '*Spectrum* in the exact shape and habit of the deceased' appeared.[18] Although this undead being could not appear in direct sunlight, it could nevertheless manhandle and stifle the living, and was reputed to have powers of shape-shifting – variously appearing as a hen, dog, cat, goat and a woman. The shoemaker's corpse was exhumed eight months after being buried and was found to still be fresh. After an unsuccessful attempt to rebury it at the gallows, it was exhumed a second time and dismembered, decoronated (had its heart removed) and cremated; the ashes were scattered in a river.

More also gives an account of Johannes Cuntius, another Silesian, who was fatally trampled by horses. A black cat appeared at his deathbed and a tempest raged from the moment he died until he was interred. He then rose as a *Spiritus incubus* – again a violent and aggressive spectre: noisy (in manducation) and malodorous, frequently attacking citizens by breathing fire on them, biting and tearing at their throats, his unearthly presence heralded by candles burning blue. Cuntius was an abductor of babies, a strangler and a rapist; he sucked cows dry and ate live chickens; he was also a shapeshifter (into a dwarf or even a long wooden staff), and could turn milk into blood. Six months after being buried his corpse was exhumed and found to be wholly fresh, his eyelids batting. The corpse was duly cut into small pieces and, with great difficulty, cremated; his ashes were likewise cast into a river.

There is an emphasis here on these proto-vampires feasting on the living and drawing vitality and nourishment from them, as distinct from the activities of immaterial ghosts that haunt and terrify. Such cases therefore have a material and physical basis, allowing for forensic examination and ratiocination. More's aim is to prove the existence of the divine world of spirits and miracles through experimental philosophy and empirical evidence, with a strong emphasis on legal frameworks (a combination that Stoker later adopted for his own definitive vampire). It was the beginning of rational theology. The natural philosopher Joseph Glanvill argued in *Saducismus Triumphatus* (1680), going beyond Protestant orthodoxy, that ghosts existed, although they could not yet be explained. An intellectually informed doubt lay at the heart of this belief.

While the uniqueness of Christ's resurrection and God's sole authority in raising the dead at the Day of Judgement was apparently questioned by vampirism and posed intriguing questions for Protestant theologians regarding the extent of the Devil's powers (whether actual or counterfeit), vampires presented further difficulties for Catholic theologians. The key thinker here is Dom Augustin Calmet, a Benedictine abbot renowned for his twenty-six-volume commentary on the Bible. Calmet's *Dissertations upon the Apparitions of Angels, Dæmons, and Ghosts, and concerning the Vampires of Hungary, Bohemia, Moravia, and Silesia* was published in French in 1746 and in English in 1759. In one sense a pioneering collection of ghost stories, his book was also a comprehensive body of antiquarian research and philosophical debate that examined the conditions and extent of popular belief in the supernatural and methods for ascertaining the actual existence (or otherwise) of vampires and their ilk. Initially Calmet adopted the position that vampires existed as a form of divine punishment, but by the second edition of 1749 he had come to the conclusion that they were fantasy – though his discussion retains many of the arguments of his earlier conviction, and his change of opinion may in any case have been influenced by Pope Benedict XIV. The Pope also rejected vampirism in 1749, writing a chapter to the handbook on canonisation attacking the 'vanity of vampire beliefs' – *De vanitate vampyrorum.*

Like More, Calmet mixed evidential history, theories of natural philosophy and disputations into theological truth, making his investigation the first sustained analysis of vampires using deductive reasoning. Vampires were embodied – tangible revenants rather than intangible spectres (although they had spectral qualities too) – which had implications for Catholic traditions of the materiality of human flesh. The fresh corpse of a vampire was a direct reflection (or evil twin) of the incorruptible body of a saint, and, like the multiple deaths of megalomartyrs such as St George or St Catherine of Alexandria, had to be killed repeatedly. Vampires were also an inversion of the Eucharist: the sucking of blood was a perversion of the communion sacrament (turning blood into wine, rather than wine into blood), yet they were dispelled rather than transubstantiated by ingestion (bread from vampiric blood was meant to give protection). In fact, Calmet comes close to reading vampires as a symbolic attack on the Church, and Marie-Hélène Huet accordingly reads the whole Arnod Paole case as the life of Christ in reverse, emphasising the forty days spent wrestling with the Devil before being raised. For the vampire Paole this is a reanimation into secular society rather than a resurrection into eternal life, gorging rather than fasting and abstinence, and infecting his victims with ghastly corruption rather than converting them into disciples.[19]

Calmet notes that recent accounts of vampirism are detailed and consistent, attested by professional witnesses and investigators, and that the depositions are legally sound and reliable. He observes that vampires are a comparatively recent phenomenon, although wizards were sometimes bloodsuckers and excommunicants sometimes rose from the dead. He notes that spectres have sometimes been resuscitated after months or years to torment the living by sucking their blood and causing death, often appearing in their former clothes to their own families – a small but significant detail of attire that is adopted by Stoker in *Dracula*. Calmet in particular wrestles with the question of how vampires can leave and return to their graves, ultimately deciding that this is impossible and that vampires are therefore not really dead.

So while some Catholic commentators such as Giuseppe Davanzati argued that vampirism was a mass hallucination, Calmet remains doubtful and undogmatic – even inconsistent – and his work was heavily criticised because it did not explode vampires as a modern myth, despite his scepticism mirroring the caution of medical researchers. Moreover, his plurality of methods also cast considerable doubt on the value of testimony. Calmet was subsequently roundly attacked by Voltaire and the French *philosophes* for prioritising testimony, thus rewarding credulity and superstition. Voltaire treated Calmet's moderation as gullibility, distorting his argument to present Calmet as believing in vampires rather than simply weighing evidence and entertaining doubt. Jean-Jacques Rousseau duly questioned vampire testimonials in rather droll terms:

> There is not an historical fact in the world more fully attested, than that of the Vampires. It is confirmed by regular information, certificates of Notaries, Surgeons, Vicars, and Magistrates. And yet, with all this, who believes in Vampires? And shall we be all damned for not believing?[20]

This emphasis on testifying is a reminder of the legal methods that under-pinned these vampire investigations. Vampirism extends the workings of crime and punishment into the hereafter. The vampire is an inflection of the exercise of post-mortem power, insisting that even beyond the grave bodies are governed by discourses such as the medical, legal and theological. So as well as being medically and theologically aberrant, the vampire is also a criminal – a grave-robber (of themselves), usually violent, often sexually abusive and consistently a mass murderer. Hence the horrified fascination with vampiric bloodletting is comparable to the appetite for crime writing at the time, known in Britain as 'Newgate Calendars'.

Meticulous accounts of shocking homicides were particularly popular, and shared the same bloodcurdling details as the vampire narratives. In 1708, Ann Edgbrook was murdered by John Barns: 'with her throat cut from ear to ear, her stomach cut down throughout like a sheep, and her bowels and heart taken out and put into a tub'. In 1717, Richard Davis was murdered by Richard Griffith: 'the deceased was found in a dunghill without a head'; the skull was subsequently recovered, 'picked clean to the very bone, which … might have been done by the hogs, which were in the field'. In 1726, Catherine Hays and her two lovers murdered her husband John, decapitated and dismembered the body and scattered his remains. The head was discovered and, so as to identify the victim, was displayed – first on a post in the street and then pickled in a jar; Mrs Hays was burnt at the stake for her pains. Even more suggestive was the celebrated case of James Hall who murdered his master, John Penny, in 1741. Hall crushed in Penny's skull. Then, to avoid staining his clothes, he stripped himself stark naked, drained Penny's blood into a chamber pot (filling the vessel five times) and threw the withered body into the privy or 'bog-house'.[21] A souvenir etching of the crime included a graphic frame of the bloodletting: Hall is positively vampiric, crouching naked in the candle-light over the prone body. He bears a diabolical expression, watching gleefully as the blood pours into the pot from a livid gash in his Penny's throat.[22] Ironically, though, in all these grisly cases it is the victim who, through the agency of the law, ultimately reaches back from beyond the grave to condemn the living murderer and consign them to execution; for the killers themselves there is no return from the dead.

These vampiric debates and depictions took place in a highly charged political atmosphere – nowhere more so than in Britain, which had weathered civil war and regicide, restoration and rebellion to lead the global economy through free enterprise and colonial exploitation. In the overpowering and incendiary context of British party politics, it was inevitable that the vampire too would be politicised. In the earliest full discussion of vampirism in Britain, Caleb D'Anvers introduced the case of Arnod Paole to a fashionable salon. D'Anvers describes how the case provoked a spirited debate between a fashionable lady and a doctor of physic, the lady pointing out the authenticating devices of the piece (names, dates and testimonies) to the sardonic doctor. D'Anvers is called on to adjudicate, and contextualises the Paole report by pointing out that in eastern Europe narratives are often allegorical:

> it deserves our Consideration that the States of *Hungary* are, at present, under the Subjection of the *Turks*, or the *Germans*, and govern'd by Them with a pretty hard Rein; which obliges Them to couch all their Complaints under *Types, Figures* and *Parables*. I believe you will make no Doubt that this Relation of the *Vampyres* is a Piece of that Kind, and contains a secret Satire upon the Administration of *those Countries*, when you consider the following Particulars.

D'Anvers (in reality Nicholas Amhurst, a satirist and political writer for the opposition) accordingly argues that '*sucking out all their Blood*' is a 'common Phrase for a *ravenous Minister* ... who preys upon human Gore, and fattens Himself upon the Vitals of his Country'; likewise, 'a *plundering Minister*' oppresses from beyond the grave through such practices as continued taxation, obliging remaining citizens to sell or mortgage their property and hence turning them into vampires too. D'Anvers' conclusion is – remarkably – to read vampirism figuratively. They are common across Europe, including Britain: 'In former Times, the *Gavestons, Spencers* and *De la Poles, Empson* and *Dudley, Wolsey, Buckingham* and an Hundred more were *Vampyres* of the first Magnitude, and spread their Cruelties far and wide through this Island'.[23] Thus he sees all sharpers, usurers, stockjobbers and other corrupt officials such as South-Sea Bubble projectors as vampiric.

The next year in an open letter to the Prime Minister Robert Walpole, the political pamphleteer Charles Forman depicted government tax revenue as a device 'to indulge the Luxury, and gratify the Rapine of a fat-gutted *Vampire*'.[24] Forman returned to the image in another open letter to Walpole (written in the same year but not published until 1741), seeing the country being bled by foreign companies, primarily the Dutch East India Company:

> Out Merchants, indeed, bring Money into their Country, but, it is said, there is another Set of Men amongst us who have as great an Address in sending it out again to foreign Countries without any Returns for it, which defeats the Industry of the Merchant. These are the *Vampires* of the Publick, and Riflers of the Kingdom.[25]

Although vampires became mordantly fashionable (by 1751 the Earl of Sandwich had a bay gelding racehorse called 'Vampire'), such emblematic uses were enthusiastically taken up by opportunists such as Voltaire, who observed:

> We never heard a word of vampires in London, nor even Paris. I confess that in both these cities there are stock-jobbers, brokers, and men of business, who sucked the blood of the people in broad daylight, but they were not dead.[26]

But the most influential political usage of vampirism (and indeed the Gothic more generally) is undoubtedly Karl Marx, who argued that capital is 'dead labour, that, vampire-like, only lives by sucking living labour'.[27] Marx does little more with the vampire than D'Anvers had done some 130 years previously, but the longevity of the metaphorical figure of the political vampire is striking. Not only does politics saturate *Dracula*, it has remained an abiding feature of portrayals of the vampire from their very first appearance in Britain to the present day.

The vampire was, then, already an established political trope before it appeared in literature. The first instance of the figure in English poetry is probably a passing reference in David Mallet's poem 'Zephir: or, The Stratagem' (1762), which is footnoted 'A certain mischievous demon that delights much in human blood; of whom there are many stories told in Hungary'.[28] By that time the vampire had already entered German poetry: Heinrich August Ossenfelder's poem '*Der Vampir*' appeared in 1748 and, most famously, Gottfried August Bürger's 'Lenore' was published in 1773 with a hugely influential English translation by William Taylor of Norwich appearing in the *Monthly Review* (1796). By then vampires had become a staple of travellers' tales of central and eastern Europe, particularly where local folklore could be connected to the ancient Scythian or 'Gothic' race – a lineage to which Van Helsing himself alludes to in *Dracula*: 'He have follow [*sic*] the wake of the berserker Icelander, the devil-begotten Hun, the Slav, the Saxon, the Magyar' (*D*, 222).

Unsurprisingly, then, British poets rapidly took up the character: Coleridge began 'Christabel' in 1798 and Southey *Thalaba the Destroyer* in 1799. Later works inspired by vampirism include Byron's 'The Giaour', and Keats's 'Lamia' and '*La Belle Dame Sans Merci*'. Elsewhere, Mary Shelley could not resist alluding to the creature in *Frankenstein* (1818) – 'my own vampire, my own spirit let loose from the grave, and forced to destroy all that was dear to me'.[29] Her novel was of course inspired on the same trip that led to Dr John Polidori writing the first fictional narrative of vampirism in English: *The Vampyre* was published in 1819. The vampire Lord Ruthven described by Polidori may not have been a Hungarian peasant, but he emerged from a highly specific phenomenon that had had its genesis in the tensions of international politics and regional identity, the militarisation of borders, the aspirations of medical science and the hybrid methods of rational theology.

The vampire has since of course become universalised – primarily through Stoker's *Dracula* – into a figure that questions the very being of what it is to be human. In its rapid (and anti-Darwinian) evolution the vampire combined fears and fantasies of consumption (refined into bloodsucking cannibalism and sexual deviancy), theological contradictions of the supernatural (especially in inverting communion and sanctity) and legal and philosophical problems in defining selfhood and authenticity (for example by challenging testimony and legitimacy). It evokes questions of sociopolitical governance (limitations of core-periphery models of internal colonialism), the exigencies of medical science (governing secular definitions of life and death, physical and psychological pathologies and the ethical and hygienic treatment of cadavers), and the articulation and exercise of domestic politics.

Among all this, the vampire retains its eerie allure. It is an incarnation of ancient Gothicism, which proved to be the nemesis of classical civilisation. The vampire confronts Enlightenment rationality and political ideology by confirming rather than questioning western prejudices against Serbia, Wallachia, Transylvania and their neighbours – places imagined as barbaric, baleful and unnatural. Though these territories have forcibly become European, they bring with them dire problems. The complexities of lands annexed from the East and the tangled lore and legend of alien and contested regions are generalised and exoticised into an uncanny realm of otherness that spawns an unholy threat. It is from this chaos, this whirlpool of berserkers and werewolves, witches and devils that the undead rose. So this threat came not from afar, not even from the Habsburg borders with the Ottoman Empire: it was already eastern Europe – already incorporated. The barbarians were no longer at the gate; they had already been compelled to cross the threshold into the West as vampires and, like the Goths of old, would swiftly become more sophisticated, more cultured and more refined. They would also become immeasurably more monstrous.

Notes

1 Claudian, *De Bello Gothico: The Gothic War*, trans. Maurice Platnauer, 2 vols. Loeb Classical Library (Cambridge: Harvard University Press, 1963), 2, 143.
2 Quoted by John Man, *Attila the Hun: A Barbarian King and the Fall of Rome* (London: Bantam, 2006), 144.
3 Jordanes, *The Gothic History*, trans. Charles Christopher Mierow (Princeton: Princeton University Press, 1915), 123.
4 Thomas Middleton, *A Tragi-Coomodie, Called The Witch; Long Since Acted by His Majesties Servants at the Black-Friers* (1778), 24.
5 James VI, *Daemonologie* (Edinburgh, 1597), vol. 3, as cited in *The Witchcraft Sourcebook*, ed. Brian P. Levack, 2nd edn. (London: Routledge, 2015), 160–61.
6 Quoted by Summers, *The Vampire in Europe* (1929; New York: University Books, 1968), 196.
7 Joseph Pitton de Tournefort, *A Voyage into the Levant: Perform'd by Command of the Late French King*, 2 vols. (London, 1718), 1, 103.
8 Klaus Hamberger, *Mortuus Non Mordet: Dokumente zum Vampirismus 1689–1791*, trans. Bräunlein and Emma Spary (Vienna: Turia and Kant, 1992), 9–10.
9 Dom Augustin Calmet, *Dissertations upon the Apparitions of Angels, Dæmons, and Ghosts, and Concerning the Vampires of Hungary, Bohemia, Moravia, and Silesia* (1759), 202. This has also been published in English as *The Phantom World: Concerning Apparitions and Vampires* (London: Wordsworth Editions, 2001). See Paul Barber, *Vampires, Burial and Death: Folklore and Reality* (New York: Yale University Press, 1988), 5–9, 15–20.
10 Letter of 13 Feb 1732 to the editor of *Commercium Litterarium*, quoted in Peter J. Bräunlein, 'The Frightening Borderlands of Enlightenment: The Vampire Problem', *Studies in History and Philosophy of Biological and Biomedical Sciences* 43, no. 3 (2012), 714.
11 Quoted by Montague Summers, *The Vampire: His Kith and Kin* (London: Kegan Paul, Trench, Trubner and Co., 1928), 1.
12 See Caleb D'Anvers [Nicholas Amhurst], 'Extract from a Private Letter from Vienna', *The Craftsman* 9, no. 307 (20 May 1732), 120.
13 'The Travels of Three English Gentlemen, from Venice to Hamburgh, being the Grand Tour of Germany, in the Year 1734', in *The Harleian Miscellany or, A Collection of Rare, Curious, and Entertaining Pamphlets and Tracts, as well in Manuscript as in Print, found in the late Earl of Oxford's Library*, 8 vols. (London, 1744–46), vol. 4, 348–59 and vol. 5, 321–45, with quotation from vol. 4, 358–59.
14 *The Gleaner* 9 (1733), quoted by Calmet, *Dissertations*, 213; John Bond, *Essay on the Incubus, or Night-Mare* (London, 1753), vi.
15 Bräunlein, 'Frightening Borderlands', 717.

16 Lorraine Daston, 'Marvelous Facts and Miraculous Evidence in Early Modern Europe', *Critical Inquiry* 18 (1991), 100.

17 Hamberger, *Mortuus Non Mordet*, 167.

18 Henry More, *An Antidote against Atheism or, An Appeal to the Naturall Faculties of the Minde of Man, Whether There Be Not a God*, 2nd edn. (London, 1655), 210.

19 Marie-Hélène Huet, 'Deadly Fears: Dom Augustin Calmet's Vampires and the Rule over Death', *Eighteenth-Century Life* 21, no. 2 (1997), 227.

20 Jean-Jacques Rousseau, *An Expostulatory Letter from J. J. Rousseau, Citizen of Geneva, to Christopher de Beaumont, Archbishop of Paris* (London, 1763), 56.

21 All sources in this paragraph come from *The Bloody Register*, 4 vols. (1764), ed. Nick Groom (London: Routledge/Thoemmes Press, 1999), vol. 1, 135; vol. 1, 343; vol. 3, 23; vol. 3, 190.

22 Anon, *James Hall Footman to John Penny of Clement's Inn* (British Library Manuscript, 1741), 1953, 0411.

23 D'Anvers, 'Extract from a Private Letter', 124 and 127.

24 Charles Forman, *A Second Letter to the Right Honourable Sir Robert Walpole* (London, 1733), 38.

25 Charles Forman, *Some Queries and Observations upon the Revolution in 1688, and Its Consequences: Also a Short View of the Rise and Progress of the Dutch East India Company; with Critical Remarks* (London: Olive Payne, 1741), 11n.

26 Voltaire, 'Philosophical Dictionary: Vampires', in *Works*, ed. Tobias Smollett (Paris: E. R. Du Mont, 1901), vol. 14, pp. 143–49.

27 Karl Marx, *Capital: A Critique of Political Economy*, vol. 1, trans. Ben Fowkes (1867; Harmondsworth: Penguin, 1976), 342.

28 David Mallet, *Poems on Several Occasions* (London: A. Miller, 1762), 54.

29 Mary Shelley, *Frankenstein or The Modern Prometheus: The 1818 Text*, ed. Marilyn Butler, rev. Nick Groom (Oxford: Oxford University Press, 2018), 57.

2

WILLIAM HUGHES

Dracula's Debts to the Gothic Romance

Biographers of Stoker have concurred about the lingering influence of the macabre stories related to the impressionable infant during his long period of childhood illness and convalescence. These unrecorded tales of ghosts, decomposing corpses and staked bodies captivated Stoker, no doubt, but their origins are folkloric, demotic and localised rather than literary. There is, however, concrete as well as anecdotal evidence that Stoker was familiar with the generic standards of the literary Gothic. Indeed, the author's mother – the primary source of these gruesome childhood entertainments, according to Stoker's biographers – provides the most explicit acknowledgement of a shared taste in, or at least familiarity with, canonical Gothic fiction. Writing on 20 July 1897, shortly after receiving a copy of *Dracula* from the author, Charlotte Stoker indulgently informs her son that

> no book since Mrs Shelley's *Frankenstein* or indeed any other at all has come near yours in originality, or terror ... Poe is nowhere. I have read much but I have never read a book like it at all in its terrible excitement.[1]

The extensive catalogue produced by Sotheby's for the public sale of Stoker's library on 7 July 1913 contains comparatively little of interest to those scholars attempting to comprehend the author's taste in supernatural fiction. The auctioneers, perhaps, deemed Stoker's collection of novels far less attractive to potential purchasers than the diverse volumes he had accumulated on topics of artistic, historical or political import. The author's own manuscripts, indeed, were catalogued with far less emphasis than some of the other properties summarily and rapidly disposed of by his widow. These treasures included manuscript letters and autographed presentation copies gifted, amongst others, by Walt Whitman, Mark Twain, Hall Caine, J. L. Toole, Winston Churchill and W. B. Yeats.[2]

A reading of the catalogued remnant of Stoker's once sizeable library – it was reduced when the author moved from Durham Place to St George's Square in London in 1910 – does betray a quantum of Gothic volumes that survived in the author's collection up until his death. Amongst these are an illustrated 1894 edition of *The Watcher and Other Weird Stories* (1894) by Sheridan Le Fanu – a posthumous anthology of the Dubliner's ghost stories which does *not*, however, include the 1872 vampire novella, 'Carmilla' – and Rudyard Kipling's 1904 collection *Traffics and Discoveries*, which contained the ghost story 'They' and the ambivalent mystery 'Mrs Bathurst'. Stoker also owned a folio copy of 'The Body Snatcher' by Robert Louis Stevenson, 'as it appeared in the *Pall Mall Gazette*, Jan. 31, 1895'. There were earlier works, including an 1813 edition of Robert Blair's 1743 Graveyard-School poem *The Grave*, illustrated by William Blake, an 1888 illustrated edition of Washington Irving's 1819 short story, *Rip Van Winkle* and a two-volume translation of Hoffman's *Weird Tales*. The early interface between Gothic and Romanticism was represented by a Victorian edition of *Frankenstein*, two volumes of poetry by Percy Shelley and a First Edition of Cantos 1–2 of Byron's *Childe Harold's Pilgrimage*. Two separate lots contained translations of the Faust narrative from the German and, addition to several Victorian studies of British and Irish folklore, Stoker also owned a copy of *Byways of Ghost Land* (1911) by Elliot O'Donnell, a prolific recorder of purportedly 'true' hauntings.

Though some of these named editions postdate the publication of *Dracula*, their presence is surely an index of the author's abiding interest in the Gothic. Their selective nature, though – their inclusion in the sale being determined by the auctioneer's economic eye rather than the former owner's aesthetic sensibilities – leaves open to speculation the potential extent of Stoker's interest in Gothic stylistics. Critics have long speculated regarding the generic archive upon which the author of *Dracula* drew when writing as well as researching that novel. Their speculations, though, have from the mid-1970s tended to suggest that the generic context of *Dracula* ought to rightly be located primarily in the relatively small corpus of vampire fictions within the nineteenth-century Gothic tradition. Whilst much of this consensus crystallises around the plausible connections between *Dracula* and 'Carmilla', the un-dead protagonists of other fictions have on occasions been implicated as more or less explicit ancestors of Stoker's Count. Robert Eighteen-Bisang and Elizabeth Miller frame *Dracula* as little more than a *bricolage* of scenes derived from other vampire narratives – Polidori's 'The Vampyre' (1819), Gautier's 'La Morte Amoureuse' (1836), Prest and Rymer's *Varney the Vampyre* (1847) and 'The Mysterious Stranger' (1853), an anonymous translation from the German published in *Chambers' Repository*.[3] The relationship between the Count and Harker follows a similar pattern to that of Polidori's vampiric Lord Ruthven and his associate Aubrey. The scene in which Harker cuts himself in Transylvania, inciting the

Count's bloodlust, is likewise associated with a corresponding incident in Gautier's work, whilst in *Varney the Vampyre* the staking of Clara could almost be a scene from *Dracula*. Again, with regard to the eponymous Gothic Hero of 'The Mysterious Stranger', the parallels with *Dracula* seem obvious.

One effect of such a stance is to atomise *Dracula*, imposing upon the novel an episodic and blood-focused structure which overshadows those crafted and protracted scenes that separate – and frame – the novel's sporadic and relatively short, bloody crises. It is this connective tissue that implicates *Dracula* not within the minor tradition of vampire fiction but with the much larger archive of the Gothic novel. The specific priority historically granted to vampire precedents in literary criticism, indeed, occludes the much greater influence of Gothic fictions *not* involved with the blood-sucking un-dead. *Dracula* is a Gothic novel, as much as it is a vampire novel. Its significant (and admittedly spectacular) scenes of blood transference and ritual disposal are joined together with generic insight and a consistent awareness of what the Gothic *is* as a genre.

Inevitably, given the paucity of explicit information on Stoker's know-ledge of earlier Gothic works beyond *Frankenstein* (1818), any attempt to develop a generic context for *Dracula* beyond vampire fiction will be neces-sarily speculative. Nonetheless, the content of *Dracula* may be taken as a plausible index to its own generic origins. Those origins are as intimate to the Gothic fictions of the eighteenth century as they are to those of the nineteenth. Indeed, certain aspects of Stoker's novel are decidedly not 'nine-teenth century up-to-date with a vengeance' (*D*, 37), to recall Harker's words about his record-keeping. After all, Harker goes on to remark that 'the old centuries had, and have, powers of their own which mere "modern-ity" cannot kill' (*D*, 37). In *Dracula*, the power, or influence, of the earlier Gothic coexists with its fin-de-siècle counterpart.

For all its avowed modernity, *Dracula* draws upon an eighteenth-century paradigm from the Gothic romance popularised by Ann Radcliffe in the 1790s. The connections between these two authors, whose best-known works are separated by almost exactly a century, are extensive. The very discourse of Gothic customarily deployed by Radcliffe, her mode of conveying her characters through space, time and moral development antici-pates much of what happens in Stoker's later fiction – most especially in its meticulous depiction of the journey made to Transylvania by Jonathan Harker, and the events which take place upon his arrival at Castle Dracula.

'The "Gothic" by definition is about history and geography', Robert Mighall argues.[4] In *Dracula*, the two are peculiarly intimate, for a journey in space is simultaneously one in time. Perversely, the journey undertaken by

Jonathan Harker to Transylvania inverts the predictable progress of linear time by plunging the traveller into an encounter with a cultural past reminiscent of the European milieux frequently found in the fiction of Ann Radcliffe and her contemporaries. The inefficient railways of Continental Europe give way, at Bistritz, to an even more primitive mode of public transport, the archaically named diligence, which carries the disorientated solicitor to his appointment with the Count's private calèche (*D*, 13). The diligence recalls those stagecoaches rendered obsolete in England by the coming of the railways. Its casual regard for timetables – the diligence's driver arrives early to avoid meeting the Count – facilitates the discharge of its passenger not at a scheduled halt or named inn but at the no-place and no-time that is the Borgo Pass. At this juncture, time – already thrown into confusion by the faulty schedules of Harker's journey from Munich – becomes hopelessly disrupted. Day and night, past and present, are curiously elided on the confused nocturnal coach journey, which seems to the weary traveller to cover the same ground and witness the same peculiar actions of the driver again and again. Once incarcerated in the castle, such is the progressive nature of Harker's temporal confusion that he neglects to wind his pocket-watch following the evening on which he is menaced by the Count's female consorts (*D*, 44). His own commitment to regulated time and punctuality is increasingly compromised by immersion in the eternal past-present of Transylvania.

Journeys across unfamiliar countryside, spanning the hours of daylight and darkness, under the control of horsemen who know the dangers of the route are a staple of eighteenth-century Gothic. Jonathan Harker is progressively feminised whilst resident at the Count's castle, where he writes letters in the persona of a retiring damsel. This process of feminisation, though, arguably begins much earlier than Simmons envisages. It is initiated during Harker's journey, where he experiences not merely a disorientation that parallels that of the abducted Gothic heroine, but much of her acute sensibility also. *Dracula*, in many respects, revives not merely the convention of powerless abduction but also the vigil of consciousness that characteristically accompanies it in earlier Gothic – the intensity of a gaze fixated upon sublime landscapes capable of offering up a pathetic fallacy to the elation or depression experienced by the perceiving, powerless self.

The narrative of Harker's journey playfully balances his preferred (though occasionally shaky) identity as a dedicated, competent, modern professional with a more naïve and curious selfhood that is frequently overawed by the novelty of his environment. If Harker is comically obsessive in his documentation of local peculiarities of cuisine and dress, he is less certain in his own personal comprehension both of an alien culture, the conventions of which he has to ascertain in imperfect English from his fellow travellers, and of a regional geography uncharted in word or image, for 'I was not able to light upon any map or work giving the exact locality of the Castle Dracula' (D, 5). Harker's journey to the arranged meeting point with the Count's calèche has an underlying sense of unease, the 'crowd of picturesque figures' (D, 10) at the inn make the sign of the cross as a protection against the evil eye. His observations of the daylight countryside between Bistritz and the Borgo Pass partake of all the recuperative sensibility characteristic of an abducted Radcliffean heroine carried away through unfamiliar terrain. Harker recalls:

> I lost sight and recollection of ghostly fears in the beauty of the scene as we drove along ... Before us lay a green sloping land full of forests and woods, with here and there steep hills, crowned with clumps of trees or with farm-houses, the blank gable end to the road. There was everywhere a bewildering mass of fruit blossom – apple, plum, pear, cherry; and as we drove by I could see the green grass under the trees spangled with the fallen petals. In and out amongst those green hills of what they call here the 'Mittel Land' ran the road, losing itself as it swept round the grassy curve, or was shut out by the straggling end of pine woods, which here and there ran down the hillside like tongues of flame.
> (D, 10)

Specifically, this vision of seasonal plenitude comforts the uncertain traveller. This is a convention of early Gothic and may be exemplified, for example, in Ann Radcliffe's *The Romance of the Forest* (1791), where a friendless heroine traverses an unfamiliar landscape in the company of unknown (though, at least, not hostile) travelling companions. Radcliffe's narrator notes how the spring landscape, with its budding trees, temporarily eclipses the heroine's earlier fears and revives her strength prior to its testing in the pathetic fallacy of a darker landscape of which she is, as yet, unaware:

> The fresh breeze of the morning animated the spirits of Adeline, whose mind was delicately sensible to the beauties of nature. As she viewed the flowery luxuriance of the turf, and the tender green of the trees, or caught, between the opening banks, a glimpse of the varied landscape, rich with wood, and fading into blue and distant mountains, her heart expanded in momentary joy.[5]

For both Adeline and Harker, 'the charms of external nature were heightened by those of novelty': the two likewise, as their respective novels progress, demonstrate 'that elastic energy, that resists calamity'.[6] In Harker's first-person account, it is as well also to acknowledge the influence, however oblique, of Edmund Burke's conception of beauty (rather than sublimity) in the manner in which the road is made to deviate captivatingly away from the brutality of the straight line, its bordering vegetation eschewing the 'dark and gloomy' in favour of a landscape both 'light and delicate'.[7]

It is the rather emphatically described pine woods that initiate a disruption of this pastoral lowland landscape in a way that is, again, strikingly reminiscent of Radcliffean stylistics. The dominant convention here is one of a transition to Burkean obscurity imbricated with arboreal wildness. Structurally, in Radcliffe's fiction and in *Dracula*, the aesthetically pleasing terrain of the familiar lowlands is characteristically succeeded by an ascent into a more rugged and terrific environment – the perception of which necessarily impacts upon the emotions of the traveller, and indeed accelerates the erosion of their already compromised sense of self-possession and self-determination. The ascent itself is frequently vertiginous – in Radcliffe's *The Italian* (1797), the heroine endures a 'road … carried high among the cliffs' that 'seemed as if suspended in air' – and the journey almost invariably embraces the richly symbolic chiaroscuro of a 'rocky defile' or 'shadowy pass'.[8] This geographical feature literally, as well as figuratively, obscures the beautiful and uplifting scenery of the mundane lowlands. A final contemplation of these latter, be it literal or figurative, is apt to concentrate the mind more upon what has been lost as much as upon what may lie ahead, as the narrator of Radcliffe's *The Mysteries of Udolpho* (1794) suggests through the heroine's parting vision of the panorama of the Italian Campagna bounded by the distant Adriatic:

> Emily gazed long on the splendours of the world she was quitting, of which the whole magnificence seemed thus given to her sight only to increase her regret on leaving it …
>
> From this sublime scene the travellers continued to ascend among the pines, till they entered a narrow pass of the mountains which shut out every feature of the distant country.[9]

After the pass has been entered there is no looking back, either at the land that has been left behind or to the emotions it has momentarily stirred. The pass is the gateway to the sublime and to a quite different empathy with the landscape. As Harker notes, as he enters the opening of the Borgo Pass, 'It seemed as though the mountain range had separated two atmospheres, and that now we had got into the thunderous one' (*D*, 12). Such places are far more than just spectacular scenery.

The pass, moreover, is intimate with the natural woodlands that surround it, and which serve to obscure the path behind and the way ahead as much as the overhanging rocks that fringe these hostile gorges and valleys. Unlike the blossom-bedecked fruit trees of the Mittel Land, the 'deep shades' and 'melancholy boughs' of a confining forest will likely lower the spirits at the contemplative hour of twilight.[10] Evergreen forests of pine and fir are, indeed, productive of a deeper and more richly symbolic gloom than deciduous greenery, as Harker himself notes after his own journey has passed from the fruitful lowlands to the wild, indigenous forest:

> As the evening fell it began to get very cold, and the growing twilight seemed to merge into one dark mistiness the gloom of the trees, oak, beech and pine, though in the valleys which ran deep between the spurs of the hills, as we ascended through the Pass, the dark firs stood out here and there against the background of late-lying snow. Sometimes, as the road was cut through the pine woods that seemed in the darkness to be closing down upon us, great masses of greyness, which here and there bestrewed the trees, produced a peculiarly weird and solemn effect, which carried on the thoughts and grim fancies engendered earlier in the evening. (D, 11)

Harker's reactions here resemble those of Radcliffe's abducted heroine, Emily, in *The Mysteries of Udolpho*. She, like Stoker's hero, ascends a road fringed by 'immense pine-forests' which 'excluded all view except of the cliffs aspiring above' other than where 'the dark woods allowed the eye a momentary glimpse of the country below'.[11] This is clearly a parallel to Harker's own momentary glimpse of light streaming through 'a cleft in the hills' (D, 12) at the inception of the Borgo Pass. Emily's reactions are characteristically shot through with exquisite sensibility:

> The gloom of these shades, their solitary silence, except when the breeze swept over their summits, the tremendous precipices of the mountains, that came partially to the eye, each assisted to raise the solemnity of Emily's feelings into awe; she saw only images of gloomy grandeur, or of dreadful sublimity, around her; other images, equally gloomy and equally terrible, gleamed on her imagination.[12]

For both travellers, the obscured pathways of the forest and the mountain pass fuel a sense of dread associated with the conclusion of the traveller's journey. In *The Mysteries of Udolpho* and *Dracula*, this destination is a castle (though it may, in Radcliffe's other fiction and that of her contemporaries be equally as likely a convent, an abbey, the retreat of kidnappers or the secret resort of banditti). The generic castle, though, is a further example of Stoker's deployment of eighteenth-century Gothic conventions in his fin-de-siècle Victorian fiction. As with the natural backdrops utilised by the author in *Dracula*, the castle is freighted likewise with the residual values of the eighteenth century, values that the author readily adapts to an age politically and socially estranged from the world of Radcliffe and her contemporaries.

The Gothic castle may be literally a haunted edifice, but its ominous potential is as much connected with the archaic cultural attitudes that it emblematises as with the dead beings that tenant its chambers. Horace Walpole's *The Castle of Otranto* (1764) initiated these protocols, and many of those who followed, such as Clara Reeve's *The Old English Baron* (1778), continued to insert eighteenth-century domestic preoccupations into the historical space of the castle. Similarly, Stoker imbues Victorian middle-class contemporaneity with a feudalism encoded in both the Count's residence and his aristocratic title.

Castle Dracula has the ambience of the battlements and ruins so familiar to the readers of those Gothic novels whose plots depicted events in the distant or near past. Like Radcliffe's eponymous Udolpho, Castle Dracula is approached from beneath, and the perceiver experiences a Burkean sense of awe regarding its ponderous size and a more sensible or emotional response to its ruined condition. Emily 'gazed with melancholy awe upon the castle' of Udolpho, comprehending 'the gothic greatness of its features, and its mouldering walls of dark grey stone, [that] rendered it a gloomy and sublime object'.[13] Harker, whose imperfect vision is further compromised by uneasy sleep, likewise perceives 'a vast ruined castle, from whose tall black windows came no ray of light, and whose broken battlements showed a jagged line against the moonlit sky' (*D*, 17). The shadowed vastness of the edifice is bound up with Burke's conviction 'That to make anything very terrible, obscurity seems in general to be necessary'.[14] Harker, showing unusual clarity of thought, notes on the day of his arrival that the castle 'perhaps seemed bigger than it really is', having 'not yet been able to see it by daylight' (*D*, 17). Those external details that are broken, jagged or worn speak of the sublime.

If the ruination of the edifice inspires melancholy, an emotion at times akin to nostalgia, then the actual meaning of castellated structures more forcefully complicates their place in Stoker's economy of the sublime. As a ruin, the castle is a survival from earlier times, and though its association with feudalism may be appropriate to the historical epochs of *The Old English Baron* (set in the fifteenth century) or *The Mysteries of Udolpho* (set in the sixteenth century), it is perceptively anachronistic in Stoker's romance of the contemporary. Even when structurally ruined, the power culturally invested in the castle remains as a residual emblem of absolutist power. Just as the abducted heroines of the eighteenth century find themselves at the mercy of their noble (or, on occasions, ecclesiastical) captors within the walls of these isolated bastions, so too does Harker come to realise that, for all his technological and legal knowledge, he has no power once he has crossed the cultural threshold that separates employment from serfdom. His submission is in part based upon deficient knowledge. As a newcomer to the Count's castle – like Emily in Udolpho – Harker is disempowered through ignorance of the internal configuration of his new residence. His maps, photographs and legal oversight of properties located far to the west have no significance here. The rooms into which he may enter are restricted, and even his right of egress to the outside world is suspended.

More than this, he is induced, through rhetoric, to become a participant in his own restricted existence, his desire being subsumed beneath the Count's own imperative. Harker recalls, having discovered for himself the castle's library of English publications, how he asked his host:

> if I might come into that room when I chose. He answered: 'Yes, certainly', and added: –
> 'You may go anywhere you wish in the castle, except where the doors are locked, where of course you will not wish to go'. (D, 23)

Effectively, on arrival all his relative power and status are annulled: what acknowledgement such things receive is granted only at the behest of the feudal overlord, just like Emily when incarcerated in Udolpho. Harker's earlier status has become a memory, a superficial fiction granted to him only whilst he remains useful to his captor. It does not take Harker long to perceive his place within this mutually sustained fiction: 'The castle is a veritable prison, and I am a prisoner!', he despairingly writes, having comprehended that there are 'doors, doors, doors everywhere, and all locked and bolted' (D, 28).

As Harker recognises, escape is possible only by way of the windows that lighten the interior of his prison. His interaction with these, though, places him for once in contradistinction to the abducted eighteenth-century heroines to which he is otherwise so easily compared. To these unfortunate women, the distant prospect of an open landscape observed from some lofty window customarily functions as some compensatory form of comfort for their confinement. Witness the emotional sensitivity of Ellena, imprisoned in a convent in Radcliffe's *The Italian*:

> She ascended the winding steps hastily, and found they led only to a door, opening into a small room, where nothing remarkable appeared, till she approached the windows, and beheld thence an horizon, and a landscape spread below, whose grandeur awakened all her heart. The consciousness of her prison was lost, while her eyes ranged over the wild and freely-sublime scene without.[15]

The landscape perceived by Ellena is sublime rather than pastoral, a succession of 'vast precipices of granite', 'broken into cliffs' that arouse in the imprisoned heroine 'a dreadful pleasure'.[16] Harker is presented with a simulacrum of the same vista from his own vantage:

> I went out on the stairs and found a room looking towards the south. The view was magnificent, and from where I stood there was every opportunity of seeing it. The castle is on the very edge of a terrible precipice. A stone falling from the window would fall a thousand feet without touching anything! As far as the eye can reach is a sea of green tree-tops with occasionally a deep rift where there is a chasm. Here and there are silver threads where the rivers wind in deep gorges through the forests. (*D*, 28)

The view neither sustains nor comforts Stoker's hapless hero, however. His consciousness of the castle's impenetrable locked doors leaves him 'not in the heart to describe beauty' (*D*, 28) – but in a state of passive despair.

This is the point at which Stoker's rhetoric departs from its hitherto fairly consistent adherence to Radcliffe. Though Radcliffe's heroines are prone to faint – as is the wont of the sensible heroine – they are resolute in their moral purpose, and constant in their self-belief. Adversity tests and stabilises their character. One might note here Ellena's immanent sensibility even under the stress of present abduction and an uncertain future in the hands of her male captors:

> her spirits being gradually revived and elevated by the grandeur of the images around her, she said to herself, 'If I am condemned to misery, surely I could endure it in more fortitude in scenes like these, than amid the tamer landscapes of nature! Here, the objects seem to impart somewhat of their own force, their own sublimity, to the soul. It is scarcely possible to yield to the pressure of misfortune while we walk, as with the Deity, amidst his most stupendous works!'[17]

Harker's departure from the Radcliffean paradigm reflects the Victorian heritage of Stoker's recension of Gothic stylistics. His resolve is of a quite different order to that of the eighteenth-century heroine, and is here engaged in a process of construction rather than affirmation. In a way, the difference is quite simply one of gender. Heroines *are* something from the outset, but heroes must *become* something. This is not unknown, certainly, in Radcliffean Gothic – Vincentio di Vivaldi overcomes his youthful impetuosity whilst incarcerated in the Inquisitorial prison of *The Italian* – but in these generic precursors to *Dracula*, it is not customary for the hero to be subjected to the same protracted and sublime journey of vision and emotion as the heroine. Harker, though a hero in the making, has followed the path usually associated with the abducted and resolute heroine, being displayed in a similarly emotional manner albeit without, for the most part, her certitude or fortitude.

Though he has often shared the heroine's emotional contemplation of aweful nature, and found himself subject to a magisterial power that is reflected in the proprietorship of a cyclopean edifice, he has seen himself 'deceived, like a baby, by my own fears' (D, 29), behaving more like a superstitious servant than a resolute heroine, and certainly not like a hero. Likewise, he has cried childish or womanly 'tears of bitter disappointment' (D, 49) at his inability to leave the castle at a time of his own choosing. That Harker subsequently garners sufficient self-control and self-belief to not merely visit the Count in his daytime grave but also to descend the sheer face of the castle walls, suggests that his essence is not that of the immanent quality associated with the Radcliffean heroine but more of the latent or developmental potential associated with a Victorian vision of masculinity. In Thomas Carlyle's conception in his influential *On Heroes, Hero-Worship and the Heroic in History* (1841), Harker must undertake another journey within his journey, one which tests him physically and mentally, in order for him to persist (to borrow his final words on leaving the castle) 'as a man' (D, 53).

Stoker, whose interests in the Victorian discourse of masculine vigour and health are well documented, wrote a number of heterosexual romances in which the hero is characteristically tested by extreme physical circumstances, and proves himself worthy in the defence of the woman he loves. In *Dracula*, Harker must cast off the submissive yoke of serfdom, think for himself, emulate his oppressor's freedom in exiting the castle, and prove himself a man fit to court his wife and, ready to defend her. Only through such a personal achievement can this ordinary man aspire to an independent status comparable to that enjoyed by the adventurous band of professionals and nobles who, at the time of Harker's incarceration, unknowingly waits to defend both western culture and womanhood from the coming invader, the vampire.

Dracula is thus far more than a vampire novel. It is written in the tradition of the early, as well as the contemporary Gothic, and balances the aesthetics of the eighteenth-century fin de siècle with the cultural demands of its Victorian counterpart. It is not, though, a passive participant in, or derivative of, that earlier phase of Gothic fiction. Rather, Stoker's novel deploys that standard so often associated with the Radcliffean heroine – the empathetic qualities and emotional self-scrutiny intimate to the isolated contemplation of sublime landscapes – in order to fabricate a hero who, in a later Victorian model, is not born but made, and made in adversity. That Stoker's novel contains many other recurrent components of the genre goes without saying, from the Gothic Hero that is the Count, through comical peasants and superstitious Roman Catholics, to more serious issues of sexual ownership. These elements are not pastiches, but answer their own respective purposes at the Victorian fin de siècle.

Stoker's mindfulness with regard to the appropriation and deployment of these standards of earlier Gothic is, however, a matter of debate rather than certainty. Nonetheless, note that the author followed *Dracula* some twelve years later with a further vampire narrative, *The Lady of the Shroud* (1909). This work – which is a pseudo-vampire novel, the heroine being mortal, a Balkan noble merely posing as a vampire out of political expediency – draws heavily, and in places ironically, upon the conventions of vampirism proposed in *Dracula*. Indeed, the hero, who – like Harker – has been a participant in his own developing masculinity, tabulates these, from her wearing a shroud, to crossing the threshold upon his invitation and disappearing hastily at cock-crow. If Stoker's playfulness here is perhaps indulgently self-referential, one small detail recalls the generic heritage that links *The Lady of the Shroud* not merely to *Dracula* but also to the tradition in which Ann Radcliffe and her contemporaries participated in the eighteenth century. It is not the hill-top castle, nor indeed the evergreen forests that encircle it. Nor is it the supposed presence of ghosts or vampires, or even the incense-scented Orthodox Christianity that here takes the place customarily reserved for Roman Catholic ceremonial in the Gothic novel. It is the small reference to the Italian port from which the hero's aeroplane is despatched across the Adriatic – the commercially insignificant harbour of Otranto, its adjoining commune the site of a castle whose name would surely be familiar to any reader of Gothic fiction, then or now.[18]

Notes

1 Quoted in Paul Murray, *From the Shadow of Dracula: A Life of Bram Stoker*, Revised Edition (Dublin: Fitzpress, 2016), 195.

2 *Catalogue of Valuable Books, Autograph Letters, and Illuminated and Other Manuscripts … The Property of Bram Stoker, Esq. (Deceased)*, reproduced in John Edgar Browning, ed., *The Forgotten Writings of Bram Stoker* (Basingstoke: Palgrave, 2012), 222–41.

3 'Appendix VI' in Robert Eighteen-Bisang and Elizabeth Miller, eds., *Bram Stoker's Notes for Dracula: A Facsimile Edition* (Jefferson, NC: McFarland, 2008), pp. 309–10.

4 Robert Mighall, *A Geography of Victorian Gothic Fiction: Mapping History's Nightmares* (Oxford: Oxford University Press, 1999), xiv.

5 Ann Radcliffe, *The Romance of the Forest*, ed. Chloe Chard (Oxford: Oxford University Press, 1986), 9, cf. 13.

6 Radcliffe, *The Romance of the Forest*, 9, original punctuation.

7 Edmund Burke, *A Philosophical Enquiry into Our Ideas of the Sublime and Beautiful*, ed. Adam Phillips (Oxford: Oxford University Press, 1998), Part 3, Section 27, 113.

8 Ann Radcliffe, *The Italian*, ed. Frederick Garber and E. J. Clery (Oxford: Oxford University Press, 2008), 62.

9 Ann Radcliffe, *The Mysteries of Udolpho*, ed. Bonamy Dobrée (Oxford: Oxford University Press, 1981), 225.

10 Radcliffe, *The Romance of the Forest*, 14.

11 Radcliffe, *The Mysteries of Udolpho*, 224.

12 Radcliffe, *The Mysteries of Udolpho*, 224.

13 Radcliffe, *The Mysteries of Udolpho*, 227.

14 Burke, *A Philosophical Enquiry*, Part 2, Section 3, 54.

15 Radcliffe, *The Italian*, 90.

16 Radcliffe, *The Italian*, 90. Emily perceives a similar 'scene of wild grandeur' from her casement at Udolpho, see Radcliffe, *The Mysteries of Udolpho*, 241.

17 Radcliffe, *The Italian*, 62–63.

18 Stoker, *The Lady of the Shroud*, ed. William Hughes (Westcliff-on-Sea: Desert Island Books, 2001), 292.

3

ALEXANDRA WARWICK

Dracula and the Late Victorian Gothic Revival

For an age that valued the new and the modern, the Victorian period is surprisingly undercut with forms and ideas of revival, survival and return. *Dracula* is no exception; in fact, with its juxtapositions of new technologies, New Women, ancient lineages and old superstitions, it could be seen as the epitome of such complex crossings of the old and the new. It is never quite clear on which side the novel, or Stoker, falls. While modern technologies like the railway, telegraph, shorthand, the phonograph and typewriter are part of the success of the struggle against Dracula, other contemporary developments, such as the New Woman, seem hardly celebrated and there is a persistent sense that 'progress' may be, at best, ambiguous. Trapped in Dracula's castle, Jonathan Harker sits to write his diary at a small table where he imagines 'some fair lady' once wrote her love-letters and is struck by the fact that he is writing in modern shorthand in his diary. It is, he says, 'nineteenth century up-to-date with a vengeance. And yet, unless my senses deceive me, the old centuries had, and have, powers of their own which mere "modernity" cannot kill' (*D*, 37).

This is the key question of *Dracula*: what are those powers, and what is their relation to 'modernity'? The publication of the novel in May 1897 coincided almost exactly with the grand spectacle of Queen Victoria's Diamond Jubilee in June, but it was only three years from the end of the century and four from the death of the Queen who gave the age its name. 'Victorian' indicates a peculiarly British perspective, and *Dracula* speaks of, and speaks to, the very 'Victorian' forms and currents of industrial capitalism, imperialism and intellectual and social change that preceded it.

In considering *Dracula* in 1897, perhaps the first question is whether there actually was a Gothic revival in the years between 1880 and 1900. There was certainly no conscious or deliberate revival of Gothic in literature and what is now rather broadly referred to as the late Victorian Gothic revival is to some considerable extent a retrospective identification of a group of texts from the perspective of a different fin de siècle: the end of the twentieth century rather than the nineteenth. On its publication, no reviewers of *Dracula* describe it as Gothic; it is most frequently called 'weird', 'uncanny', 'ghastly', 'gruesome', even 'a ghost-story'.[1] Nor are other texts, such as *The Strange Case of Dr Jekyll and Mr Hyde* (1886) or *The Picture of Dorian Gray* (1891) identified as Gothic at the time, by their authors or by critics; that labelling takes about another hundred years and the emergence of Gothic as a critical category during the late 1980s and early 1990s. There was a move then from the earlier studies that examine the eighteenth-century Gothic novel as an historically located and bounded phenomenon to a more trans-historical and psychological approach. This tended to focus on fear and cultural anxiety, widening the range of texts that are drawn into a 'Gothic' net.[2]

This is not to say that *Dracula* in 1897 was thought to be without precedent; its forebears are quickly recognised by reviewers. The *Daily Mail*, for example, noted that 'in seeking for a parallel to this weird, powerful, and horrorful story our mind reverts to such tales as "The Mysteries of Udolpho", "Frankenstein", "Wuthering Heights", "The Fall of the House of Usher" and "Marjery of Quether", thus picking out a neat lineage that spans a century from Ann Radcliffe's *Udolpho* in 1794 to Sabine Baring Gould's novella *Margery of Quether* in 1891.[3] *The Spectator* likewise puts Stoker in 'the domain of the horrible', noting his relationship to 'Sheridan Le Fanu, and all the other professors of the flesh-creeping school'.[4] The reviewers of the 1890s seem to suggest that a certain kind of 'horrid' novel had not died out at all during the Victorian age. The *Athenaeum* also saw *Dracula* as part of a widespread phenomenon:

> Stories and novels appear just now in plenty stamped with a more or less genuine air of belief in the visibility of supernatural agency. The strengthening of a bygone faith in the fantastical and magical view of things in lieu of the purely material is a feature of the hour.[5]

So while the particular designation of 'Gothic' may be in question, the fin de siècle does see a proliferation of 'flesh-creeping', 'fantastical' and magical narratives. From about 1880 to just past the turn of the century there are many that immediately appear to fit the description. Some of them, like Robert Louis Stevenson's *Strange Case of Dr Jekyll and Mr Hyde* (1886) or Oscar Wilde's *The Picture of Dorian Gray* (1891), remain well known. Others, like Arthur Machen's *The Great God Pan* (1894) and *The Three Impostors* (1895) were subsequently less famous. Richard Marsh's *The Beetle* is an interesting example of critical revival. It first appeared under a different title, *The Peril of Paul Lessingham: The Story of a Haunted Man*, as a serial over fifteen weeks from March to June 1897 in the penny magazine

Answers. Dracula came out in May, and Marsh's novel was published in a single volume with its new title in the autumn. Reviewers also described it as 'weird' and 'horrid', noting the relationship, and implying the competition, between the two: 'Mr Bram Stoker's effort of the imagination was not easy to beat, but Mr Marsh has, so to speak, out-Heroded Herod' and 'Dracula, by Mr Bram Stoker, was creepy, but Mr Marsh goes one, oh! many more than one better'. It sold very well for some decades, as much as *Dracula*, went out of print by the 1950s, and was brought back to life in the 1990s with the new interest in the fin de siècle.[6]

Beyond these cases there is a further list, not entirely of the flesh-creeping school but magical, supernatural and some way from domestic Realism. Marie Corelli's *The Sorrows of Satan* (1895) was the most successful of her many attempts to reconcile mysticism, mesmerism and Christianity. George MacDonald, who was already known for his Christian stories for children, published his last novel *Lilith*, a very strange mystical fantasy for adults, in 1895. There were other odd novels that were not necessarily typical of the rest of their authors' works, such as George Du Maurier's *Trilby* (1894) or Florence Marryat's *The Blood of the Vampire* (1897). The burgeoning British Empire provided rich settings for not-quite-realist fictions, most notably Henry Rider Haggard's adventure tales *King Solomon's Mines* (1885) and *She* (1886) and Rudyard Kipling's stories of strange occurrences in India like those in *The Phantom 'Rickshaw and other Eerie Tales* (1888). Entirely fictional states were also full of adventure and there were many 'Ruritanian' kingdoms after Anthony Hope's *The Prisoner of Zenda* (1894). The real world cut through by the fantastic also character-ises H. G. Wells's set of what he called 'scientific romances': *The Island of Dr Moreau* (1892), *The Time Machine* (1895), *The Invisible Man* (1897) and *The War of the Worlds* (1898). The latter draws strongly from the trend for invasion novels set slightly in the future that started with George Chesney's *The Battle of Dorking* (1871). William Le Queux produced many versions of invasions, including *The Great War in England in 1897* (1894) and a variety of other utopian and dystopian future Britains apppeared, like Richard Jeffries's *After London* (1885) and William Morris's *News From Nowhere* (1890).

Weirdness was not limited to novels; there were hundreds of short stories with curious subject matter, some published in collections, such as Vernon Lee's *Hauntings* (1890), Grant Allen's *Strange Stories* (1884), *Ivan Greet's Masterpiece* (1893) or M.P. Shiel's *Shapes in the Fire* (1896). There was a resurgence in ghost stories: Henry James published eighteen ghost tales between 1868 and 1908 but twelve were in the last decade of the nineteenth century. Detectives also prospered in the short story; Sherlock Holmes appeared first in the novella *A Study in Scarlet* (1887) and by 1900 had solved twenty-five more cases and died, only to be revived to tackle another thirty-four more after the turn of the century. Arthur Conan Doyle admired *Dracula*, but reviewers compared Stoker's novel far more frequently to Holmes's antecedents in Wilkie Collins's work, picking out the use of the forensic form of the diary or witness statement, but also the legacy of the sensation fiction of the 1860s and 1870s.

Print Culture

So while it was not necessarily a 'Gothic' revival, there was a proliferation of heterogeneous fiction that departed from what might be called domestic Realism. The explosion, in the 1890s especially, can be accounted for in part by the changing conditions of print culture and technology in the late nineteenth century. Middle-class Victorian reading was dominated by 'triple-deckers': novels published in three volumes. Each volume cost 10s 6d, so the complete work cost 31s. 6d – more than the weekly wage of a working person (a survey of poverty carried out by William Booth in the 1890s described 22 to 30 shillings per week as standard earnings). Availability and readership of the triple-decker increased with the establishment of subscription circulating libraries in the 1850s. Libraries became powerful forces because they would purchase many, sometimes hundreds, of copies of new works, so authors and publishers conformed to their demands, both in form and acceptable content.

Although the circulating library dominated middle-class reading, there was still a good deal of fiction that was not published in expensive volumes and the horrid sensations of the eighteenth-century Gothic flourished there. New developments in printing presses had enabled much more rapid printing and cheaper fiction was available in monthly or weekly part-publication; there were many very long-running instalment works. One of the most popular, George W. M. Reynolds's *The Mysteries of London*, started in 1842 and ran for 624 instalments over twelve years, selling as many as 250,000 penny copies a week. *Varney the Vampire* (started in 1845) and *The String of Pearls* (1846) introduced Sweeney Todd, the Demon Barber of Fleet Street. As a comparison, Dickens's novels came somewhere in between the triple-deckers and penny bloods: *Dombey and Son* was published between 1846 and 1848 in nineteen monthly issues costing a shilling each. The form also influenced the content as the narrative pace of instalment works tended to the dramatic at more regular intervals, and exaggerated crime and urban low-life provided more promising material than romantic or society subjects. 'Railway reading' emerged in mid-century as publishers tried to exploit the expanding market of train travellers with fiction and non-fiction volumes costing one or two shillings. It has been suggested that the experience of reading by train also had a profound effect on both narrative mode and content and that it directly contributed to the popularity of the sensation novel. Fiction often filtered through various forms; once a serial had been completed, it might be reprinted in a cheaper (usually six shillings) single volume edition and then again even more cheaply for the railway bookstalls for one or two shillings and later as little as sixpence.

The gradual removal of the so-called 'taxes on knowledge' between 1849 and 1869 – the taxes that were collected on newspapers and journals – coupled with further increased rapidity of printing technology, contributed to greater expansion and diversification of print culture and by the end of the century the changes were evident. In 1880, 380 new novels were published; in 1891 this had more than doubled to 896; in 1895 there were 1,315. The flourishing magazine and periodical market provided a venue for instalment publishing and the short story as well as reviews of fiction and publicity for new works. The publishing history of some of the fin de siècle fictions illustrates the market. The first edition of *Dr Jekyll and Mr Hyde* was only 140 pages long, cost a shilling and sold 40,000 copies in six months. *King Solomon's Mines*, costing 6s, sold 31,000 copies in six months; Haggard's next book *She* was serialised in the *Graphic* (at sixpence an issue). The *Graphic* positioned itself as a superior competitor to the very successful *Illustrated London News*, which was a penny cheaper, but still published writers like George Eliot, Hardy and Trollope. *Dracula* was first published in a single volume priced at six shillings, with a simultaneous edition for distribution in British colonies. A sixpenny edition, abridged by Stoker himself, was published in 1901. *Answers*, where *The Beetle* first appeared as a serial, was Alfred Harmsworth's first publishing venture, having been founded 1888 as a deliberate response to new reading publics and the huge success of *Tit-Bits*, a magazine that concentrated on stories of sensational human interest and that published, in instalments, Haggard's 'lost world' novel *The People of the Mist* (1893). Harmsworth went on to assemble a huge publishing corporation that included the *Daily Mail* (founded 1896). *The Beetle* also cost 6s on first volume publication. *The Time Machine* came out as an unfinished series of seven articles in the *National Observer* in 1894 then, with changes, in five instalments in the *New Review* and then with further changes in six-shilling volume form in Britain and America in 1895. *Dorian Gray* first appeared in the American *Lippincott's Magazine* in 1890 and then in a rewritten version as a single 6s volume in 1891.

Just these few examples show the late Victorian 'Gothic revival' as closely enmeshed in a frantic print culture that provided many different avenues for authors and that was both creating and responding to the public interest in the dramatic and sensational.

Realism *versus* Romance

Many magazines contained non-fiction essays and reviews too, and the proliferation of fiction coincides with a renewed debate about the form and function of the novel itself. The eighteenth-century Gothic novel appears very early in the history of the novel form and shares in the persistent uncertainty about what its proper purpose might be. In the eighteenth century, the debate circles the tensions between truth, instruction and delight and at the end of the nineteenth century it is re-articulated in an opposition between Realism and Romance. The terms are tricky, but in this debate 'Realism' rather means Naturalism (most frequently represented by the work of Émile Zola, or George Gissing in a British context) and 'Romance' tends to refer to more imaginatively expanded narratives of adventure or mystery. The poles were caricatured as 'serious' against 'escapist' writing, though the debate was more subtle and the parties on either side would have rejected such characterisation. The argument was also entangled in the personal friendships and professional rivalries of the intensely competitive literary world of the 1880s and 1890s and was further complicated by questions about the function of literary criticism as that too began to formalise as a more recognisably professional intellectual activity.

Through the 1880s the debate took shape. Grant Allen and Robert Louis Stevenson pitched in early: Allen with 'The Decay of Criticism' in the *Fortnightly Review* in March 1882; Stevenson's 'A Gossip on Romance' appeared in *Longman's Magazine* in November of the same year. Walter Besant's 'The Art of Fiction' appeared in May 1884 and both Henry James (in September) and Stevenson (in December) responded in *Longman's Magazine*. One of the most influential of late Victorian men of letters, Andrew Lang, weighed in with 'Realism and Romance' in the *Contemporary Review*, where he concludes:

> The dubitations of a Bostonian spinster may be made as interesting, by one genius, as a fight between a crocodile and a catawampus, by another genius. One may be as much excited in trying to discover whom a married American lady is really in love with, as by the search for the Fire of Immortality in the heart of Africa. But if there is to be no *modus vivendi*, if the battle between the

crocodile of Realism and the catawampus of Romance is to be fought out to the bitter end – why, in that Ragnarôk, I am on the side of the catawampus.[7]

The defence of his friend Haggard and the jibes at Henry James and William Dean Howells can be detected here, though Lang also contested the notion that Romance is 'only met with in Central Africa or on the Spanish Main'. Rather, Lang says is it 'that element which gives a sudden sense of the strangeness and the beauty of life; that power which has the gift of dreams'.[8] Lang didn't like *Dracula* however; he only read it when it came out as a sixpenny edition in 1901 and having 'inexpensively perused, and thrown away' the novel, concludes that 'the rules of vampiring, as indicated by Mr. Stoker, are too numerous and too elaborate', it is too 'butcherly' and missing the 'clash of honest steel'.[9] Clearly, it evoked the wrong kind of strangeness, or the wrong kind of dreams. Other writers like Vernon Lee, Thomas Hardy, Edmund Gosse and George Saintsbury, continued what James called the 'era of discussion' during the 1880s and 1890s, but for Howells, writing in 1912, it seemed that Realism had lost: 'the monstrous rag-baby of romanticism was as firmly in the saddle as it was before the joust began, and that it always will be, as long as the children of men are childish'.[10]

Modern Readers

As implied in Howell's remarks, much of the Realism and Romance debate is articulated as a concern for the reader and what he or she 'deserves'. Questions of class and gender are never far from the surface and show the consciousness of a new readership that had emerged after the Elementary Education Acts of 1870 and 1880. *Longman's*, for example, where Lang reigned for twenty years, addressed itself directly from its first appearance in 1882 to the new reading public. The cheaper price of Charles Longman's magazine (at sixpence it was half the price of other monthly journals) did not attract the literate working classes as hoped and, under pressure from contemporary social problems, the enthusiasm of *Longman's* and others was displaced onto a 'nostalgic, pastoralized populism'.[11] The Realism versus Romance debate was the last moment before the divisive differentiation of mass culture and modernism. The displacement of popular culture from the canon of English Literature as an emergent university discipline was also a crucial element in this response. Literature in an era of empire and war was increasingly expected to carry a heavy freight of nationalism, class, gender and the education of imperial subjects.[12] *Dracula* was published in this decisive phase of the estrangement of mass culture and 'Literature'.

The *Athenaeum's* lofty review suggests this: '*Dracula* is highly sensational, but it is wanting in the constructive art as well as in the higher literary sense ... Isolated scenes and touches are probably quite uncanny enough to please those for whom they are designed'.

Other reviews are critical, but they all seem to agree on a similar point. Lang's review remarks that 'A vampire with a cheque-book, a solicitor, and a balance at the bank, is not a plausible kind of creature'; the *Spectator* says that the 'up-to-dateness of the book – the phonograph diaries, typewriters and so on – hardly fits in with the medieval methods which ultimately secure the victory for Count Dracula's foes'. *The Stage* remarked:

> In surrounding his gruesome and fantastically supernatural root idea with a framework plainly matter-of-fact and purely of 19th Century structure, Mr Stoker has, we think, gone too far in the introduction of complicated details. As the book also contains much about hypnotism medically employed, semi-medieval philosophy, and applications of the latest information concerning the workings of the abnormal brain, it must be conned very carefully indeed if the reader wishes to grasp all the threads in the author's elaborately constructed argument.

The juxtaposition of the old and the new is clearly identified but is given as the weakness of the book rather than its strength. Another feels it is a deception:

> It is a bold attempt to concentrate the fables and superstitions which have existed in eastern Europe especially for many centuries into a shape sufficiently like reality to cheat the imagination of the nineteenth century.[13]

What makes the reviewers uneasy is making the flesh-creeping modern. Although one of the distinctive features of the late Victorian fantastic is the contemporary urban setting none of the other texts enact quite so explicitly the movement from the past to the present as *Dracula* does. The purpose of Jonathan's journey to Transylvania is to close the deal on the purchase of Carfax, the estate that he has selected for the Count. He takes with him photographs snapped with his portable Kodak camera of the old building 'of all periods back, I should say, to medieval times' (*D*, 25). Carfax, its name as Jonathan speculates, a corruption of an older French title, is the staging post for the Count's transport of boxes of earth from his crumbling feudal castle. From Carfax the boxes are spread across the social and geographic range of London from Piccadilly to Bethnal Green.

The medieval origin of Carfax is important, as is the fact that it has been built upon in subsequent periods. The vague 'medieval', which is also the term picked up by the reviewers, stood for a recognisable body of ideas by

1897, derived from the developments of antiquarianism through the course of the century. Antiquarianism in the eighteenth century was an eclectic practice of collection, most obvious in the legacy of the Grand Tour and the acquisitions by Grand Tourists of paintings, sculpture, vases and other objects that eventually formed the core of Victorian museums. Tourists collected mainly foreign items, especially Greek, Italian and Egyptian artefacts. Egyptian objects were especially productive of a type of 'museum gothic' in which antiquities wreak some terrible revenges. There was also a strain of British antiquarianism. This had an important literary base in the collections of ballads, songs and other early written and printed texts, and in 1765, almost simultaneously with Horace Walpole's *The Castle of Otranto*, Thomas Percy's influential collection *Reliques of Ancient English Poetry* was published. The architectural and the literary are pinned together from the first. Walpole's book arose from a dream of giant armour in the staircase of his extraordinary house: Strawberry Hill. The house was theatrically conceived, but it was very accurate to its sources, a product of meticulous antiquarianism, and was an important stage in what was actually called a Gothic Revival – in architecture and design.

Revival

The controversy of the Victorian 'Battle of the Styles' between the neoclassical and the Gothic is not about matters of taste, but about nationalism, politics and religion. We see here again the idiosyncrasy of the British (collapsed into English) position. Britain's medieval past is Catholic, but the radical break of the sixteenth century means that Catholicism was not, for most, a living present so much as a set of ruins or a persistent problem of rebellious populations. In the later seventeenth century, Gothic begins to be named as specifically English and characterised as a natural, untutored inventiveness that differs from the contained and learned classical form (as in, say, Richard Hurd's 1762 book, *Letters on Chivalry and Romance*). Manifest in the love of freedom that caused the English to resist the Roman imperial yoke, Gothic is also evident in its native poets: Spenser, Shakespeare and Milton.

The architectural Gothic Revival, as it gathered pace during the course of the nineteenth century was itself an increasingly explicit consideration of the place of the past in the present, not as an alien, disruptive force but a natural survival, and an endeavour to mobilise the power of past ages. For its passionate champions, like architect Augustus Pugin and writer John Ruskin, Gothic style carried a truth and in both there was a kind of magical thinking at work in which stone can embed and transmit values and principles that mere modernity cannot do without. Ruskin, in 'The Nature of Gothic' (1853), describes the Northern 'Gothic heart' as having 'strength of will, independence of character, resoluteness of purpose, impatience of undue control, and that general tendency to set the individual reason against authority, and the individual deed against destiny', in contrast with Southern 'languid submission of thought to tradition and purpose to fatality'.[14] England's spirit is free, individualistic and resistant to tyranny, unlike the lazy, superstitious and submissive character of the southern nations. In *Contrasts* (1836) and *An Apology for the Revival of Christian Architecture in England* (1843), Pugin argues for a return of medieval Gothic architecture and with it a return to the religious practices and social relations of the Middle Ages. He identifies 'revived Paganism' (by which he means the neo-classical) and 'Protestantism' as the 'two monsters' of the fifteenth century that had ravaged both the true faith of England and the social and material expression of it.[15] For Pugin and his followers, Gothic was English, and in England the use of any other style was a betrayal of national character. Pugin's triumph was the rebuilding of the Houses of Parliament. The medieval buildings had been spectacularly destroyed by fire in 1834 and Charles Barry and Pugin won the design competition. Both were dead before it was completed in 1860 but it is true Victorian Gothic: medieval detail over a skeleton of modern cast iron. It exposes too the split between conservatism and radicalism at the root of English Gothic. It is a space that holds together the 'traditions of feudal authority and the gothic liberty, in one British people are subjects whose rights are concessions; in the other fellow-citizens whose rights are inherent'.[16]

The force of this revival, though much of it departs from Pugin's own strict style, is such that it transforms the material landscape, mostly noticeably in the urban environment in churches as well as in landmarks like the Albert Memorial (designed by George Gilbert Scott, 1872) or Royal Courts of Justice (George Street, 1882). The style was exported to the empire, as in Mumbai's Victoria Station (Frederick Stevens, 1887). The 1880s, however, were the last stand of the Gothic Revival; by the 1890s the style was a leftover as the boom of industrial capitalism that had furnished both patronage and materials was entering one of its periodic crises. The end of the architectural revival coincides almost exactly with the explosion of the fantastic in literature. So when contemporary reviewers described *Dracula* as 'the revival of a medieval superstition' and 'the bold adaptation of the legend to such ordinary spheres of latter-day existence' they are noticing more than the set-dressing.[17]

For neither Pugin nor Ruskin is the Gothic empty or inert, it is a force acting upon the world. It is an invisible force that can be made material, but the material is more than just representation, it is the thing itself. This echoes the religious belief in transubstantiation, or real objective presence, where in the Eucharist the wine and wafer *become* the blood and body of Christ and do not simply symbolise it. It is one of the most finely detailed of theological arguments but variations of real objective presence do not only exist in Roman Catholic doctrine. Nineteenth-century church history is very complex, but the Roman Catholic Relief Act of 1829 had repealed much of the remaining disenfranchising legislation and there had also been, under the influence of the Evangelical Revival, a de-emphasising of the importance of liturgical practice such as the Eucharist in the Church of England. The Gothic Revival in architecture accompanied and often expressed (as it did in the building of Keble College, Oxford in 1870) the rise of the deeply controversial Oxford Movement in the Church of England and the schismatic formation of Anglo-Catholicism. The movement had a powerful influence that led to the reintroduction of many medieval practices in worship, principally in the communion.

In *Dracula* the assertion of real objective presence is clear, not only in emphasising the verb in Renfield's repeated assertion: 'the blood *is* the life', but in Seward's account of the confrontation with Dracula in the house in Piccadilly. 'Instinctively', he says, he thrusts the crucifix and wafer forward and 'felt a mighty power fly along my arm; and it was without surprise that I saw the monster cower back before a similar movement made spontaneously by each one of us' (*D*, 284). What matters here is not just the fact that the crucifix and wafer are not symbolic, but that the gestures made are 'instinctive', 'spontaneous' and the effects do not 'surprise': they are somehow natural survivals of true faith. Stoker, an Irishman, had been brought up in the Church of Ireland, and his treatment of religion in *Dracula* is an illustration of the tangle of religion and politics in Victorian Britain. By the 1890s questions of religious identity were deeply embedded in the anti-imperial struggle for Home Rule, but the problem was not so much one of doctrines as of politics. *Dracula*, in its assertion of tradition as radicalism returns to the tension between conservatism and free independence and some of the over-determinism of the text comes from that irreconcilable difference at the core of the English Gothic.

Survival

If Stoker tends to the conservative side, it is William Morris who asserts most strongly his claim to the other. As well as *News from Nowhere*, he wrote eight other fantasy romances between 1880 and his death in 1896, styled on medieval versions of northern sagas and expressing what Morris called 'one of the very few necessary and inevitable utterances of the century': Ruskin's 'Nature of Gothic', an essay that was deeply influential on a generation of socialists.[18] In Morris and other socialist writers, Ruskin's work is elaborated by readings of Karl Marx. Marx's political imaginary has often been proposed as Gothic, but it is interesting to note exactly where he employs his monstrous figures. Marx died in 1883, so the vampire that he would have been acquainted with would have been the peasant of superstition or the feudal aristocrat of popular culture. Although there are many discussions of feudalism in *Capital*, the vampire does not appear in them and Marx reserves his monsters for the nineteenth century. In the most famous analogy, 'capital is dead labour which, vampire-like, lives only by sucking living labour'.[19] As in the other invocations, the vampire is never the tyrannical aristocrat, nor indeed the bourgeois capitalist, but capital itself. This is arguably the first modern vampire, far beyond one that simply has a cheque book and a bank balance, the vampire is entirely disembodied as capital, the invisible phenomenon that constitutes all contemporary social relations. Marx's analysis of the commodity also draws its explanatory mechanisms from the same field as *Dracula*. In characterising the commodity as the new feature of the nineteenth century, Marx deploys references to spiritualism and the anthropological idea of fetish worship. This is more than just history weighing 'like a nightmare on the brains of the living' but the power of old centuries from much further back in the past.[20]

Anthropology had partly come from exposure to other cultures and the nexus of curiosity, taxonomical effort and the imposition of disciplinary regimes that fuelled many of the Victorian human and social sciences. It also has deep roots in the new consciousness of time that had arisen in the wake of geology and Darwinian biology. Where antiquarianism had sharpened a sense of history in relation to recorded time, the expansion of the notion of 'record' to the non-human stretched time far back to unimaginable distances. As phenomena like rock strata and fossils came to be seen as records of processes, 'pages of ancient history' as John Lubbock called them in *Pre-Historic Times* (1865) rather than natural occurrences without a past, the challenge became to read unwritten records, to give deep time a sequence, to investigate its contents and, increasingly, to establish the moment of the appearance of humanity and the nature of the strange world of human existence before words.

The full title of Lubbock's book was *Pre-Historic Times as Illustrated by Ancient Remains and the Manners and Customs of Modern Savages* and it clearly considers the place of the past in the present. In the section on 'Modern Savages' Lubbock counters the view that they are the degenerate remnants of previous Golden Ages, asserting instead that they have always been as they are: unchanged survivals of earlier times. Time is sequential but moving, as it were, at different speeds in different places; some parts of the globe, while apparently sharing a 'present', were in fact still in the past. Such 'survivals' become the focus of intense interest, not least because as Edward Tylor suggests in *Primitive Culture* (1871)

> superseded habits of old-world life may be modified into new-world forms still powerful for good and evil. Sometimes old thoughts and practices will burst out afresh, to the amazement of a world that thought them long since dead or dying; here survival passes into revival, as has lately happened in so remarkable a way in the history of modern spiritualism, a subject full of instruction from the ethnographer's point of view.[21]

Pre-historians and anthropologists were not a unified field, but it is possible to trace much of fin-de-siècle debate to the interchange of their ideas. Tylor's notion of the stages of development from primitive to savage to civilised was easily mapped elsewhere: the analogy of childhood, adolescence and adulthood worked neatly and with far-reaching consequences in the formation of new hierarchies of race and class in social and political thought. The first edition of J. G. Frazer's *The Golden Bough* was published in 1890. Its influence ensured that its Tylorian perspective was carried into the twentieth century, not least via the influence of writer Jessie L. Weston on T. S. Eliot's key poem *The Waste Land* (1922). The racialisation of class is apparent in more localised mapping. 1890 also saw the publication of William Booth's *In Darkest England and the Way Out*, which drew deliberately on the explorer Henry Morton Stanley's travelogue *In Darkest Africa* to locate the 'modern savages' in London's East End. Racist imperialism lies, too, behind some of the antipathy to the non-realist fiction of the fin de siècle. For its great champion Andrew Lang, Romance is sublimated anthropology, and the accusations of the childishness of the genres often fold rather neatly into the parallels established between children, the working class and savages, all of whom are credulous and gullible, made rational only with much effort, if at all, and constantly in danger of reverting to their 'natural' state and taking others with them.

Stoker repeats this thinking in Van Helsing's explanation of Dracula: 'In him the brain powers survived the physical death ... In some faculties of mind he has been, and is, only a child' (*D*, 280), his 'child-brain' has been 'learning new social life; new environment of old ways, the politic, the law, the finance, the science of a new land and a new people who have come to be since he was' (*D*, 298). It isn't just Dracula: the primitive survives in all the characters. Jonathan may have learned the 'mere modernity' of shorthand, but it is his *senses* that enable him to detect the powers of the 'old centuries'; the primitive part of Mina's brain allows telepathic connection; Lucy would embrace polygamous practices if she could. Stoker could well have summarised his novel as Tylor asserts: 'Progress, degradation, survival, revival, modification, are all modes of the connexion that binds together the complex network of civilization'.[22] *Dracula* is an intensely serious book, and far from it being an attempt to 'cheat the imagination of the nineteenth century' and simply make its flesh creep, what gives it its power and its seriousness, is that Stoker really is asking 'What if these things are true?' He does not treat the reader, as H. G. Wells said the writer of fantasy must, and 'trick him into an unwary concession to some plausible assumption and get on with his story while the illusion holds'; the narrative begins from believing those assumptions and the reader watches as the characters come to believe them too.[23] *Dracula* does not cheat the late-Victorian imagination but describes it.

So although there may not have been a late Victorian Gothic revival in literature, other revivals, survivals and novelties in the crucible of the fin de siècle serve to produce some very dense and enduring crystals of fictional figures. It isn't, however, a Gothic novel tradition that ensures the continued existence of those figures but two others of their companions in the last decade of the nineteenth century. In 1897, one of the first panning cameras filmed Victoria's Jubilee. The small audiences who watched the films of the 1890s swelled rapidly into thousands and millions and the early film-makers, seeking narratives, turned very quickly to the popular fiction of the fin de siècle. Alexander Butler directed *The Beetle* in 1919, having already filmed Conan Doyle's *The Valley of Fear* in 1916 and *The Sorrows of Satan* in 1917. *Trilby* was adapted twice, in 1914 and 1915; *Dorian Gray* six times between 1910 and 1918 and *Jekyll and Hyde* eight times between 1908 and 1920. The last of the 1920 versions of *Jekyll and Hyde* was an unauthorised one by F. W. Murnau, who changed the setting and names of the characters to avoid copyright infringement, just as he did with Stoker's text for *Nosferatu* in 1922.

And in the very last breath of the 1890s, December 1899, Sigmund Freud published an 'endeavour to elucidate the processes which underlie the strangeness and obscurity of dreams'.[24] *The Interpretation of Dreams* was no Victorian best-seller and it took eight years to shift its first edition of 600 copies, but its assertion of the ways in which fantasy has reality came to convince the twentieth century that monstrous rag-babies of many kinds were truths much stranger than fiction. It is in the modernity of the film screen and the analyst's couch that the vampire survives the twentieth century, ready to revive the Gothic in Britain in time for Queen Elizabeth's fin de siècle.

Notes

1 See, for example, *Daily Mail* (1 June 1897); *Bristol Times and Mirror* (8 June 1897); *Manchester Guardian* (15 June 1897); *Country Life* (19 June 1897); *Athenaeum* (26 June 1897); *Punch* (26 June 1897). See 'Contemporary Reviews of Bram Stoker's *Dracula*' collected on *Vampire over London* (blog), beladraculalugosi.wordpress.com.

2 For discussion of the trajectory of Gothic criticism see Chris Baldick and Robert Mighall, 'Gothic Criticism' in David Punter, ed., *A Companion to the Gothic* (Oxford: Blackwell, 2001), pp. 209–28.

3 Review, *Daily Mail* (1 June 1897).

4 Review, *Spectator* (31 July 1897).

5 Review, *Athenaeum* (26 June 1897).

6 Quotations cited from Minna Vuohelainen, 'Richard Marsh's *The Beetle* (1897): A Late Victorian Popular Novel', *Working with English: Medieval and Modern Language, Literature and Drama* 2 (1) (2006), 89–100, quote on p. 94.

7 Andrew Lang, 'Realism and Romance', *Contemporary Review* 52 (November 1887), 693.

8 Andrew Lang, 'Romance and the Reverse', *St. James's Gazette* (7 November 1888), 3.

9 Andrew Lang, 'At the Sign of the Ship', *Longman's Magazine* 38 (October 1901), 570–72.

10 *William Dean Howells, Criticism and Fiction*, eds. Clara and Rudolf Kirk (New York: New York University Press, 1952), 381.

11 Julia Reid. '"King Romance" in *Longman's Magazine*: Andrew Lang and Literary Populism', *Victorian Periodicals Review* 44 (4) (Winter 2011), 361.

12 See Chris Baldick, *The Social Mission of English Criticism 1848–1932* (Oxford: Oxford University Press, 1983).

13 Reviews from *Athenaeum* (26 June 1897); *Spectator* (31 July 1897); *The Stage* (17 June 1897); *Argus* (6 November, 1897).

14 John Ruskin, 'The Nature of Gothic', *The Stones of Venice* (Kent: George Allen, 1885), vol. 2, 205.

15 Augustus Pugin, *Contrasts* (Edinburgh: John Grant, 1898), iii.

16 Chris Brooks, *The Gothic Revival* (London: Phaidon, 1999), 219.

17 *Hampshire Advertiser* (5 June 1897).

18 William Morris, Preface, *The Nature of Gothic* (London: Kelmscott Press, 1892), i.

19 Karl Marx, *Capital: A Critique of Political Economy*, trans. Ben Fowkes (1867; Harmondsworth: Penguin, 1976), vol. 1, 342.

20 Karl Marx, *The Eighteenth Brumaire of Louis Napoleon* (Moscow: Progress Publishers 1937), 10.

21 E. B. Tylor, *Primitive Culture*, 2 vols. (London: John Murray, 1873), vol. 1, 16–17.

22 Tylor, *Primitive Culture*, vol. 1, 17.

23 H. G. Wells, *The Scientific Romances of H. G. Wells* (London: Victor Gollancz, 1933), ix.

24 Sigmund Freud, *The Interpretation of Dreams*, trans. James Strachey (London: Hogarth Press, 1953), 35.

PART II

Contexts

4

CHRISTINE FERGUSON

Dracula and the Occult

The role of the occult in *Dracula* is curiously ambiguous. On the one hand, the novel stands as a veritable compendium of occult beliefs, sciences and figures, riven through with allusions to alchemy, necromancy, lycanthropy, geomancy and the Eastern fakir practices that had become familiar to late Victorian audiences through the rise of comparative religious studies and the contemporary occult revival. In fact, so frequent are such references in the 1897 Gothic classic that Stoker's biographer Barbara Belford has suspected him of membership of the actual occult organisation, the Hermetic Order of the Golden Dawn, although no evidence for such an affiliation has ever been found.[1]

On the other hand, scholars have proved reluctant to read *Dracula*'s pervasive occult signs *as* occult, preferring instead to recognise its plot of vampiric menace and telepathic resistance as an extended allegory for a series of non-supernatural anxieties allegedly endemic to the fin-de-siècle cultural landscape: the fear of a renewed outbreak of the imperial insurgency; the production of bourgeois subjects; or the dangers of gender anarchy. As these examples demonstrate, the plight of the occult within cultural studies of *Dracula* is like that of religion generally, often interpreted as a symptom or pathology. This tactic of sublimation might well lead us to question whether *Dracula*, despite its heavy machinery of magical ritual, supernatural visitation and esoteric lore, should be considered an occult novel at all.

There are important reasons, however, why we should resist the temptation to allegorise away the novel's engagement with the occult. These have less to do with the issue of Stoker's possible membership in a magical society than with the novel's fascinating relationship to fin-de-siècle theories of vampirism and its complex meditation on esoteric or occult knowledge systems. To honour the non-allegorical ambitions of *Dracula*, we need to consider it as working directly with, rather than at a metaphorical remove from, the context of the late Victorian occult milieu. Such an approach allows us to recognise both its modernity and also the marked anachronism of Stoker's fiendish vampire-initiate in a period when occult believers of various types were attempting to transform popular understandings of vampirism and the esoteric wisdom that might defeat it.

Victorian Esotericism and the Occult Revival

Dracula appeared in print at a time when the occult revival that had been underway in Britain since the 1840s was reaching a new apogee. Incubated in the eighteenth-century heterodoxy of Emanuel Swedenborg and Richard Payne Knight, it emerged in full force with the advent of the modern spiritualist movement.[2] The revival encouraged its participants to seek out a hidden, spiritual world that lay beyond the confines of both scientific modernity and Church orthodoxy, one in which the dead continued to exist and communicate with the living, the future might be foretold through clairvoyance, and adepts could commune with elementals and enact their magical will on the world after an intense period of initiation.

The *exoteric* side of the revival included those practices that were accessible and non-exclusive, designed to appeal to as wide an audience as possible in a language or style that did not require specialised interpretation; the *esoteric* side, by contrast, comprised activities which were geared at restricted, uniquely prepared and sometimes secret audiences who studied texts whose production and circulation had been deliberately limited. To penetrate this realm, seekers adopted a myriad of new and established occult sciences such as palm reading, crystal gazing, alchemy, ritual magic and spirit mediumship, sometimes deploying these techniques within an exoteric spiritualist context open to everyone regardless of their social status or education, and at others within esoteric orders whose members required some level of training or attested spiritual purity.

The final decades of the nineteenth century witnessed an explosion of occult activity and institutionalisation in Britain and America, with the establishment of the Theosophical Society in New York in 1875 and, in London, of the Hermetic Society in 1884 and the Hermetic Order of the Golden Dawn in 1888. Linked to and catalysed by the revival were secular initiatives such as the Society for Psychical Research, founded in 1882 by a group of Cambridge intellectuals to investigate paranormal phenomena such as telepathy and haunting from a scientific point of view and seemingly with no pre-formed assumption as to the essential veracity or fraudulence of such manifestations.

These different currents of the revival can often be difficult to tease apart and their constituencies were by no means mutually exclusive, but we can nonetheless identify several characteristics that often if not always distinguished self-professed occultists in nineteenth-century Britain from casual séance attendees or psychical investigators. In addition to a belief in the existence of spiritual intermediaries and realms, these include a desire to reconcile rather than oppose science and religion, a rejection of Church orthodoxy, an openness to Eastern faith traditions, an emphasis on active spiritual self-development rather than passive doctrinal acceptance and a perennialist belief in an ancient wisdom tradition suppressed by religious authorities but preserved by initiates.[3] All of these have a presence in *Dracula*, but perhaps more important to the narrative than any discrete occult belief or practice is its adoption of the structure foundational to Western esotericism, namely its reliance on a dialectic of concealment and revelation in which the need for secrecy and initiatory control is balanced and given force through a countervailing urge towards revelation. *Dracula*, in other words, can be classified as a novel of the occult revival not only by virtue of the supernatural phenomena and ancient wisdom discourse it contains, but also in the ways it imagines the project of exposing and then re-concealing esoteric knowledge amongst a closed band of anti-vampiric initiates whose numbers will ultimately include the reader themself.

Dracula and Esotericism

The occult revival had a massive impact on British fiction at the fin de siècle, with many fictions (not only Gothic ones) featuring spectres, trance, possession, somnambulism and weird supernatural moments. This relationship was by no means unidirectional. Just as writers who, like Stoker, did not publicly affiliate themselves with occult belief laced their plots with esoteric tropes, so too did prominent occultists such as Helena Petrovna Blavatsky, Mabel Collins and Aleister Crowley produce Gothic novels and theatrical spectacles as a way of proselytising new audiences and inducing in them a sense of mystical awe. This pattern of reciprocal appropriation did not necessarily indicate a mutual endorsement. Indeed, *Dracula*'s occult plot can be read as religiously orthodox in ambition and effect, working to critique challenges to established Christianity, even as its mode of doing so ultimately retains the beliefs it seeks to suppress. Christopher Herbert has called *Dracula* 'very likely the most religiously saturated popular novel of its time', and argues that its true target is not atheism, but rather 'the alarming upsurge of superstition and black magic that is symbolized by the vampiric invasion of England'.[4] In enlisting the scholarly necromancer Dr Van Helsing as the vampire's central antagonist, however, the novel compounds the intermingling of religion and magic it opposes, reminding its readers of the primitive and fetishistic nature of Christianity itself. What returns in Stoker's sensational Gothic plot is thus, for Herbert, the occultic alterity that Western Christianity had extruded in order to shift its status from cult to religion.

Victorian occult believers would not necessarily have shared Herbert's equation of the supernatural with the primitive, and indeed this alliance flies in the face of Count Dracula's understated but significant backstory of occult initiation. While nineteenth-century spiritualists and occultists regularly collected and championed global superstitions as evidence of a universal spiritual reality, they saw themselves in these endeavours not as magical thinkers but as rational actors who were simply abstracting a logical conclusion from a wealth of evidence. In *The History of the Supernatural* (1863), for example, Quaker and spiritualist William Howitt claimed to have assembled 'a mass of evidence from every age and people ... so overwhelming' that its rejection would 'inevitably reduce all history to a gigantic fiction'.[5] To reject such testimonials, in other words, was to abrogate the possibility of ever knowing the past or trusting empirical data. Viewed from the inside, then, spiritualism and occultism looked not like erratic fantasies or relativistic indulgence but rather science-based faiths, albeit very different ones from what believers viewed as the soulless scientific naturalism of prominent professionals such as John Tyndall and T. H. Huxley.

This positioning of the occult as both scientific and to a certain extent mundane is reflected in the Count's scholastic route into vampirism, one that differs markedly from the aetiology of infection. Unlike Lucy or Mina, the Count has not been transformed by a bite, nor, as some contemporary occult theories of vampirism would have argued, by the iniquity of his character alone. This in fact conforms to occultist explanations of vampirism as the product of extreme moral transgression, as in the famous magical text by Eliphas Lévi, *Transcendental Magic* (first translated into English in 1896). Count Dracula enters the realm of the undead through his study of alchemy. In the first of two very fleeting discussions of the Count's genesis as a bloodsucker, Van Helsing explains that Dracula, like all of his race, was a student at the Scholomance, 'where the devil claims the tenth scholar as his due' (*D*, 224). Later, we learn that he has been a distinguished alchemist, a skill he presumably picked up at the notorious institution. Rather than deliberately setting out to make a pact with the devil then, Dracula has simply lost a statistical lottery in his quest to gain the knowledge that would allow him to maintain his imperial dominance over the Turks. This suppressed alchemical past is signposted in the novel in the piles of obsolete gold coins that litter Castle Dracula (*D*, 47) and which spill out like blood from his coat when he is stabbed (*D*, 284). As with the pitiful protagonist in

William Godwin's 1799 alchemical novel *St Leon*, Dracula's ability to transmute base metals into gold – and later, blood into immortal life force – has come with a heavy price, serving to alienate him irrevocably from the human community in which currency and knowledge have value.

If Dracula's proficiency in the occult sciences – and in alchemy in particular – seems redundant in Transylvania, it is perhaps because these skills, and his own vampirism, are not esoteric there. Transylvania is not yet sufficiently modern enough to conceal or discard such phenomena in a way that, as we later see in England, ultimately empowers the occult through suppression. When Harker arrives in Bistritz, it is immediately clear that everyone there knows who and what the Count is. The technique for his repulsion with the crucifix is common knowledge, successful even when, as critics routinely point out, the wielder has no faith in the talisman. In the coach to the Borgo Pass, a cacophony of voices warns Harker of '*ordog*', '*pokol*', '*stregoica*', '*vrolok*', and '*vlkoslak*' (*D*, 9). Their counsel falls on deaf ears not because the Englishman cannot understand the words – he is equipped with a dictionary – but because for him these terms only have metaphoric meaning. For the denizens of Transylvania, however, vampirism has never ceased to be a real fact of everyday life, no more unnatural than the dense green foliage that covers their mountain landscapes. Indeed, this physical environment and Dracula's undeath are inextricably linked, with Van Helsing suggesting that the Count's condition might owe as much to the 'strangeness of the geologic and chemical world' (*D*, 296) in the region as it does to his commerce with the black arts.

Little wonder, then, that Dracula seems to have had so little success in vampirising a region he has occupied for centuries, with the three vampire maidens being the only full converts in evidence. Vampirism is simply too exoteric a phenomenon to pose much threat. In transplanting it to England, Stoker's novel does not so much infect the rational West with an occult menace, but rather enacts a process of esotericisation in which something explicit and common becomes hidden through geographic shift, gaining the considerable benefits and cultural capital of secrecy as a result. Read in this light, *Dracula* becomes a central text of the literary occult revival in its enactment of the structuring processes which demarcate exoteric from esoteric knowledge and its simultaneous depiction of the ease with which these categories might morph into each other.

Occult Vampirism and Textual Initiation

In bringing the vampire to Britain, Stoker places him in a space in which he can become truly esoteric, hidden from the secularists and orthodox

Christian believers who will become his prey, and conquerable only through the occult lore contained in Van Helsing's library and the equally scientifically marginal technique of telepathy. Dracula is thus occulted by movement rather than by his own vampiric characteristics, ones that are, it is worth noting, significantly out of step with the new theories of vampirism being contemporarily pioneered by occult believers in Britain and on the continent. By the 1890s, occultists in and beyond the Theosophical Society, founded by Madame Blavatsky in the 1870s and very active in London, had largely relegated the folkloric figure of the blood-drinking vampire to the past, replacing it with two equally dangerous but less sanguinary alternatives: the psychic vampire, usually a mortal human who, wittingly or not, drains the life force of those around them, and the astral vampire, a disembodied entity on the spirit plane who possesses the corpses of the recently dead to effect a similar enervation.[6] Psychic vampirism forms the central plot focus of 1897's other major British vampire novel, Florence Marryat's *The Blood of the Vampire*, in which the hapless and emotionally impulsive protagonist Harriet Brandt kills herself after learning that her vampire constitution, inherited from her degraded mixed-race parents, brings death to everyone she loves. Marryat was a noted spiritualist, who had published the influential testimonials, *There Is No Death* (1891) and *The Spirit World* (1894). Her vampire is a tragic rather than demonic figure, and Brandt seems to derive from contemporary occultist treatises on social and sexual parasitism such as Paschal Beverley Randolph's *Eulis: The History of Love* (1874), which defines the vampire as 'a person born *love-hungry*, who [sic] have *none* themselves, who are empty of it, but who fascinate and literally suck others dry who *do* have love in their natures'.[7] The Christian arsenal of crucifixes, holy water and communion wafers held no danger to increasingly secular occult vampires such as Brandt whose aberration was not theological and whose threat was to the social nexus rather than the individual human soul.

While *Dracula* does not embrace the modernised discourses of occult vampirism that might have diminished its old school Gothic effects, it does however feature a mode of group identification via closed knowledge transmission that suggestively parallels the structures of initiation-based esoteric societies such as the Hermetic Order of the Golden Dawn.

The novel's narrative action brings together a group of almost-exclusively male vampire hunters united in their possession of a secret knowledge with which they cannot go public lest they be accused of insanity. Nicholas Daly has described this band as a reflection of the period's emergent culture of professionalism, designed to legitimate the culture of the expert rather than to replicate contemporary anxieties about imperial decline and degeneration.[8] The group represents a productive rather than a simply reactive or negative response to the fin-de-siècle milieu, but the professional status Daly claims for it seems more debatable. It is obvious that none of the vampire hunters make money or gain prestige from the activity about which they are sworn to secrecy. Nor does their experience allow them to institutionalise a form of discrete anti-vampiric professional knowledge that they might pass on to others. As Harker states in the closing note, '[w]e could hardly ask anyone, even did we wish to, to accept these ... proofs of so wild a story' (*D*, 351).

Rather than an exoteric professional one, then, the affiliative homosocial structure promoted in *Dracula* is instead, esoteric and secret, the goal of its secret society of vampire hunters as much about creating bonds of initiation between its members as expunging the vampire curse.[9] After all, the latter could have been achieved without the formation of a male fraternity. Speaking about the necessary exorcism rites for Lucy, Van Helsing tells Seward 'If I did simply follow my inclining, I would do now ... what is to be done ... to act now would be to take danger from her forever' (*D*, 188). Why wait, one wonders, if Lucy's soul could be saved with a solitary, furtive act? Van Helsing answers his own question by saying that the potential future need of a larger secret group, one whose members, like Arthur, will only believe if they have seen, outweighs the immediacy of Lucy's present suffering. The requirements of group identity here trump those of individual salvation, and Lucy's redemption is deferred, and even deliberately jeopardised, by Van Helsing's need to stage her staking as a piece of participatory ritual theatre in which Seward, Holmwood, and Morris are initiated into the secret knowledge of undeath already possessed by Jonathan Harker, and soon to be shared by Mina.

This is not the only place in the novel where the practical goal of vampire destruction is sidelined to the importance of fostering esoteric associative ties between characters. When Mina's vamping is belatedly discovered, the group reacts with ritual precision, dropping to their knees and joining hands as they pledge their mutual commitment to her purification. Should they fail, Harker writes, Mina 'shall not go into that unknown and terrible land alone. I suppose it is thus that in old times one vampire meant many' (*D*, 276). What strikes one immediately about this avowal is its redundancy. By this stage in the novel, a very efficient and relatively easy cure has already been established for vampirism, one that clearly restores the victim's soul despite the continued existence of the original parasite (Stoker's solution is still not so easy as that proposed by contemporary Theosophists such as Henry Steel Olcott and A. Osborne Eaves, both of whom claimed that vampirism would disappear with the mass uptake of cremation).[10] Were this not so, Lucy Westenra could not have recovered her 'unequalled sweetness and purity' (D, 202) after her staking. The men's ambition to follow, if need be, Mina into the land of the undead makes no sense at all if we believe the narrative goal is to eliminate vampirism and heal its sufferers. It only acquires a logic if the real impetus is to maintain the connections between Van Helsing's initiates at all costs, whether in the land of the living or the dead.

Even if not *au fait* with contemporary esoteric theory in its construction of the vampire, *Dracula* nonetheless comes to the fore as an occult text in its championship of initiatory bonds and the power of secrecy and, perhaps most of all, its self-presentation as a collection of arcane texts. *Dracula*'s authenticity, like that of the magical cipher manuscripts of the Hermetic Order of the Golden, cannot be verified. Proof of status is not in any case required for initiates who already know the truth. 'We want no proofs', concludes Harker, 'we ask none to believe us!' (D, 351). The narrative functions not only to eliminate the source of vampirism, but to provide a series of platforms from which Van Helsing as scholar-adept can teach occult truths wrapped in modern scientific language and ritually test his restricted band of initiates.

What triumphs is nothing less than the principle of esotericism itself, one fascinatingly, even paradoxically, endorsed through the accessible style and familiar popular genre trappings of the mass-market Gothic. The secrecy that Dracula seeks in England as a means of continuing and extending his reign amongst a more supernaturally-ignorant population is appropriated by his antagonists, who are simply better than him at transmitting and deploying covert knowledge.

In light of its endorsement of esoteric knowledge structures and textual strategies, it is not entirely surprising that at least one reader has argued for *Dracula* as a sacred occult text in itself. Referring to the novel as *The Book of Stoker*, Nöel Rarignac extolls *Dracula* as a work of 'high mysticism' that was not 'generated as a commodity, but as a prayer'.[11] We need not share Rarignac's bombastic effusion for the novel's spiritual qualities in order to recognise that *Dracula*'s occult purview and strategies are more than just metaphoric substitutes for mundane fin-de-siècle concerns, and well worthy of investigation in their own right as products of and responses to a period of unique activity and openness in the history of British esotericism. Future research on the novel's occult currents will help to shed light both on the literary reach of the occult revival, and on the complex relationship between literary Gothicism and esotericism more broadly.

Notes

1 Barbara Belford, *Bram Stoker and the Man Who Was Dracula* (Cambridge: Da Capo Press, 1996), 213.

2 For more on the pre-Victorian history of Britain's occult revival, see Joscelyn Godwin, *The Theosophical Enlightenment* (Albany: State University of New York Press, 1994).

3 Marco Pasi, 'Occult/Occultism', in Robert Segal and Kocku Stuckrad, eds., *Vocabulary for the Study of Religion* (Leiden: Brill, 2015).

4 Christopher Herbert, 'Vampire Religion', *Representations* 79 (2002), 100–27, quote on p. 101.

5 William Howitt, *The History of the Supernatural, In All Ages and Nations, and in All Churches, Christian and Pagan: Demonstrating a Universal Faith* (London: Longman, Green, Longman, Roberts, & Green, 1863), vi.

6 This evolution is discussed in Joseph Laycock, *Vampires Today: The Truth about Modern Vampirism* (London: Praeger, 2009). Laycock traces the origin of these two types to Eliphas Lévi's *Dogme et Rituel de la Haute Magie* (1856), 50–52.

7 Paschal Beverly Randolph, *Eulis: Affectional Alchemy; The History of Love: Its Wondrous Magic, Chemistry, Rules, Laws, Moods, Modes, and Rationale*, ed. R. Swinburne Clymer (Quakertown, PA: Confederation of Initiates, 1930), 87.

8 Nicholas Daly, *Modernism, Romance, and the Fin de Siècle: Popular Fiction and British Culture, 1880–1914* (Cambridge: Cambridge University Press, 1999), 36.

9 Katie Harse, '"Power of Combination": *Dracula* and the Secret Societies', in David Ketterer, ed., *Flashes of the Fantastic: Selected Essays from the Nineteenth International Conference on the Fantastic in the Arts* (London: Praeger, 2004), pp. 195–202.

10 H. S. Olcott, 'The Vampire', *The Theosophist* 12, no. 7 (April 1891), 386–93, quote on p. 385; A.Osborne Eaves, *Modern Vampirism: Its Dangers and How to Avoid Them* (Harrogate: The Talisman Publishing Co., 1904), 52.

11 Nöel Montague-Étienne Rarignac, *The Theology of Dracula: Reading the Book of Stoker as Sacred Text* (London: McFarland and Company, 2012), 117 and 154.

5

ROGER LUCKHURST

Dracula and Psychology

Sigmund Freud's psychoanalytic theory, first formulated as a distinct thera-peutics in the 1890s, has proved an irresistible mode of interpretation for readers of *Dracula*. Freud's basic theory of psychological disorders was to regard them as the result of the conflict of unbounded unconscious wishes and desires that are repressed by the more socially oriented conscious ego. The most intensive conflicts, Freud controversially suggested to his conserva-tive medical colleagues in fin-de-siècle Vienna, were around the sexual instincts. In the struggle of the pleasure principle to express its desires against the constraints of the reality principle, all manner of weird and disguised symptoms leak out, in disguised or distorted forms that marked the act of repression that they had undergone. Freud interpreted dreams, slips of the tongue and compulsive behaviours as enigmatic but meaningful markers of this conflict. He also unusually looked to classical myth, folklore and litera-ture for further support of his highly unorthodox libidinal theory.

Freud speculated (in the manner of a nineteenth-century anthropologist) that the superstitions of 'savages' about the dead returning as ghosts or spirits that must be placated by ritual had never really been superseded but were beliefs that remained coiled in the primitive recesses of the modern, rational mind. These beliefs flooded back when triggered at moments of extreme emotion. He read vengeful ghosts or demons as projections of repressed ambivalent feelings of love and hate for the recently dead.[1] Freud also raided Gothic literature for evidence, using Wilhelm Jensen's ghost story *Gradiva* to explore sexual neurosis or E. T. A. Hoffmann's 'The Sandman' for his formulation of the uncanny, that spooky feeling of the dead or inanimate returning to life.[2]

Although Freud was an avid reader of Rider Haggard's exotic romances, and particularly admired the undead, immortal *She*, there is no evidence that he read Stoker. Nevertheless his theory that psychic sexual development can be arrested around oral fixation, or that childhood fantasy mistakes sex as a violent act of animalistic biting or devouring, which he explored in his

'Three Essays on the Theory of Sexuality' (1905) and in his case history of the 'Wolf Man' (1918), lend themselves to a psychoanalytic reading of Stoker's blood-sucking vampire as a creature created by desire bent into allegorical shape by the force of psychic repression.

Freud's earliest and most ardent British follower, Ernest Jones, devoted a whole chapter to the vampire in his psychoanalytic study *On the Nightmare*, although this book relied on the anthropological collection of folklore and peasant superstition rather than cheap sensation fiction. Stoker was too lowly a source to even get into Jones's footnotes. Jones understood the vampire as an ambivalent figure of both guilt and angst of the living for the dead and a projection of limitless desire of the dead for the living, since 'a dead person who loves will love for ever and will never be weary of giving and receiving caresses'.[3] 'Love Never Dies' ran the strapline of Francis Ford Coppola's film version of *Dracula*, encapsulating this fantasy. From Stoker's novel, recall Jonathan Harker's paralysed ambivalence before the female vampires in the castle:

> I was afraid to raise my eyelids, but looked out and saw perfectly under the lashes. The fair girl went on her knees and bent over me, fairly gloating. There was a deliberate voluptuousness which was both thrilling and repulsive, and as she arched her neck she actually licked her lips like an animal.   (*D*, 39)

'Thrilling and repulsive' captures the supernatural vampire as a symbol of a compromise formation forged by the conflict between desire and its repression. In Freudian terms, Harker is broken not just by objective terror at the monster that imprisons him but also by the subjective conflicts that motor his neurotic reactions to the sexual advances of the vampires. This same ambivalence attaches to Lucy Westenra, the young beauty who chafes against social restraint and who is corrupted by her libidinal weakness to become another voluptuous vamp, all repression lifted from her insatiable, asocial desire. Her brutal staking in her coffin by her fiancée, surrounded by his band of brothers, is a barely disguised conflictual expression both of sexual longing and the very extermination of that longing. The female vampire, intertwining allure and repulsion, sex and death, was a privileged symbol in the fin de siècle, not just in literature but frequently figured in painting, too.

Freud stumbled towards his distinct psychodynamic theory of mind in the first decades of his career as a Viennese doctor, and only coined the term 'psychoanalysis' in 1896, around the same time that Stoker was completing *Dracula*. Freudian theories have come to dominate readings of *Dracula*, and still inflect contemporary feminist and queer theory readings, but it is a mistake to see psychoanalysis anywhere in the composition of the text *itself*. When one critic suggests that the novel 'draws liberally on psychoanalytic concepts' and that the medics in the book are 'psychoanalysts of a kind', this is not just inaccurate but obscures the recognition that *Dracula* is in fact generated from the very clash of distinct psychological paradigms at the end of the Victorian era, put into dramatic conflict by Stoker's Gothic plot.[4]

Dracula is a Gothic rendition of psychology on the cusp of shifting paradigms. It is full of hysteria, mental and physical collapse, trance, somnambulism and dream states, wasting illnesses that might be psychosomatic or the product of weak heredity, mania and madness and conditions that shade from the psychological into the supernatural. Stoker develops a driving narrative that stages drama from the debate between the paradigms of 1) psycho-physiological parallelism of body and mind, 2) degenerative theory, 3) emerging psychodynamic theories of mind, of which Freud's psychoanalysis was only one version and 4) the new science of psychical research that explored the border zone of the subliminal mind, seeing folkloric figures like the vampire as existing in a vanishing point between the natural and supernatural. Let's take these four different paradigms in order.

In *Dracula*, the asylum superintendent Dr Seward starts out as an orthodox representative of the dominant Victorian *psycho-physiological* paradigm, which regarded disorder of the mind as a result of a disease of the body. Seward is a mad-doctor, a dubious line of work considered little better than a gaoler until it was professionalised with the Lunacy Act of 1845 (a law reframed and extended again in 1890). A system of county asylums was built across England to house and treat the insane separately from prisoners or paupers, and the medical superintendents of asylums became *alienists*, supposedly authoritative experts in taxonomising and treating the 'alienated' mind.[5]

In the first half of the nineteenth century, alienists placed their hopes in the moral treatment of the mad, pioneered by Quaker reformists who refused to treat the insane as barely human but instead argued that moral persuasion could revive the lost will and redeem the soul of the patient and bring them back to reason and civility. The reader can see traces of this method in Seward's endless willingness to reason with his patient Renfield, his constant attempts to appeal to any remnants of rationality that survive beneath the manic behaviour. His confidence in objectively categorising this form of 'homicidal mania' is typical.

Therapeutic persuasion partly understood mental disorder as a loss of control of the will over bodily impulses, a disruption of psycho-physical balance. It was the role of the doctor to lend his own will to the patient for a time, effectively compelling them to return to health. This leant itself to sinister narratives of compulsion and control by mad-doctors, material for the Sensation Fiction boom of the 1860s, which often featured Gothicised

stories of wrongful committal by corrupt asylum doctors. Dr Seward is not
the locus of horror in *Dracula*: he is presented as an earnest, actually rather
repressed, professional man whose psychological approaches are destined to
be of limited effect because he is not at first able to grasp the genuine occult
forces at work around him.

By the 1850s, optimistic moral treatment was falling out of favour as the
numbers of the insane seemed to continue growing, and the rise of 'incur-
able' patients requiring permanent incarceration appeared inexorable. Alienists who hoped to legitimise their psychology as a science increasingly
propped their theories of mind on the authority of developmental biology
and the emergent science of neurology. Materialists suspected the speculative
and metaphysical methods of psychology and instead promised an empirical
investigation rooted in physiology. In this modern approach, 'mind' was
almost an accidental product of the physiology of the brain; consciousness
was considered epiphenomenal. As the prominent advocate of this position,
John Hughlings Jackson stated: 'psychical symptoms are to medical men
only signs of what is wrong in a material system'.[6] This is classic Victorian
reductionism of mind to body in the hope of finding objective ground for
scientific assertion.

Stoker, using knowledge gleaned from his brother, Sir Thornley Stoker, an
eminent brain physiologist, makes Seward an ambitious young materialist in
this mould. He names as his medical heroes thoroughgoing materialists, such
as the pioneering brain surgeons Sir John Burdon-Sanderson and Sir David
Ferrier (*D*, 69). Early on, the solution to Renfield seems to require only the
correct label (a monomania or zoophagous disorder), and Lucy's strange
dissociated states are symptoms that result from weak heredity or an unusual
kind of anaemia.

The psycho-physical parallel theory allowed some alienists to speak with
the authority that had accrued to evolutionary psychology after Charles
Darwin's epochal book *On the Origin of Species* in 1859. Darwin's framework allowed the chaos of insanity to be organised into a developmental
series, which arranged all organisms along a spectrum from the most simple
to the most complex biological forms. For the leading alienist in England,
Henry Maudsley, madness was a sliding down the evolutionary scale. When
mental illness struck, he argued in *Body and Will*, 'the moral feeling is the
first to show it, and it is the last to be restored when the disorder passes
away … In undoing a mental organisation nature begins by unravelling the
finest, most delicate, most intricately woven and last completed threads of
her marvellously complex network'.[7] Disintegrations of the ego were horri-
fying descents into man's animal inheritance: this is why Dr Jekyll comes to
be truly appalled by his bestial alter-ego Mr Hyde, and why the monstrous

Dracula is always associated with feral creatures, such as rats and wolves. Renfield again offers a lunatic's parody of developmentalism as he builds the chains of creatures he devours in his asylum cell, from flies to spiders to birds to cats.

The problem with this psycho-physical theory was that legitimacy came by the ceding of authority to the new biology. In the 1870s, there was a concerted effort by neurologists in Britain and America to dismiss the groundless speculations of the metaphysical claims of untrained alienists. The other, related effect was a turn from optimistic moral treatment to a far more pessimistic and deterministic understanding of madness. If madness inhered in the flaws of biology, there was little hope of cure and the chance of only marginal amelioration.

This shaded into a new paradigm, the theory of biological degeneration, a general account of cultural decline given the patina of scientific authority by a loose, metaphorical appropriation of Darwin's developmentalism. After years of being propounded by specialists in biology and psychology, degeneration became very influential in the 1890s when the German writer Max Nordau popularised it in his best-selling *Degeneration* (published in German in 1892 and in English in 1895). Nordau's book was a moral jeremiad against the cultural decadence and perceived onrushing collapse of civilisation rendered in pseudo-scientific terms. The evidence of the so-called Dusk of Nations was visible everywhere from modern art and literature to the epidemic of perversity and madness. Such a theory even allowed the Italian Cesare Lombroso to speak of born criminals and detect the predisposition to crime in physiognomy, which carried the stigmata of degenerate criminality. Lombroso promised a predictive science that could read crime in the shape of a skull or the size of the ears. This negative determinism crept into late-century alienism too. Maudsley ended *Body and Will* with the apocalyptic view that the increase in insanity was merely an early sign of something much more serious. 'Nations that have risen high in complexity of development', he said, 'will degenerate and be broken up, to have their places taken by less complex associations; they in turn will yield place to simpler and feebler unions of still more degraded beings'.[8]

Dracula picks up on the ambiguities of degenerationist theory. On the one hand, Stoker's novel is full of portents on the Dusk of Nations. It was published in the year of Queen Victoria's Diamond Jubilee in 1897, but installs the Count in a house on Piccadilly about as close to Buckingham Palace as it is possible to get, a canker at the heart of empire. The defenders of the British state seem weak or subject to bouts of debilitating hysteria. Harker's early collapse, from which he never really recovers, is followed by virtually all of the men suffering fits of hysteria at key moments of the plot.

Lucy Westenra is portrayed with a hereditary predisposition that dooms her from the start. With 'too supersensitive a nature' she 'feels the influences more acutely than other people do' (*D*, 87). Her mother dies of a weak heart, and Lucy's disorderly desire for three men and her spontaneous sleepwalking indicate a possibly hereditary psychic morbidity that makes her susceptible to vampirism. Her undead nymphomania (another medical coinage of the era that invented an abnormal sexual pathology in women), and her awful inversion of the maternal instinct in supping on the blood of children, are markers of an accelerating degeneracy. The doom of English womanhood was much feared by conservative thinkers in the 1890s.

On the other hand, it is Dracula's degenerate weaknesses that eventually allow the Christian band to rally their meagre resources and defeat the vampire. Dracula is praised early on for having a 'mighty brain' (*D*, 224), but in the last phase of the book he is pushed out of England and into headlong flight because, as Mina Harker defines him, 'the Count is a criminal and of the criminal type. Nordau and Lombroso would so classify him, and *qua* criminal he is of imperfectly formed mind' (*D*, 317). The close of the novel alters the capacities of the Count to ensure the conclusion is a rousing, restorative tonic against degenerative accounts of inevitable decline and fall.

Even so, *Dracula* exposes the fatal limits of Dr Seward's Victorian maddoctoring paradigms. He never successfully diagnoses or treats Renfield, and indeed breaks the law to falsify his patient's death as an 'accident' on the death certificate. He cannot save his beloved Lucy either, because he is constrained by the exercise of 'normal science', unable to see beyond established psycho-physical, reductionist conventions.

In contrast, his mentor Professor Van Helsing moves quickly outside these limited frameworks, recognising that the data presented compel conclusions that break the bonds of 'normal science' and demands the recognition of 'extraordinary' propositions.[9] Van Helsing does not simply trump the natural with the supernatural, though. Instead, he points to emergent psychological theories that at the time were investigating how the boundary between the natural and the supernatural might be redefined. Arriving from the European mainland, Van Helsing brings with him new psychodynamic paradigms that astonished and troubled so many in the 1890s.

Professor Van Helsing is heterodox in both his medical and psychological practice. He is far beyond the cutting edge of experimental medicine, for his use of multiple blood transfusions on the ailing Lucy is extremely risky in an era before blood groups had been identified (only fatal blood clotting or renal failure would have been expected by his medical contemporaries). Yet at the same time, he also seems to give credence to ancient superstitious beliefs and marginal folk remedies, such as the use of garlic flowers. He reads the wrong kind of books to be a proper materialist and is ominously called 'a philosopher and a metaphysician' by Seward (D, 106).

Van Helsing's interest in hypnotism is ancient and modern, outdated yet ahead of the materialist curve. After his medical treatment of Lucy, he offers more psychological solutions for Mina, once she has been contaminated by the Count. Van Helsing uses passes of his hands over Mina's face to put her into a trance state, using the discredited methods of the eighteenth-century Franz Anton Mesmer, repeatedly denounced as a fraudster, who in the 1780s claimed to be able to cure patients by sending them into a dissociated state of consciousness with these passes and then topping up their depleted reserves of energy with an invisible transfer of what he named animal magnetism. After Van Helsing hypnotises Mina, *Dracula* then enters a strange phase in which Mina's hypnotic *rapport*, her psychic connection to Dracula, means that she can be put into an artificial trance state at dawn and dusk to gain clues about the Count's location. They soon realise that this peculiar 'dial up' of Dracula is dangerous, since vampires have demonstrated their own powers of Mesmeric control: Harker in the Castle recalls wonderingly 'I was being hypnotized!' (D, 44), Lucy is compelled into sleepwalking states that makes her highly suggestible to Dracula and on fateful night of her death the whole household is found in artificial slumber. Renfield has also proved, too late for the literal-minded Seward to understand, to have been remotely controlled by Dracula. The novel might seem to enter the supernatural realm with this exploration of occult *rapport* and yet Stoker was only following the furious contemporary argument amongst psychologists over the status of hypnotic phenomena.

In France, from the mid-1870s, a new generation of psychologists returned to Mesmer's treatments, but dispensed with the theory of a physical transfer of some kind of magnetic fluid between doctor and patient. Instead, they revived James Braid's forgotten idea of 'nervous sleep' or 'hypnosis', first coined in 1841. Braid was a medic who verified the artificial inducement of trance as an objective physiological phenomenon, yet this area was so bound up with sensational claims and accusations of fraud that his work was ignored. However, a provincial French medic, Eugène Azam, published in 1875 a sober yet incredible account of his use of hypnosis on a hysterical patient known as Félida X. He found that Félida's personality was transformed if put into a trance, something he had demonstrated not once but over decades, prompting him to propose that she had a double or 'alternating' personality. Fascinatingly, patients like Félida and others who soon became celebrated case histories, seemed to have different memory chains attached to each state.

These explorations led to the emergence of new psychodynamic theories of mental disorder. In this model, hysteria was not necessarily the by-product of organic disease or hereditary weakness but a disorder of autonomous psychic processes, a dissociation of memory. These sciences of memory were explored in France experimentally through the use of hypnosis, and the leading neurological authority of the day, Jean-Martin Charcot, declared that hypnosis had been proven an objective physiological fact in 1882.[10]

Controversy flared over the next ten years, for the idea that alternating or multiple states of consciousness could co-exist was nonsensical to the dominant psycho-physical paradigm. Treatment of the mad was about unifying and reinforcing the moral will, not fracturing it or wilfully suspending it. In the 1890s, the editor of the *British Medical Journal* Ernest Hart denounced the dangers of hypnotism, aiming to debunk 'a prevalent system of imposture'.[11] Yet when Joseph Breuer and his colleague Sigmund Freud published 'On the Psychical Mechanism of Hysterical Phenomena' in 1893, they argued that the symptoms of hysteria (the paralyses, altered behaviours and mental dissociations) were not the result of physical disorders but had largely psychical origins. Famously, they concluded: '*Hysterics suffer mainly from reminiscences*'.[12] This was a quintessentially psychodynamic statement.

If Freud claimed to abandon hypnosis shortly afterwards to create 'psychoanalysis', this was partly to distinguish his own work from rival theories, but also because hypnosis never quite escaped its associations with the weird or supernatural. From the very earliest demonstrations of Mesmerism, it was claimed that the *rapport* was uncanny, with doctors and patients able to read each other's minds, or establish mental connections that could operate over vast distances. A fear of one will dominating another (and particularly of male doctors controlling submissive female patients) was the alarm that caused the suppression of Mesmerism in pre-Revolutionary France in the 1780s.

In the return of Mesmeric states as hypnotic trance, these associations recurred. Just a few years before *Dracula* was published, the literary sensation was George du Maurier's novel *Trilby* (1893), which introduced the menacing foreign Jewish impresario Svengali, who exerts Mesmeric control over the young English rose, Trilby. Count Dracula's power over Lucy (and Renfield and others) is a direct echo of this fear. Stoker was not picking up casually on this trope: he later included a study of Franz Mesmer in his book *Famous Impostors* (1910).

Dracula shows Stoker well versed in the uncanny aspects of hypnosis that were amplified in the emergent science of psychical research. This fourth psychological paradigm was promoted by the Society of Psychical Research (SPR), founded in London in 1882 by a group of eminent gentlemen to explore supernatural phenomena such as haunted houses, Mesmeric treatments and the spirits allegedly called up by mediums at séances. Although the SPR adopted the tone of disinterested science, they hoped to prove the objective existence of these phenomena, and thus naturalise the supernatural. They invented a whole new quasi-scientific terminology that often overlapped with psychodynamic psychology. Ghosts became crisis apparitions; mind-reading became telepathy. Hypnotic phenomena were also key sources of evidence for the society, and in fact the acceptance in England of this aspect of Continental psychodynamic theories of mind was largely down to the work of two key psychical researchers, Edmund Gurney and Frederick Myers, acknowledged pioneers in this field.

The shading of new psychodynamic theories into the supernatural is exactly where Van Helsing hopes to lead his dutiful but dull student Dr Seward. Seward latches on to a reference the professor makes to the neurologist Jean-Martin Charcot – a man of science in this swirl of superstition. Van Helsing then argues, in his execrable English: 'Then tell me – for I am a student of the brain – how you accept the hypnotism and reject the thought-reading' (D, 178–79). Here is exactly the vanishing point, hovering between the natural and the supernatural, in the hyphen of the psychophysical, from which Stoker produces his shivery effects on his readers, as Dracula emerges from the shadowy margins of the driest psychology textbooks, a creature created in the transitions in the late Victorian paradigms of psychology.

Notes

1 See Sigmund Freud, *Totem and Taboo* (1913), particularly pp. 59–67 in the *Standard Edition of the Complete Psychological Works of Sigmund Freud*, vol. 13 (London: Hogarth, 1955).
2 Sigmund Freud, 'Delusion and Dream in Jensen's Gradiva' (1907) and 'The Uncanny' (1919), both collected in the Penguin Freud Library, vol. 14, *Art and Literature* (Harmondsworth: Penguin, 1990).
3 Ernest Jones, *On the Nightmare* (New York: Liveright, 1950), 110.
4 Ken Gelder, *Reading the Vampire* (London: Routledge, 1994), 66.
5 Andrew Scull, *Madness in Civilization: A Cultural History of Insanity, from the Bible to Freud, from the Madhouse to Modern Medicine.* (Princeton: Princeton University Press, 2015).
6 John Hughlings Jackson cited in Michael J. Clark, 'The Rejection of Psychological Approaches to Mental Disorder in Late Nineteenth-Century British Psychiatry', in Andrew Scull, ed., *Madhouses, Mad-Doctors and Madmen: The Social History of Psychiatry in the Victorian Era* (London: Athlone, 1981), p. 283.
7 Henry Maudsley, *Body and Will, Being an Essay Concerning Will in Its Metaphysical, Physiological and Pathological Aspects* (London: Kegan Paul, 1883), 266.
8 Maudsley, *Body and Will*, 320.

9 The breach of paradigms of 'normal science' in phases of 'extraordinary science' is the proposed in Thomas Kuhn, *The Structure of Scientific Revolutions* (Chicago: Chicago University Press, 1970).

10 Ian Hacking, *Rewriting the Soul: Multiple Personality and the Sciences of Memory* (Princeton: Princeton University Press, 1995).

11 Ernest Hart, *Hypnotism, Mesmerism and the New Witchcraft* (1896; New York: Da Capo Reprint, 1982), viii.

12 Sigmund Freud and Joseph Breuer, *Studies in Hysteria* (Harmondsworth: Penguin, 1986), 58.

6

HEIKE BAUER

Dracula and Sexology

Queer Gothic, Straight-Up

Bram Stoker's *Dracula* was published at that moment in time when the modern concept of sexuality started to gain traction in scientific, cultural and political debates. A 'correlative', in Michel Foucault's well-known phrase, to the formation of the *scientia sexualis*, the notion of sexuality emerged out of political and cultural efforts for the decriminalisation and affirmation of same-sex sexuality. Related scientific and legal practices also sought to identify perceived transgressions from an implicit reproductive norm.[1]

The *scientia sexualis*, more commonly known as sexology or sexual science, was a new field of research that developed out of nineteenth-century medical sciences and related forensic work. Initially dominated by the work of psychiatrists and other medical doctors as well as criminologists, it was concerned with studying all aspects of 'sex', which in this context was primarily understood as sexual behaviour. Broadly speaking, the early sexologists aimed to establish whether certain sexual acts were the products of illness or criminal intention, a distinction that mattered when trying to establish if a person had broken the law or needed medical treatment. But sexuality was not merely the product of the clinic and the courtroom. Sexual debates including within sexology were shaped from the outset by the contributions of writers, poets, philosophers and literary and cultural critics who presented imaginative evidence of the long history of same-sex desire and its naturalness, coining a new vocabulary that included terms such as inversion, contrary sexual feelings, and, most lastingly, homosexuality.[2]

Fiction in turn served as a kind of sourcebook for some of the medical sexologists who were inspired by literary narratives to conceptualise phenomena such as sadism and masochism, both terms coined by the influential psychiatrist Richard von Krafft-Ebing and derived from the works of the Marquis de Sade and Leopold von Sacher-Masoch respectively. There are many influences between sexology and literature, especially in relation to the constructions of sexual deviancies and the formation of affirmative same-sex discourses and counter-discourses. Literature is key to the genealogies of certain sexual concepts and their relationship to the lives of nineteenth-century subjects, fictional and real.

Sexology and its fictions are often aligned with realism and life-writing via their focus on the sexual life of the subject. But the Gothic has come to be understood as a 'queer' genre because of its concern with the crossing of boundaries. Clearly, the Gothic's emphasis on fluidity and transgression echoes the concerns of queer theory, which are conceptually informed by the linguistic roots of the word queer in a vocabulary of movement. As Eve Kosofsky Sedgwick has so influentially noted, 'the word "queer" itself means *across*', derived from 'an Indo-European root – *twerkw*, *which* also yields the German *queer* (traverse) [and] Latin *torquere* (to twist)'.[3] Like queer theory, the Gothic's concern with transgression offers more than insights into the conception of deviancies. It also brings to light the fears, ideals and social expectations that forge the implicit norms against which deviancies are measured. In the nineteenth century, it was an emerging yet little mentioned heterosexual ideal that shaped the explosion of discourses about 'perversion' and 'corruption'. Coined in relation to the neologism of homosexuality, the term heterosexuality was first introduced into English in the 1892 translation of Krafft-Ebing's *Psychopathia Sexualis*. It did not enter popular discourse until much later in the twentieth century, and remained under-theorised in sexological debates despite – or rather because – sexual deviancies were tacitly read against it. While sexological writings paid little attention to heterosexuality, then, the formation of a modern notion of heterosexuality can nevertheless – and somewhat paradoxically – be charted via the queer Gothic genre. Novels such as *Dracula* represent anxieties about the implications of sexual transgression, anxieties that may have publicly targeted same-sex subjects (including via legal persecution) but which de facto revealed fears about the impact of improper opposite-sex acts on the future of the national body.

Dracula addresses key concerns in discourses of sexuality at the fin de siècle including questions about the integrity, violation and potentially dangerous reproduction of certain bodies, and anxieties about an increasingly unstable gender binarism that was nevertheless considered crucial to social life. The novel seems less about sexual orientation than about desire as such, and pulses with fears and fantasies clustered specifically around the implications of reproductive sex. Reading *Dracula* in proximity to sexological discourses of the time reveals the complexity of fin-de-siècle attitudes to sex, showing that the possibilities and impossibilities of heterosexuality came under scrutiny as much as perceived deviations from that norm.

From Perversions to Heterosensibilities

Dracula's place in the history of modern sexuality is often taken to be where it intersects with emerging sexology, particularly with *Psychopathia Sexualis*, that key work of sexology, a text that has come to epitomise the pathologisation of sexual acts and the classification of sexual types. Robert Mighall, for instance, has argued that the proximity of *Dracula* with *Psychopathia Sexualis* marks the moment when older, mythological formations of 'deviancy' were replaced by a modern concept of the 'sexual pervert'.[4]

But the development of a modern vocabulary of sex cannot merely be understood in terms of discipline and repression. Count Dracula, the iconic vampire of Western modernity, entered the English literary scene in the same year in which Havelock Ellis and John Addington Symonds's *Sexual Inversion*, the first work of English sexology, was published. Unlike scientific works such as *Psychopathia Sexualis*, which catalogued a wide range of sexual 'perversions', *Sexual Inversion* dealt specifically, and broadly affirmatively, with the history and present-day experiences of same-sex desire. The work's same-sex focus to some extent reflected the authors' own personal investments in the topic. Ellis, a medically trained literary critic and editor, was at the time working on a larger study on *The Psychology of Sex*, which was partly motivated by the discovery that his wife, the feminist activist and writer Edith Lees, was in a relationship with another woman. Symonds in turn, an influential Victorian literary critic and married father of four, had several affairs with men and a long-lasting relationship with a Venetian gondolier, Angelo Fusato, whom he supported financially.[5] Ellis's and Symonds's personal investments combined with their literary-philosophical, rather than medico-forensic, conception of 'sexual inversion' signal a broader shift in sexual debates in the 1890s when the pathologising discourses of early sexology increasingly came to compete with more positive, identitarian claims in support of the naturalness and long history of same-sex sexuality.

The greater visibility of male same-sex cultures in particular came at a cost. In 1895, at the height of his fame, Oscar Wilde was tried for indecent conduct with other men and sentenced to two years' imprisonment with hard labour in Reading Gaol. These events mark the moment when homosexuality first entered public discourse in England, as well as many other countries in Europe and North America, where Wilde's trials received considerable attention. The Wilde scandal surely influenced Stoker, who knew Wilde well from Dublin, attended the salon of the controversial Sir William and Lady Wilde, and even shared Florence Balcombe as a love object (she rejected Wilde and married Stoker). Nina Auerbach claims that 'Dracula was one particularly debased incarnation of the fallen Wilde, a monster of silence and exile, vulnerable to a legalistic series of arcane rules [who as Dracula] could be isolated by diagnoses and paralyzed by rules'.[6] Auerbach's reading, which aligns Wilde with Dracula and Stoker with the Count's foe, Jonathan Harker, suggests that the first public homosexual trial and scandal produced a clear-cut division between those sympathetic to homosexuality and those who rejected it outright. Yet boundaries of identification were often blurred. Talia Schaffer argues that *Dracula's* proximity to the Wilde trial, and Harker's own anxieties about the 'ever-widening circle of semi-demons' that surround Dracula, reflect not merely anti-homosexuality attitudes but broader fin-de-siècle concerns with 'corruption'.[7] While this reads 'corruption' mainly in terms of what we might call 'bad' influence, the term was also used in nineteenth-century sexual debates to describe what we might today call child sexual abuse.[8]

The double-connotations of corruption as a both immoral influence and criminal act are picked up within *Dracula* when Mina Harker, following Professor Van Helsing and Dr Seward's diagnosis, claims that 'the Count is a criminal and criminal type. Nordau and Lombroso would so classify him' (*D*, 317). This much-cited quotation refers to two of the most notorious figures in fin-de-siècle socio-sexual debates: the polemist Max Nordau, who would become an influential figure in the emerging Zionist movement, gained infamy for his work *Entartung* (1892), translated as *Degeneration* (1895), in which he claimed that nineteenth-century cultural production was evidence of Western civilisation in decline. Cesare Lombroso in turn gained fame for his typologies of criminality which sought to trace the hereditary characteristics of supposed criminals via studies of their cranium and other facial features. Alluding to their work on degeneration and heredity, *Dracula* firmly moves beyond a specific concern with homoeroticism towards broader contemporary fears about the decline of Western civilisation, fears that centred specifically on the reproductive body. If Seward's classification of the Count as a degenerate criminal places great emphasis on the importance of taxonomic identification, which here is figured as a crucial step in the attempt to capture and contain the Count, it also serves as a reminder that vampirism within the novel serves a metaphor both for sexual acts and the transmission of undesirable, dangerous traits.

Vampire Sexuality

Over the course of the nineteenth century, the mythological figure of the vampire was increasingly dragged into all kinds of scientific debates about the boundaries of human life. Against the backdrop of brutal imperial expansion post-evolutionary discourses, which reimagined the human body as the repository of a past that will shape its future, increasingly centred on questions about sexual reproduction and related concerns with contagious influences and their transmission. In this context vampirism came to serve as a metaphor for the leaky boundaries of human existence, used to conceptualise all kind of violations of the body that were feared to push the subject into the spaces between life and death, and between the animal and the human.

How these debates were racialised is indicated, for instance, by the claims of Edward B. Tylor, one of the founders of English anthropology, who argued in his *Anthropology: An Introduction to the Study of Man and Civilisation* (1881) that it was 'Slavonic countries' specifically which suffered from 'blood-sucking nightmares whose dreadful visits the patient is conscious of in his sleep'. Tylor's observations on the Slavonic 'demon-souls dwelling in corpses' [which are known as] vampires' picks up on the older cultural stereotyping of certain parts of eastern Europe, which in the twentieth century would replace the generic mythology of vampirism with the specific story of Dracula.[9] Daniela Olărescu has pointed out that when West Germany forged new links with Romania in the late 1990s several publishing houses in the country immediately reissued new editions of *Dracula*.[10] Perhaps even more significantly, Tylor's words are a reminder that up until the nineteenth century many observers located the existence of the vampire outside of the realm of English civilisation.

Towards the end of the nineteenth century, however, vampirism was increasingly invoked in debates about British health. For example, in a book entitled *Cremation and Urn-Burial, or The Cemeteries of the Future*, which was published in 1889, the influential Irish gardener and horticulturalist William Robinson, who was an avid advocate of cremation, turned to the vampire to conceptualise issues of hygiene. Robinson, citing members of the Cremation Society of England, argued that by adhering to the common practice of burying bodies 'we are continually producing vampires' because while 'we bury our dead, decay does not take place, and the vampires spread from our burial grounds, attacking the population and producing disease'.[11] 'Vampire' here served as a name for germs and diseases transmitted from the rotting flesh of the dead into the living world, a discursive sleight of hand that recurs in *Dracula*, most famously perhaps in the description of the fate of the upstanding Mina Harker, 'that sweet, sweet, good good woman' who is corrupted by 'the Vampire's baptism of blood' (*D*, need pages: Penguin 328/343).

While vampires came to stand in as a metaphor for corruption in all kinds of scientific writing, then, they are curiously absent from the sexological literature of the time. Instead scientists and other cultural commentators concerned with sexual violations and the transmission of vice tended to draw indirectly on the 'life-sucking' discourses associated with vampirism.

This was especially the case in discussions of all kinds of non-reproductive sexual acts, such as masturbation or same-sex sex acts, that were figured as parasitic activities with a weakening effect on the national body. The few sexual commentators who did mention vampirism did so primarily to comment on the nature of women. Iwan Bloch, for example, author of *Sexual Life of Our Time* (1909), in a chapter on 'Obscene Art', mentions in his analysis of Wagner's *Tristan* 'a horde of frightful, half-nude vampire women [who are] half-crazed with delight, neighing, necrophilic'.[12] The controversial French journalist Léo Taxil in turn claimed in his study *La Prostitution Contemporaine: Étude d'un Question Sociale* (1884) that 'vampire' was a name given in antiquity and during the Middle Ages to someone who had has sex with corpses ('passion du cadavre').[13] This practice entered the modern catalogue of sexual perversions as 'necrophilia', a term coined by the Belgian physician Joseph Guislan in 1850. It was made famous by Krafft-Ebing, who adopted it in his *Psychopathia Sexualis* where he argued that 'this horrible kind of sexual indulgence is so monstrous that the presumption of a psychopathic state is, under all circumstance, justified'.[14] Taxil's discussion stands out not only because he used the term 'vampire' to distinguish sex with corpses from 'exhibitionists, pederasts, people who have sex with animals', but also because he considered vampirisim as part of a study of prostitution and sapphism, aligning it with female sexuality in particular.[15]

The alignment of vampirism and predatory female same-sex practices was famously explored by Sheridan Le Fanu in 'Carmilla' (1871–72). Although Stoker was a friend and neighbour of Le Fanu in Dublin, *Dracula* in contrast is less concerned with female same-sex sexuality. Instead it redirected the parasitic fantasies about sexuality that preoccupied so many Western observers into more specific concern with the effects of the colonial encounter, especially in relation to fears that the perceived inferiorities of other races might infiltrate Western society via reproduction. The novel picks up on discourses that figured the body in sexual terms, influenced by the colonial expansion efforts and on the psychic strains colonial violence brought back into fin-de-siècle life in unacknowledged ways. The impact of individual sexual behaviour on collective wellbeing especially came under intense scrutiny in the later nineteenth century when European state-building efforts and their colonial expansion redrew the political boundaries of the modern world. As major European nations, such as the recently founded German and Italian states, France and Britain, struggled to subjugate peoples and territories in Africa, Asia and the South Pacific, questions about the strengths and weaknesses of the individual body became the focus of anxious theorising, and legal and medical interventions that were ostensibly aimed at protecting or improving the collective body of the nation. Intimate practices here became fantastic sites onto which fears about the wellbeing and future progress of social, national and racial health were projected.

But if Dracula and his entourage of vampires offered a perfect metaphor for the racial anxieties of the time, as the sexualised act of blood-sucking came to symbolise both the forbidden thrills and overt fears of a loss of power that marked the colonial encounter, the figure of the Count also raises questions about how the struggle against oppression was perceived by the dominant powers. Count Dracula initially claims kinship with the Székely, a Hungarian-speaking people whose distinct culture in Transylvania is threatened.[16] While Dracula's nationality – his origins, becoming, belonging – are never fully revealed, he is thus firmly identified as on the margins, out-of-culture, a figure that according to Viragh stands for the cultural extinction of minority culture in a globalising world. Viragh's reading runs counter to the established arguments that *Dracula* represented Victorian fears about 'reverse colonization' and the integrity of English identity under foreign influence.[17] Instead it alerts us to a queer characteristic of the text: that the novel, produced at a historical point in time when national, racial, gender and sexual identities were being forged, left Dracula's identity unfixed. This unfixedness to some extent reflects the discursive circumstance of opposite-sex sexuality at the time, which, unlike its same-sex counterpart, remained a difficult to pin down phenomenon. Dracula's unclear allegiances, as much as his vampiristic pursuits, reflect fin-de-siècle fears about the reproductive sexual body, a new kind of heterosensibility that conceived of the sexual body simultaneously as fundamental to the future of the empire and one of the biggest threats to it.

A Violent Conclusion

If *Dracula's* Gothic form problematises the possibilities of realist representation, it also raises questions about the relationship between fantasy and the social. I want to conclude with a brief consideration of what the novel can tell us about sexual violence, a twentieth-century concept that slowly started to come into view at the fin de siècle. Sexologists described all kinds of what we would now call non-consensual sexual behaviours, typically categorising them under the headings of 'fetishism' or 'perversion'. Yet their focus on classification all too often obscured the real violence they thus documented. Much of the modern catalogue of 'abuse', especially around child abuse, emerged in fin-de-siècle debates about sexuality, but only gradually entered social as well as legal contexts over the course of the twentieth century. It is partly against this long history of the denial and obscuring of sexual violence against women and children that some feminist critics have examined *Dracula* specifically for the insights if offers into the relationship between violence and sexuality.

One of the most famous passages of *Dracula* appears in chapter 16 when Lucy, now a vampire, is staked by her beloved Arthur. Arthur is entreated by the group of male vampire hunters to drive 'deeper and deeper the mercy-bearing stake' (*D*, 201). While many critics have discussed this scene as a symbolic rendering of sexual intercourse, this ignores the violence represented. Macy Todd distinguishes between two types of violence in the text – the 'mythical' violence ascribed to Count Dracula and the 'terrestrial' violence of his adversaries. Todd argues that 'Dracula materializes the impossible fantasy of violence-that-disappears in his magical ability to inflict wounds that vanish'.[18] Yet if this is a violent wish-fulfilment – the ability to inflict injury and get away with it – it also has a social reality. Sexual violence, in particular, all too often still disappears, if not from the lives of those who suffer it, then from public and political life where for instance rape remains underreported and unpunished even when brought to trial. *Dracula*'s narrative turns, which are built around violent encounters, draw attention to the erasure of sexual violence from many accounts of modern sexuality, be they fictional, scientific or critical.

Considering *Dracula*'s representation of opposite-sex practices and the fears and concerns that gathered around them brings to light some of the violence of the gender norms that governed what counted as permissible sexual behaviour around 1900. Reading *Dracula* and sexology in proximity reveals some of the gaps and silences in nineteenth-century discourses about sexuality, especially in relation to the emerging heterosensibilities of the time: the norms and expectations that centred on opposite-sex acts. In an influential queer reading of *Dracula*, Jack Halberstam has argued that the novel 'calls into question all scientific and rational attempts to classify and quantify agents of disorder. Such agents, Gothic literature makes clear, are invented, not discovered, by science', in other words they challenge the authorial function of sexology.[19] Yet science – including the *scientia sexualis* – is a contingent discipline, less a rigid inventor of norms than one of the ways normativity enters into the everyday. Or to say this differently, while sexology no doubt played a formative role in the establishment of certain sexual norms, the questions that motivate sexual study reflect the social anxieties and aspirations of fin-de-siècle Britain. So, rather than reading *Dracula* against sexology in the way many critics have done, I have read them together, as documents of the discursive and social transformations that occurred around sex towards the end of the nineteenth century. The gaps and tensions between fiction and sexology reveal how modern heterosensibilities began to take shape at a time when public discourses centred on the vagaries of same-sex desire.

Notes

1 Michel Foucault, *The History of Sexuality Volume 1: An Introduction*, trans. Robert Hurley (London: Penguin Books, 1990), 68.

2 Heike Bauer, *English Literary Sexology: Translations of Inversion 1860–1930* (Basingstoke: Palgrave Macmillan, 2009).

3 Eve Kosofsky Sedgwick, *Tendencies* (Durham, NC: Duke University Press, 1993), xii.

4 Robert Mighall, *A Geography of Victorian Gothic Fiction: Mapping History's Nightmares* (Oxford: Oxford University Press, 2003), 227.

5 Ivan Crozier, 'Introduction', in Havelock Ellis and John Addington Symonds, eds., *Sexual Inversion: A Critical Edition* (Basingstoke: Palgrave Macmillan, 2009), pp. 1–95 and Sean Brady, *John Addington Symonds (1840–1893) and Homosexuality: A Critical Edition of Sources* (Basingstoke: Palgrave Macmillan, 2012).

6 Nina Auerbach, *Our Vampires, Our Selves* (Chicago: University of Chicago Press, 1995), 102.

7 Talia Schaffer '"A Wilde Desire Took Me": The Homoerotic History of Dracula', *ELH: A Journal of English Literary History* 61 (1994), 381–415, quote on p. 400.

8 Louise Jackson, *Child Sexual Abuse in Victorian England* (London: Routledge, 2000), 3.

9 Edward B. Tylor, *Anthropology: An Introduction to the Study of Man and Civilisation* (London: Macmillan, 1889), 356.

10 Daniela Olărescu, *Die Rezeption der rumänischen Literatur in Deutschland zwischen 1945 und 1989* (Frankfurt: Peter Lang, 2008), 82.

11 William Robinson, *Cremation and Urn-Burial, or The Cemeteries of the Future* (London: Cassell, 1889), 184.

12 Iwan Bloch, *The Sexual Extremities of the World* (New York: Book Awards, 1964), 301.

13 Léo Taxil, *La Prostitution Contemporaine: Étude d'un Question Sociale* (Paris: Librairie Populaire, 1884), 132 and 449.

14 Richard von Krafft-Ebing, *Psychopathia Sexualis: With Especial Reference to the Antipathic Sexual Instinct*, trans. by Francis Joseph Rebman from the 12th German edn. (New York: Eugenics Publishing Company, 1934), 611.

15 Taxil, *La Prostitution Contemporaine*, 132.

16 Attila Viragh, 'Can the Vampire Speak? Dracula as Discourse on Cultural Extinction', *English Literature in Transition, 1880–1920* 56, no. 2 (2013), 232.

17 Stephen D. Arata, 'The Occidental Tourist: Dracula and the Anxiety of Reverse Colonization', *Victorian Studies* 33, no. 4 (1990), 621–45.

18 Mary Todd, 'What Bram Stoker's *Dracula* Reveals about Violence' *English Literature in Transition, 1880–1920* 58, no. 3 (2015), 361–84, quote on p. 375.

19 Judith Jack Halberstam, 'Technologies of Monstrosity: Bram Stoker's *Dracula*', *Victorian Studies* 36, no. 3 (1993), 340.

7

DAVID GLOVER

Dracula in the Age of Mass Migration

In the third of his secret journal entries while confined in the Castle Dracula, Jonathan Harker describes 'a long talk' with his host in which 'a few questions on Transylvanian history' prompt an impassioned lecture from 'the Count', who paces up and down the room as he proudly narrates and at times violently acts out 'the story of his race', a tale of pitched battles and an unending flow of blood. It is a curiously intimate moment: Harker is utterly absorbed, as though mesmerised, desperately trying to remember every last detail, while the Count expressively seizes hold of anything that comes to hand 'as though he would crush it by main strength' (*D*, 30). Although he has not yet encountered the three young female vampires, nor heard the Count angrily release him from their clutches, Harker already knows that he is a prisoner and recognises that he is in real danger. Still, he is captivated by Dracula's tribal self-identification with the Szekelys, the feudal aristocratic guardians of the Carpathian borderlands against the incursions of such ethnic rivals as the Magyars, Bulgars or Ottoman Turks. And, despite the Count's earlier insistence that 'you dwellers in the city cannot enter into the feelings of the hunter', Harker is clearly beginning to be pulled towards a more bellicose alter ego (*D*, 21). Only when he has learned to close the gap between his urban and combatant selves will *Dracula*'s tale finally be told.

The Count's martial pedigree has led some critics to read the novel as the story of a conquest that almost succeeds, aligning Stoker's supernatural shocker with other popular invasion novels from the period, including the works of George Chesney, William Le Queux and H. G. Wells. But as Stephen Arata argues in what remains the most searching discussion of this theme, *Dracula* is not merely a symptom of growing inter-imperial competition, drawing its energy from the widespread fear of a confrontation with Britain's resurgent military adversaries. What made the threat imagined in Stoker's novel so disturbing was the implicit suggestion that the nation's stock had sunk so low that Britain now risked being overrun by the very same archaic or primitive forces that had once been powerless to resist the spread of empire. Arata identifies this second scenario as 'the period's most important and pervasive narrative of decline, a narrative of reverse colonization', strongly motivated by a sense of 'cultural guilt' in which Britain 'sees its own imperial practices mirrored back in monstrous forms'.[1] On this view, *Dracula* was closer to H. Rider Haggard's *She: A History of Adventure* (1887) than to Chesney's bestseller *The Battle of Dorking: Reminiscences of a Volunteer* (1871). However, Arata's own careful reading of *Dracula* shows that in practice these twin narratives substantially overlapped. For while he entrusts the menial aspects of his expedition overseas to the fearsome Slovaks, regarded by Harker as 'more barbarian than the rest' of the indigenous population, the Count's personal aspirations appear to be those of a liberal English gentleman, 'at liberty to direct myself', with the 'knowledge and acumen' of someone who 'would have made a wonderful solicitor' – in addition to his prowess as a professional soldier (*D* 7, 32–33).

No matter how it is finessed, Arata's 'reverse colonization' inevitably evokes a military venture, a feat of strategy and stealth, cunning and confrontation. Scenes of war can be glimpsed throughout *Dracula*: in night watches, reconnaissance missions, terrorism, raiding parties, armed forays and, finally, hotfoot pursuit. Serious weaponry is frequently and ostentatiously on display: from Jonathan Harker's antique Kukri knife to the American frontiersman's bowie knife wielded by Quincey Morris and an assortment of pistols, revolvers and modern Winchester rifles. By the novel's close even the endangered Mina Harker is amongst those pointing a gun at Dracula's leiter-waggon. Indeed, in a deleted paragraph from Stoker's original annotated typescript, the dissolution of the Count's body is followed by the final destruction of his already ruined castle in a kind of volcanic convulsion in which the whole edifice, including its mountainous base appear 'to rise into the air and scatter into fragments while a mighty cloud of black and yellow smoke ... in rolling grandeur was shot upwards with inconceivable rapidity', like some lurid tableau from a nineteenth-century battlefield.[2] But these resonances are far from being the only manner in which the sound of the contemporary war machine can be heard in Stoker's novel. In this chapter I want to take a somewhat different tack and look at the complex ways in which *Dracula* drew its inspiration from the fallout or after-effects of war and armed conflict, particularly as evidenced by the displacement and movement of peoples.

Stoker first encountered his Balkan setting via the exploits of his younger brother George who, as a newly qualified doctor, had signed up with the Red Crescent, an Islamic counterpart to the Red Cross that offered humanitarian medical aid to the Turkish army in the Russo-Turkish War (1877–78). After an armistice was agreed early in 1878 George Stoker returned from eastern

Europe and lodged with Bram and Florence Stoker at their house in Chelsea, publishing a diary of his military experiences later that same year, provocatively entitled *With 'the Unspeakables'; or, Two Years Campaigning in European and Asiatic Turkey*.[3] The book predates Bram's earliest preparatory notes for *Dracula* by more than a decade, but the parallels between memoir and novel are striking, despite the fact that Romania, and especially the bleak Carpathian region, lay at the periphery of the main theatre of war between the Russian and the Ottoman Empires. When George Stoker itemises the clothes of the Bulgarian peasants, for example, he notes that Christian and Muslim men are alike in sporting trousers 'worn wide and baggy like the Turkish ones', with 'white linen' or 'white homespun' shirts and brightly dyed jackets or coats, revealing a marked Oriental influence and confirming that he has now definitively left the West behind.[4] These descriptions could be taken almost verbatim from Jonathan Harker's Romanian travelogue and both Stokers use the same hackneyed Victorian term to pinpoint the impression they create: 'picturesque' (D, 7) Or again, when George Stoker expresses scepticism at the attempts of these 'backward' territories to modernise, his complaints about the slowness and lack of punctuality in the railway service are carried over into Jonathan Harker's rather similar reflections on the unreliability of his own train journey, exacerbated by the poor quality of the local maps that fall far below British Ordnance Survey standards (5).

If one brackets off the horrendous impact of the war, *With 'the Unspeakables'* portrays these northern sectors of Bulgaria as a hostile and inhospitable environment plagued by rampant disease, packs of wolves and blinding snowstorms, dangers heightened by the presence of 'cruel and lawless-looking' bands of men carrying rifles, revolvers and swords – very close in fact to the Transylvanian ecology in the opening chapters of *Dracula* (24). George Stoker reported that at times the temperatures fell so low that even the wolves were driven down from the higher parts of the mountains into the more populated areas. However, it is above all the military conflict that makes 'the busy hand of death' visible at every turn, revealing a landscape of summary executions, makeshift graves and bloody abandoned corpses piled beside the road (82).

But at this point the convergence between the two overlapping genres of writing starts to go awry. For the devastation that the war visits upon vast numbers of people in the region introduces a new element: the figure of the refugee, the forced migrant so characteristic of the second half of the nineteenth century. In George Stoker's memoir, this land of the dead is heavily imprinted with the tracks of those seeking to escape to a place of greater safety. He records that his passage across the steep Orkhanié Pass took 'many hours' solely because the roads were 'so crowded ... with refugees' fleeing from the Russian advance, at least 30,000 people with 'overloaded ... bullock waggons' pulled by 'poor half-starved cattle' (82). George Stoker closes his book with a series of pressing questions as to their likely fate and asks whether the great powers will ensure that they receive the justice they so urgently need: 'What is to become of all these refugees in the future? Will Europe, especially England, permit [that] these hundreds of thousands of unfortunate people shall be prevented from returning to their homes? ... Will England do anything to help these poor of God's great family, and put them in the way of winning their daily bread?' (124–25).

Is it possible to read *Dracula*, with its transnational cast of characters and frequent border crossings, as a kind of migrant story? Curiously enough, the one starkly deracinated figure that might arguably be said to qualify as a migrant is Count Dracula himself. True, his plight differs sharply from that of the Muslim refugees depicted by Stoker's brother, since he is neither a casualty of war nor someone who is making a desperate bid to escape from immediate danger, with the hope of returning home as soon as possible. As Professor Van Helsing insists, Dracula's urgent desire to forsake Transylvania for a distant imperial city stems from the recognition that his native land has become empty and uninhabitable, a lifeless country that is 'barren of people'; and so he plans to settle in 'the place of all the world most of promise for him', a decision with which many nineteenth-century Irishmen and women might well have sympathised in the years following their country's Great Famine (*D*, 296–97). Bram himself was amongst four of the five Stoker brothers who left Ireland in order to pursue a professional career. When Jonathan and Mina Harker return to Transylvania seven years after Dracula's defeat they find it unchanged, a virtually deserted province that is no more than 'a waste of desolation' (*D*, 351). But, of course, this bleak intractable landscape takes us directly into the bloody heart of vampirism.

At the time that Bram Stoker was researching and plotting his novel, large-scale global population shifts were rapidly increasing as long-distance, transoceanic and often permanent mass migration tended to replace traditional, short-term patterns of relocation. The Muslim refugees who slowed the advance of George Stoker's medical team were frantically fleeing to what they hoped would be a temporary home on the other side of the mountains, unlike the multitudes of Europeans seeking a better and safer life in the Americas. Between 1871 and 1900, the United States received almost twelve million new immigrants, making it arguably *the* major world destination for those in search of new opportunities.[5] This era of mass migration was regularly fuelled by wars and political crises and was accompanied by angry outcries against the persecution of minority groups. In the aftermath of the

Crimean War, this was especially true of eastern Europe – Romania being a case in point. One of the provisions of the Treaty of Paris (1856) released Romania from Turkish control and made it an independent, largely Christian nation, but with full protection for non-Christian minorities, including citizenship for Romanian Jews. However, in 1866 there was a nationalist *coup d'état* that undermined the civic and political gains achieved by the Romanian Jewish community and led to frequent anti-Semitic riots in which many Jews lost their lives.[6] This fatal alternation between violence and legal repression spread right across eastern Europe and by the early 1880s, as these areas became more and more unstable, Jews began to leave in growing numbers, a process that quickly accelerated after the Russian pogroms of 1881. According to one contemporary estimate, some twelve thousand Polish and Russian Jews had settled in Britain between 1867 and 1883, the majority in London's East End.[7]

Since Britain lacked any real border controls during this period, those Jews who in different circumstances might have sought refugee status were under no necessity to do so. Indeed, any practical distinction between 'immigrant' and 'refugee' had little administrative importance. So, for example, when Karl Marx's long-time collaborator Friedrich Engels arrived in England from Germany in 1842 to take up a managerial position in the family firm, he required no entry visa, passport, travel documents or work permit. What mattered was that the title deeds to the factory were securely in place and that a legal official like Jonathan Harker had made sure that all the paperwork relating to the company property of Ermen & Engels was in order. In this era of economic *laissez-faire*, foreigners were in principle free to come and go and work in Britain as they wished.

In fact, in the middle of the nineteenth century, Victorians were very proud of their liberal traditions of tolerance and sanctuary. When Austria, France and Prussia complained that republican leaders of the 1848 European revolutions were being sheltered by Britain, men like Lajos Kossuth and Guiseppe Mazzini whom they regarded as political outlaws, *The Times* responded with an uncompromising editorial that thundered: 'this country is the asylum of nations, and ... will defend the asylum to the last ounce of its treasure, and the last drop of its blood'. Within Britain's political culture these claims were rooted in the lofty ideals of freedom of conscience and freedom of speech and, so long as refugees did not break the law of the land, they were entitled to 'say and do what they please', whether they were trying to escape 'the fury of the people' or 'the terror of Kings'. Speaking with the all-embracing majesty of empire, *The Times* insisted that Britain was 'a nation of refugees', a place of asylum 'which none but barbarians will attempt to break, and which they will break to their own ruin'.[8]

However, by the 1880s a significant anti-immigrant backlash was brewing, dismissing the idea of freedom of movement and the old, hallowed notion of asylum as, at best, a set of grave economic and political errors, and, at worst, a series of weaknesses that were being deliberately exploited by Britain's enemies and would ultimately undermine the nation's security. The figure of the East European Jew bore the brunt of these accusations and again and again was constructed as a kind of internal adversary that had wormed its way into the imperial capital. In this process of demonisation, the vulnerable and disadvantaged were converted into aggressors, as though the presence of relatively small numbers of strangers could somehow actively destabilise the shared sense of national belonging. Two words played a crucial role in this transformation. The first entailed the redeployment of the old legal term '*alien*', which had originally referred to any person who was the subject of another country and owed only partial or temporary allegiance to an English monarch. Nevertheless, despite their status as outsiders, aliens did possess some important legal rights in the country in which they lived. In thirteenth-century England, for example, 'aliens' could serve on juries in cases involving conflicts between the laws and customs of different communities, such as Christians and Jews.[9] Yet by the late Victorian era, this word was popularly used to refer to strangers or foreigners who constituted a problem, the ultimate outsiders, particularly if they were poor. Phrases like 'destitute foreigners' or 'pauper aliens' were synonymous.

When the first anti-migrant campaign group was founded in 1886 it promptly called itself the Society for the Suppression of the Immigration of Destitute Aliens – though it took nearly twenty years before the first immigration control law was passed: the Aliens Act of 1905. As immigration from Russia and eastern Europe expanded, the arrival of steamships carrying Jewish passengers was greeted with alarmist and even hysterical headlines. One word more than any other encapsulated the feeling of danger and menace that was routinely invoked by the press: '*invasion*' – implying that the English faced the very real threat of being turned into subjects of a foreign or 'alien' power. As early as April 1887 the *St James's Gazette* highlighted what it called 'The Invasions of Foreign Pauperism' and in 1891, during another upsurge in anti-immigration politics, the *Evening News and Post*, a newspaper with the largest evening sales in London, regularly featured hostile columns on immigration with captions like 'Keep the Aliens Out!', 'Sixty Thousand Coming', 'The Alien Inrush', 'Still More Aliens' and 'Still They Come'. The headline 'The Alien Invasion' appeared more than once in the months of May and June, with references to 'aliens' and 'Jews' occurring almost interchangeably, as in the phrase 'The Jewish

Invasion'.[10] Like Dracula's own comings and goings they were associated with disaster and subterfuge, a tradition that has continued in the countless adaptations that have followed in his wake. When the vampire's ship glides eerily into harbour in *Nosferatu: Eine Symphonie des Grauens* (1921–22), F. W. Murnau's pirated silent film version of the novel, its sails eclipse the image of the city's church, a sign that the community's lines of defence have been decisively breached.[11]

If *Dracula* is in part a special kind of invasion (or reverse colonisation) narrative, then how exactly did Stoker represent these fears in the novel? And, in particular, what role does the figure of the Jew play in the text? There have been a number of attempts to give the Count a Jewish profile and to argue that anti-Semitism is integral to the forms of horror that are mobilised in the narrative. Much has been made of the Cockney carrier's description of Dracula's new home at Purfleet as a place so 'neglected that yer might 'ave smelled ole Jerusalem in it' and of the character Immanuel Hildesheim, the Jewish shipping agent in Galatz who expedites Dracula's return to Transylvania (*D*, 212, 324). But these could easily be dismissed as incidental details. That is why the fullest and most convincing case directly confronts the question of the language used in depicting the Count – as all such analyses must. Judith Halberstam argues in *Skin Shows: Gothic Horror and the Technology of Monsters* that in *Dracula* the Count 'embodies and exhibits all the stereotyping of nineteenth-century anti-Semitism'. So, by employing the pseudoscientific repertoire of a purportedly 'Jewish physiognomy' – 'peculiar nose, pointed ears, sharp teeth, claw-like hands' and a preoccupation with 'blood and money' – Stoker 'merges Jewishness and monstrosity and represents this hybrid monster as a threat to Englishness and English womanhood in particular'.[12]

This illuminating argument positions *Dracula* within the complex field of Victorian socio-biological interpretations of national decline, especially those collected around the concept of degeneration which reversed the more forward-looking aspects of evolutionary theory and replaced them with notions of atavism, decadence, hereditary pathology and cultural breakdown. While the epicentre of this strain of thought was located in continental Europe, it did have an impact in Britain. When the novel begins to turn towards explaining the vampire's inner nature in order to grasp his failings and vulnerabilities, the names of Nordau and Lombroso, two of the major European degeneration theorists, are immediately invoked by Mina Harker and Professor Van Helsing (*D*, 317–18). Some recent writers, like the philosopher and cultural historian Michel Foucault, have argued that the roots of nineteenth-century anti-Semitism are to be found in degeneration theory and Halberstam builds on this claim by suggesting that *Dracula* enacts a key transition in which the evil aristocrat in the Gothic novel is decisively transformed into 'the degenerate foreigner', tipping the emphasis from social class towards race. For Halberstam, not only are vampires indelibly associated with 'bad blood' and 'gender instability', but also, more fundamentally, they are 'a race and a family that weakens the stock of Englishness by passing on degeneracy and the disease of blood lust'.[13] From this perspective, Mina Harker's violation or rape by the Count at Carfax later in the novel can be read as an extended, twice-narrated example of perversion and degeneration in action, a scene accompanied by her assailant's 'mockingly' triumphant commentary (D, 266–68).

Although the Count's foreignness is never in doubt, the logic of Halberstam's own argument actually undermines the possibility of fixing his meaning or identity with any certainty. In *Skin Shows* to 'gothicize' is not simply to devise a 'form', it is to let that form unravel or fall apart, since 'Gothic ... always goes both ways'. While highlighting 'the plasticity or constructed nature of the monster', the Gothic mode cannot help but bring 'into question all scientific and rational attempts to classify and quantify agents of disorder'.[14] Yet, as Daniel Pick once wittily observed, *Dracula* could 'even be said to be *parasitic*, like its own villain, feeding off a social moral panic about the reproduction of degeneration, the poisoning of good bodies and races by bad blood, the vitiation of healthy procreation' – and moving on.[15] At the same time, one effect of this constant sliding between discourses is to plunge the reader repeatedly into a world of radical doubt and 'possible impossibilities' that blurs the boundary between theory and fiction (D, 180). In short, *Dracula* cannot operate outside of the borderlands of the degeneration paradigm's scientific pretensions: mesmerism, physiognomy or criminal anthropology.

But, as this essay has tried to show, Bram Stoker's *Dracula* is also inseparable from the hysteria that debates about 'alien immigration' encouraged, as much in its populist imaginary as in its pseudoscientific underpinnings. On returning to 'the great box' in the castle's chapel with the aim of destroying his captor, Jonathan Harker famously pictures the Count in London, 'amongst its teeming millions', creating 'a new and ever widening circle of semi-demons to batten on the helpless' and is again driven 'mad' by 'the very thought' that such things could be (D, 51). If, as Halberstam claims, Dracula represents 'the most telling example' of the 'monstrous foreigner', he is also 'a criminal and of criminal type' and both notions became part of the adversarial rhetoric around the figure of the 'alien' (D, 317–18).[16] One of the abiding ambiguities in the construction of what Michel Foucault has identified as the 'criminal' or 'moral monster' in the eighteenth and nineteenth centuries is that this extraordinary evildoer 'breaches the law' while simultaneously standing 'outside the law', in flagrant contravention of the laws of nature as well as the laws of society, just as the 'alien immigrant' was often thought to do.[17] This contradictory formulation helps to explain why it is so important that Van Helsing, Lord Godalming, Quincey Morris and Jonathan and Mina Harker make a 'solemn compact' to act collectively against the Count and drive him out, re-establishing or reaffirming the civic bond (*D*, 222).

Yet beyond the grave, *Dracula* endures. Unlike the immigrant paupers in the popular newspapers of the day, the Count possesses the uncanny ability to pass as a native *flâneur*, an alien invader who has become socially invisible, a face lost in the crowd. On 'a hot day' in autumn he may be glimpsed in Piccadilly, 'a dark stranger' attentively watching a 'pretty girl' pass by, 'a tall, thin man' whose presence is barely noticed (*D*, 160–61).

Notes

1 Stephen Arata, 'The Occidental Tourist: *Dracula* and the Anxiety of Reverse Colonization', *Victorian Studies*, 33, no. 4 (1990), 623.

2 Catalogue for Christie's New York sale (no. 1166) of *Bram Stoker's Dracula: The Original Typed Manuscript. Wednesday 17 April 2002*, 18.

3 Joseph S. Bierman, 'The Genesis and Dating of *Dracula* from Bram Stoker's Working Notes', in Margaret L. Carter, ed., *Dracula: The Vampire and the Critics* (Ann Arbor: UMI Research Press, 1988), pp. 51–55. He argues that Stoker's first clearly dated memorandum was written on 8 March 1890.

4 George Stoker, *With 'the Unspeakables;' or, Two Years Campaigning in European and Asiatic Turkey* (London: Chapman and Hall, 1878), 8–9; 67. Further references in the text.

5 Mae M. Ngai, *Impossible Subjects: Illegal Aliens and the Making of Modern America* (Princeton: Princeton University Press, 2004), 273.

6 Israel Davis, *The Jews of Roumania; A Short Statement of Their Recent History and Present Situation* (London: Trübner & Co., 1872).

7 Todd M. Endelman, *The Jews of Britain 1656 to 2000* (Berkeley: University of California Press, 2002), 128.

8 *The Times* (28 February 1853), 4.

9 Marianne Constable, *The Law of the Other: The Mixed Jury and Changing Conceptions of Citizenship, Law, and Knowledge* (Chicago: University of Chicago Press, 1994).

10 See the *Evening News and Post*, 9 May–15 June 1891, *passim*.

11 S. S. Prawer, *Nosferatu – Phantom der Nacht* (London: British Film Institute, 2004).

12 Judith Jack Halberstam, *Skin Shows: Gothic Horror and the Technology of Monsters* (Durham, NC: Duke University Press, 1995), 14.

13 Halberstam, *Skin Shows*, 94–95.

14 Halberstam, *Skin Shows*, 95.

15 Daniel Pick, *Faces of Degeneration: A European Disorder, c. 1848–c. 1918* (Cambridge: Cambridge University Press, 1989), 173.

16 Halberstam, *Skin Shows*, 13.

17 Michel Foucault, *Abnormal: Lectures at the Collège de France 1974–1975*, ed. Valerio Marchetti and Antonella Salomoni, trans. Graham Burchell (1999; London and New York: Verso, 2003), 55–57.

8

MATTHEW GIBSON

Dracula and the East

At the beginning of *Dracula*, when Jonathan Harker describes the scenes on his arrival at Buda-Pesth, he famously remarks: 'The impression I had was that we were leaving the West and entering the East; the most Western of splendid bridges over the Danube, which is here of noble width and depth, took us among the traditions of Turkish rule' (*D*, 5). Later in the same diary entry, when describing his movement from Klausenburgh to Bistritz, Harker remarks on his train's late departure, that '[i]t seems to me that the further East you go the more unpunctual are the trains. What ought they to be in China?' (*D*, 6).

Both these statements probably owe something to Alexander Kinglake's beginning to his celebrated travelogue, *Eothen* (1841), when he describes moving from Austria-Hungary to Turkish-occupied Belgrade as follows: 'I had come, as it were, to the end of this wheel-going Europe, and now my eyes would see the Splendour and Havoc of the East'.[1] Harker's first statement echoes the sense of crossover into a world dominated by the traditions of Turkey, a movement from Europe to an Eastern, Islamic-influenced world (with a faint echo of 'Splendour' in 'splendid'), while the second description echoes the concept of moving from order to 'Havoc' in the increased unpunctuality of trains. Harker even seems to see this movement from order to havoc on a gradually increasing scale, presumably between the two polarities – a factor which would have been all the more influenced by Stoker's own enormous esteem for the United States of America.

These statements go some way to justifying an approach to Stoker's 'East' based on Edward Said's theory of Orientalism, which seeks to understand the West's own discussion of the Near East – in particular the Arab world in the nineteenth century – as being infused with a dominant discourse that articulates 'Orientals' as being 'irrational, depraved (fallen), childlike, "different"' in contrast to Western Europeans, who are seen as being 'rational, virtuous, mature, "normal"'.[2] Said's dichotomy is evident in the idea of

Dracula's 'reverse colonization', as the Count acquaints himself with the manners and customs of the West through his library of London directories and civil lists, the better to infiltrate the society he wishes to destroy.[3] Dracula's Gypsies and Slovaks, meanwhile, deserve comment for the racial stereotyping of eastern Europe in the novel, these two groups used to construct an opposition with the orderly 'crew of light', and so act as a justification for British imperialism and Western hegemony.[4]

Dracula's portrayal of eastern Europe must address the immediate, political context of the Balkans rather than an abstract discourse of Orientalism, though. How far is the diplomacy or geopolitical policies of Liberal and Tory governments of the time towards the Ottoman and Austrian Empires reflected in the novel? Does the crew's destruction of Dracula, an embittered Eastern Christian degraded by the Ottomans, reflect Stoker's sharing of the view that the so-called 'Concert of Europe' required the destruction of the so-called 'sick man of Europe', the Ottoman Empire? This is how Eleni Condouriotis has viewed the politics of Dracula, arguing that the novel evokes 'Britain's burden as the hegemonic force behind the Concert of Europe' which was then aiming 'to create a new Europe by destroying what remained of the sick man of Europe and his antithesis, the powerful existence of a "pure" Christian Europe'.[5] Thus both Turkey, and its fanatical enemies in the form of Dracula, are symbolically expunged by the book in keeping with William Gladstone's desire for free, secular states.

The history of Britain's relations with Russia was another vital military and diplomatic front in the East during the nineteenth century, with the antagonism over the Russian rise in the Black Sea and threats to British interests in India and Central Asia. This was a long-term military and diplomatic tussle that was called 'the Great Game'. Stoker has been accused by one critic of 'Russophobia', a hatred that determines Dracula's negative portrayal as a condemnation of the Orthodox Eastern and Slavic peoples historically allied to Russia.[6] Stoker certainly manipulates his sources to alter the historical Dracula's ethnicity (turning the Dracula clan from Wallach into Szekeley chieftains), as well as the geographical reality created in eastern Europe after the Treaty of Berlin in 1878, since the political upshot of that treaty was the maintenance of an Austrian and Ottoman presence in the region.

This chapter explores the political background in eastern Europe and the Balkans in the centuries and decades preceding the publication of Dracula, and the extent of Stoker's own knowledge of this historical context. I will then analyse how Stoker manipulates his sources, and what this implies.

Political History

There are commonly two tendencies amongst nineteenth-century British travellers and politicians with regard to the Ottomans: progressively-minded Liberals, who were usually Hellenophiles and later Slavophiles, and Aristocrats and Tories, who were in general Turcophiles. To put it another way, there were those who wished to see the Turks displaced from mainland Europe and those who, for either expediency or ideological reasons, either condemned or admired the Turkish empire.[7] Support for the Ottomans in Britain – by the likes of Prime Minister Benjamin Disraeli or the long-serving British Ambassador to Turkey, Sir Stratford Canning – was fuelled by domestic needs, in particular keeping Russia away from the Mediterranean. But there was also an anti-progressive discourse amongst admirers that fêted imperial power for its own sake.

After the Treaty of Karlovics in 1699 and the Serb revolt of 1816, the Ottoman Empire was in retreat from its varied forms of government in the regions of southeastern Europe. British and French policy towards the Ottomans wished to bolster them against an encroaching Russia. Russia made various attempts to destroy Turkish rule in the Balkans on behalf of an enthusiastic Orthodox Christian community in Roumelia – the area now understood as comprising Macedonia, Greece, Bulgaria and Serbia, a complex and frequently changing patchwork of administrative regions and peoples. There were three noteworthy events in the Russians' attempted encroachment into the Balkans and the Black Sea: first, their effective occupation of Wallachia and Moldova after the Treaty of Adrianople in 1829; second, the Crimean War (1854–56), when the British and the French fought alongside the Turks to curb the Russian domination of the Black Sea; and third, the Treaty of Berlin (1878), when, after the Russians occupied virtually all Ottoman Europe, the German Chancellor Baron Bismarck, British Prime Minister Benjamin Disraeli and the French Foreign Minister William Waddington handed the Austrians occupation of Bosnia, permitted Ottoman military presence in a quasi-independent Eastern Rumelia (now eastern Bulgaria), but restored full Ottoman control to Macedonia (which then included northeastern Greece). This assured the restoration of a wide corridor of Turkish power from Constantinople to the Dalmatian coast: only Northern Bulgaria, centred around Sofia, was allowed full independence as a new Principality.[8] This renewed imposition on the Balkan Christians of Bulgaria – who months before secured a large independent kingdom for themselves that included Macedonia under the Treaty of San Stefano – led to the increasingly anti-Ottoman electorate in Britain punishing Disraeli in the election of 1880 and returning the Liberals to power under Gladstone.

The British position on the Balkans changed unilaterally after 1880 and for almost two decades Great Power politics in the region became a much greyer area. One reason was that the Crown Prince of Northern Bulgaria Alexander Battenberg annexed Eastern Roumelia in 1885, and then declared himself King of the united country in 1886, angering the Russians, who abducted him. Thus, Bulgaria itself now became a Russian enemy and possibly a British ally, and so support for the Ottomans as a bulwark against Russia was no longer necessary. However, there had been a resumption of brinkmanship in the two years before the publication of *Dracula* over the Black Sea ports, with the Tory Prime Minister Lord Salisbury attempting to dismantle the Ottoman Empire, while the Russian strategy no longer aimed to do so.[9] In 1894 and 1896 there were massacres of Christian Armenians, which drove public opinion firmly against the Ottoman Empire. In 1896 Salisbury threw his support behind Greek Cretan independence from the Sultan. As G. D. Clayton wrote, British and Russian attitudes towards the Ottoman Empire had by now completely reversed.[10]

From the evidence, it appears that Bram Stoker's own politics was Russophobic. When Stoker addressed his fellow students at the Philosophical Society of Trinity College in Dublin, he had warned of the threat to 'British India' from the 'greedy arm' of Russia.[11] Many years later Stoker recounted a conversation with the Russian anarchist Sergei Stepniak on the barbarous treatment of political prisoners in Russia.[12] In the correspondence issuing from this meeting Stepniak acknowledges that Stoker has 'read all my books', and sends Stoker copies of his journal *Free Russia* in 1892. If Stoker had read all of Stepniak's books, then he would have read *Russia under the Tsars* (1885), which describes the country as a bureaucratic autocracy.[13] If the copies of *Free Russia* were the most recent ones to be printed, Stoker would have found in the June 1892 edition a long essay by the Ukrainian Liberal Professor Dragamanev declaring that while Russia should be the promulgator of freedom for the Balkan peoples, it could not do so because of the despotism of its Tsarist government.[14]

While Stoker may have shared Salisbury's contempt for Russians, it is also likely that he held to the older, pro-Ottoman argument as to how best to contain them, as well as perhaps a pro-Austrian position. Just after his removal to London in 1878, Stoker took his brother George as a lodger in Cheyne Walk. George had just emerged from an intense experience tending the Ottoman army's soldiers in the Russo-Turkish War, which he recorded in his travel memoir *With 'the Unspeakables'*.[15] This work is entirely Turcophile in terms of attitudes to both the Turks themselves and their government, and condemns Russians and their Balkan allies amongst the Greeks and Bulgarians. George Stoker must have regaled Bram with his political opinions about the Russians and Turks, including supporting the latter's presence in the Balkans. This support can be discerned in *Dracula*.[16]

As for Transylvania, the site of Dracula's castle, there were no major changes to its borders or sovereignty over the nineteenth century, although it lay on the edge of Moldavia, an area that had recently been dominated by Russia. It had been one of the only areas of the medieval kingdom of Hungary to escape full Ottoman domination after the capitulation of King Louis II of Hungary to the Ottomans at the Battle of Mohacs in 1526, and it was ruled by a succession of Crown Princes who paid tribute to the Ottoman Sultan. Eventually allying itself with the Hapsburgs during the reign of Emperor Leopold I, it came under Hapsburg rule after the raising of the siege of Vienna in 1683 – a misfortune which led to civil wars from 1703–11, led by the Catholic Prince Ferenc Rakoczy II, aimed at reuniting all Hungarian peoples regardless of religious allegiance, but which failed and ended with the Peace of Szathmar.[17] In 1867 Emperor Franz-Josef divided the Hapsburg empire into two, giving the Hungarians the administration of Transylvania. This disgruntled the swelling Wallach or Romanian population. Aurel Popovici, leader of Transylvania's Romanian National Party, sent a list of objections to the diet to be passed on to the emperor in 1892, which was returned unopened.[18] Support for the Wallachs of Transylvania was especially fierce in France, a factor present in Jules Verne's Gothic novel of 1892, *Le Chateau des Carpathes* (published in Britain in 1893 as *The Castle in the Carpathians*), which presents the Transylvanian Wallachs as suffering from Magyar domination, and contains – somewhat like *Dracula* – a diabolical Wallach Baron in a castle, who has been demoralised by Magyar rule. The Wallach-dominated provinces next-door to Transylvania, Wallachia and Moldovia, after some decades of Russian domination (until 1858), were now part of a united Romania, under King Charles Hohenzollern, who had declared himself the first King of Romania in 1881.[19]

Working from the travel writings of Major E. C. Johnson, Stoker represented the ethnic composition of Transylvania very accurately in Harker's own description early in the diary: 'In the populations of Transylvania there are four distinct nationalities: Saxons in the south, and mixed with them the Wallachs, who are the descendants of the Dacians; Magyars in the west; and Szekelys in the east and north. I am going among the latter, who claim to be descended from Attila and the Huns' (*D*, 6). However, despite this accurate description of the ethnic and geographical make-up of Transylvania, Stoker's manipulation of his sources and the locations they describe suggests that, unlike Jules Verne, he is less interested in local political problems than in using Transylvania as a representative site to offer political commentary on the entire Eastern question.

Dracula's Place and Progeny

Stoker used three main sources in building up his principal character. These were William Wilkinson, *An Account of the Principalities of Wallachia and Moldavia* (1820), Emily Gerard's essay in the *Nineteenth Century* entitled 'Transylvanian Supersititions' (1885), and Major Johnson's *On the Track of the Crescent* (1885). The last of these texts provided most of the information concerning the two, unassimilated and treacherous groups that surround Dracula's castle, the Gypsies and the Slovaks. However, if we look at the speech that Dracula delivers to Harker describing his own history and that of his people, we can see that Stoker has drawn somewhat creatively from the first and the third of these books in creating his fiction:

> When was redeemed that great shame of my nation, the shame of Cassova, when the flags of the Wallach and the Magyar went down beneath the Crescent; who was it but one of my own race who as Voivode crossed the Danube and beat the Turk on his own ground! This was a Dracula indeed. Who was it that his own unworthy brother, when he had fallen, sold his people to the Turk and brought the shame of slavery upon them! Was it not this Dracula, indeed, who inspired that other of his race who in a later age again and again brought his forces over the great river into Turkeyland; who, when he was beaten back, came again, and again, and again, though he had to come alone from the bloody field where his troops were being slaughtered, since he knew that he alone could ultimately triumph? They said that he thought only of himself. Bah! What good are peasants without a leader? Where ends the war without a brain and heart to conduct it? Again, when, after the battle of Mohacs, we threw off the Hungarian yoke, we of the Dracula blood were amongst their leaders, for our spirit would not brook that we were not free. Ah, young sir, the Szekelys – and the Dracula as their heart's blood, their brains, and their swords – can boast a record that mushroom growths like the Hapsburgs and the Romanoffs can never reach. (*D*, 31)

Wilkinson's notes on Wallachia and Moldavia influence Stoker's portrayal of Dracula's family history. Wilkinson describes how a Wallachian Voivode Dracula was defeated along with the Hungarians at 'Cossovo' battle in 1448, but was avenged by another Dracula (presumably his son) in a skirmish across the Danube after 1460 (the exact date is not given). The Sultan Mahomet forced this scion into hiding in Hungary and then put his brother Bladus on the Wallachian throne, a move that for Wilkinson created 'foundations of that slavery' which the Wallachia of his day knew as its constitution.[20] Wilkinson explains in a footnote how Dracula can mean 'evil' in the Vlach language,[21] and thus Stoker links the mysterious attributions of Wilkinson with the exciting Transylvanian *nosferatu* described by

Emily Gerard in her article on the superstitions of that region.[22] From Johnson, Stoker learnt that the Szekelys were one of the major groups in Transylvania, but Wilkinson's Wallach Voivode has changed his nationality, and moved west. Dracula's subsequent comment that the Szekelys 'threw off the Hungarian yoke' at the Battle of Mohacs is a further misappropriation of enemies, since Johnson, his source for this detail, describes the battle (1526 AD) as being the point at which Hungarian independence fell into the hands of 'the unspeakable' – meaning the Turks.

Another reason for making Dracula a Szekely is more political. The *nosferatu* or vampire was a Transylvanian figure, but amongst Romanian rather than Hungarian-speakers and it was the latter who provided the majority of the superstitions in Emily Gerard's article. The Szekelys, according to Johnson, 'received certain privileges' from the Magyars 'for having guarded the frontier toward Moldavia and Turkey-land'.[23] The mixture of Wilkinson's Turk-hating Dracula with the Szekely people described by Johnson reinforces his identity as a guardian against the Turks. Indeed, the most important aspect of Dracula's lecture to Jonathan Harker on Transylvanian history appears to be this enduring conflict against them, as he describes how 'again and again' he went over the Danube: he pits the cross against the crescent, even though the former has by now forsaken him.

Divorcing the Magyars from the Szekelys may have been politically motivated. At the time of writing, Austria and Hungary were still part of the same dual Austro-Hungarian empire, even though the Magyars were keen to break away from Hapsburg rule, while Transylvania itself was under Hungarian jurisdiction. Effectively the Szekelys are a Hungarian-speaking people entrusted with keeping the border, but by changing the meaning of the Battle of Mohacs to an event which freed the Szekelys from the Hungarian yoke (by effectively placing them under the Turkish one), Dracula and his people are portrayed as rebels against the Magyars, with whom Szekelys in real life identified (and still do). This helps to further legitimise the Austro-Hungarian empire as a political entity of necessary control over the region, reinforced by the fact that Jonathan later finds sanctuary in a Buda-Pesth hospital named 'Saint Joseph and Sainte Mary' (*D*, 94) – a reference to the enlightened rulers of the Holy Roman Empire in the eighteenth century, the Emperor Joseph and his mother Maria Teresa. Through manipulating the history of the Wallachian warlord Vlad Dracul by turning him into a Szekely, and further rearranging the history of that people themselves to be against both Magyars and Turks, Stoker is creating a political hybrid which justifies the controlling *status quo* in the Balkans. The enemies of both the Ottoman and the Hapsburg Empires are dangerous and demonic forces in need of restraint by those imperial forces.

The extent to which Dracula's portrayal is a condemnation of Russia is more difficult to gauge. Cain suggests that Dracula's behaviour echoes that of Peter the Great, the great expansionist tsar of Russia in the seventeenth century. The exact position of Dracula's castle, on the far east of Transylvania, on the edge of Moldavia and an area recently vacated by Russia, means that Dracula is himself a representative of Russian culture, and hence a symptom of Stoker's and his brother's intense Russophobia.[24] However, while the portrayal of the Count is certainly motivated by a fear of Russian involvement in the Balkans, it seems more likely that by making Dracula a Magyar-hating Szekely, Stoker constructs him as an exemplar of those who have fought both Austria and Ottomans. The novel's manipulation of the sources is an attempt to justify an unpopular political order put in place at the Treaty of Berlin, with the maintenance of both Hapsburgs and Osmanlis in the region. This position was different from both Conservatives and Liberals in 1897.

Whatever the case, the contemporary problems of Transylvania are not prevalent in Stoker's portrayal in the way they are in Verne's novel *The Castle in the Carpathians*, although there are some shared concerns in relation to ethnography.

Conclusion

While the eastern Europe of *Dracula* draws from the accounts of that region which Stoker read, it also utilises the fantasy of the 'East within'. The novel raises questions in its representations of Ashkenazi Jews in the East, a population in flight from persecution in Russia and arriving in London in large numbers throughout the 1890s. The portrayal of the superstitious, animalistic gypsies is present in all of Stoker's major sources on the East, although these representations are in keeping with racial stereotypes throughout Victorian literature.

However, the political context of the Eastern question and the contemporary situation in which Britain found itself in relation to Russia, the Ottomans and the Austrians, also played a part in determining the portrayal of Dracula, his region and his family. Whether motivated by Turcophilia or Russophobia, Stoker's condemnation of the enemies of Turkey and Austria-Hungary stems less from a well thought-out political position than simply from general and long-held prejudices.

Notes

1 Alexander Kinglake, *Eothen* (London: George Rutledge and Sons, 1905), 1.
2 Edward Said, *Orientalism*, rev. edn. (London: Penguin, 1995), 40.

3 Stephen D. Arata, 'The Occidental Tourist: Dracula and the Idea of Reverse Colonization', *Victorian Studies* 33 (1990), 621–45, quote on p. 634.

4 Stoyan Tchaprazov, 'The Slovaks and Gypsies of Bram Stoker's *Dracula*: Vampires in Human Flesh', *English Literature in Transition* 58, no. 4 (2015), 523–35, quote on p. 531.

5 Eleni Condouriotis, '*Dracula* and the Idea of Europe', *Connotations* 9, no. 2 (1999–2000), 143–159, quote on p. 154.

6 Jimmie E. Cain, *Bram Stoker and Russophobia: Evidence of the Fear of Russia in* Dracula *and* The Lady of the Shroud (Jefferson, NC: McFarland, 2006), 125.

7 Maria Todorova, *Imagining the Balkans* (Oxford: Oxford University Press, 1997), 101, 108.

8 Robert Seton-Watson, *Disraeli, Gladstone and the Eastern Question*, (London: Macmillan, 1935), 461.

9 Cain, *Bram Stoker and Russophobia*, 118.

10 G. D. Clayton, *Britain and the Eastern Question: Missolonghi to Galllipoli*, London History Studies 8 (London: University of London Press, 1971), 184, 181–82.

11 Paul Murray, *From the Shadow of Dracula: A Life of Bram Stoker* (London: Jonathan Cape, 2004), 36–37.

12 Stoker, *Personal Reminiscences of Henry Irving*, 2 vols. (London: Heinemann, 1906), vol. 2, 55.

13 Sergei Stepniak, *Russia under the Tsars*, trans. W. Westall, 2 vols. (London: Ward and Downes, 1885), vol. 2, 277–80.

14 M. P. Dragomanav, 'Russian Policy, Home and Foreign', *Free Russia* 1 (June 1892), 10–12, 12.

15 Barbara Belford, *Bram Stoker* (London: Weidenfield and Nicholas, 1996), 128.

16 George Stoker, *With 'the Unspeakables'; or, Two Years Campaigning in European and Asiatic Turkey* (London: Chapman and Hall, 1878), 3, 6–7, 76, 90.

17 Louis Leger, *A History of Austro-Hungary from the Earliest Time to the Year 1889*, trans. B. Hill (London: Rivingtons, 1889), 315, 321, 341.

18 Endre Haraszti, *The Ethnic History of Transylvania* (Astor Park: Danubian Press, 1971), 119.

19 George Clenton Lodio, *Rumania: Its History, Politics and Economics* (Manchester: Sherratt and Hughes, 1932), 21.

20 William Wilkinson, *An Account of the Principalities of Wallachia and Moldavia: With Various Political Observations Relating to Them* (London: Hurst, 1820), 17–18.

21 Wilkinson, *An Account*, 19.

22 Emily Gerard, 'Transylvanian Superstitions', *Nineteenth Century* (July 1885), 130–50, 142.

23 Major E. C. Johnson, *On the Track of the Crescent: Erratic Notes from the Piraeus to Pesth* (London: Hurst and Blacket, 1885), 234.

24 Cain, *Bram Stoker and Russophobia*, 121, 132.

9

ANTHONY BALE

Dracula's Blood

'A Few Unmentionable Preparatory Operations'

Blood is a multifaceted sign and a vital symbol in Stoker's novel. Even those who have never read the novel will know that its key theme is blood-sucking. Blood, in *Dracula*, is not restricted just to Stoker's presentation of the Count's need for blood. Rather blood is phenomenal: sensed, perceived, experienced, lacking in an objective reality or stability: blood matters, but not in one clear, stable way. Central to Stoker's novel are productive questions about the meaning of blood: is blood a life-force or a sign of death? Is it nourishing or polluting? Is blood universal – to animals, living creatures, humans? Or is it particular, gendered, differently valued? How can blood be both a sign of horror and carry within it redemption? And what was the meaning of blood in the fraught Anglo-Irish context in which Stoker grew up and lived, as a conflicting symbol of the Eucharist between Catholics, Protestants and Anglo-Catholics?

The familiar image of the blood-thirsty vampire is at the novel's centre, but alongside it is a range of other bloody conceptions: these include the attack of gout (a painful 'drop' (French: *gout*) of morbid material in the blood) by which Mr Hawkins is afflicted (*D*, 19); the vampire bats of the American pampas, referred to by the Texan Quincey Morris (*D*, 179) and the sacramental body of the consecrated Eucharist brought from Amsterdam by Van Helsing (*D*, 196). Indeed, in the very first pages of Stoker's novel there is a striking moment in which blood-lust is quietly, and strangely, evoked. As Jonathan Harker travels eastwards into Transylvania, he eats a meal of 'Chicken Paprikash', 'a chicken done up some way with red pepper' (*D*, 5). The waiter tells Jonathan that it is the national dish, 'paprika hendl', a dish that Stoker would probably have read about in one of his sources for information on Transylvania. For example, John Paget's *Hungary and Transylvania* (1839) contains a gruesome description of the preparation of chicken paprika hendl:

the cocks and hens are in alarm; one or two of the largest, and probably oldest members of their unfortunate little community, are seized, their necks wrung, and, while yet fluttering, immersed in boiling water. Their coats and skins come off at once; a few unmentionable preparatory operations are rapidly despatched – probably under the traveller's immediate observation – the wretches are cut into pieces, thrown in a pot, with water, butter, flour, cream, and an inordinate quantity of red pepper, or paprika, and, very shortly after, a number of bits of fowl are seen swimming in a dish of hot greasy gravy, quite delightful to think of.[1]

Paget's description, with its evident and explicit pleasure in the violent preparation of the dish, foreshadows the violent exchanges in Stoker's novel, in which bodies are transformed into meals. We learn of Jonathan's enjoyment of the dish but Jonathan notes twice, in his journal, how the dish left him extremely thirsty (*D*, 5, 6). On a literal level, Stoker's knowledge of local cuisine is an authenticating device that shows how he had done his research carefully into the customs of Transylvania. But, on a figurative and allusive level, the bright-red meal can be read as a prediction of the horrors Harker will himself encounter: the Count's appetite for the food of blood and the thirst for more with which each meal leaves him. The dead chicken of Harker's meal, in its tasty, thirst-inducing red sauce, is the first instance in the book of an appetite for another body, one representation amongst many of creatures feeding on another creature.[2] As the novel's plot unfolds, it is clear that in all the characters there is a potential vampire. Quietly, and slyly, in Harker's first meal, and before we have even heard of the Count, Stoker raises the question of the divergent values placed on the transformation of living things into food and the savoury deliciousness of an animal meal.

Similarly, when Mina Harker writes in her journal about Quincey Morris that 'my heart bled for him' (*D*, 215) a metaphorical, sentimental bleeding is invoked. However, in this novel of multiple blood-lettings and transfusions, our attention is drawn to the possible literalness of the image of Mina's bloodied heart (and her bleeding body, from which Count Dracula feeds multiple times), as if to suggest her (Christ-like) offering of her own blood to sustain Quincey. In this scene, Stoker's ironic parallels are reinforced a few lines earlier by his description of Mina's 'red eyes' – a sign of sympathetic crying but elsewhere in the novel a sign of imminent vampirism. Moments later, Mina 'impulsively' bends over and kisses Quincey, upon which 'the tears rose in his eyes, and there was a momentary choking in his throat' (*D*, 215), as Mina's compassion (literally, a participation in suffering) places her in the role of vampire to the prone Quincey. Here Mina and Quincey's conventional and apparently sincere signs of emotion take on a bloodied cast, calling our attention to the ways in which normal human behaviour can be put into ironic and disturbing play through the excitable, unstable image of blood.

A parallel strand of imagery informs Stoker's presentation of blood: that of anti-Semitic representations of blood-sucking and blood-lust, long-standing in European culture. Judith Halberstam has influentially identified the 'Jewish Dracula' through 'his peculiar physique, his parasitical desires, his aversion to the cross and to all the trappings of Christianity, his blood-sucking attacks, and his avaricious relation to money', and identified Stoker as a likely anti-Semite via his friendship with Richard Francis Burton (1821–90), who, in the 1870s, wrote luridly of the 1840 blood libel in Damascus.[3] As Halberstam writes, she complicated her own understanding of Dracula as a Jew, realising that in equating vampirism with Jewishness she had 'unwittingly essentialised Jewishness' and instead sought to show how Gothic monsters like Dracula 'produce monstrosity as never unitary, but always as an aggregate of race, class, and gender'. Halberstam asserts that 'Gothic anti-Semitism makes the Jew a monster with bad blood and it defines monstrosity as a mixture of bad blood, unstable gender identity, sexual and economic parasitism, and degeneracy'.[4] It is hard to refute this assertion; it is, however, applicable to more characters than Dracula alone, and parts of Halberstam's statement could be applied to almost all the novel's characters.

'The Blood Is the Life': Stoker's Medievalist Sacramentalism

The opening sections of *Dracula*, set in Transylvania, are described as a journey to a past coloured by Victorian medievalism. As Jonathan Harker says as he goes into Transylvania,

> All day long we seemed to dawdle through a country which was full of beauty of every kind. Sometimes we saw little towns or castles on the top of steep hills such as we see in old missals; sometimes we ran by rivers and streams which seemed from the wide stony margin on each side of them to be subject to great floods. (*D*, 6)

Harker's invocation of an 'old missal', a medieval manuscript containing the service for the Mass, is a not just a picturesque Gothic touch but quietly invokes the Eucharist of the Christian Mass that will, at the novel's climax, help to save Harker. Stoker is signalling that Harker's thoughts have already turned to the Catholic Mass and the elevation of Christ's body and blood in it; Harker rides into Transylvania with a Catholic conception of sacramental, redemptive blood already in mind. Pre-Protestant temporality is likewise invoked in the shape of the anxious locals, who warn Harker that it is 'the eve of St George's Day' (D, 8), recalling a traditional belief in the potency of evil on the night before saints' days; Harker states that 'it was all very ridiculous, but I did not feel comfortable' and then, apologetically and awkwardly, he takes a rosary and crucifix offered to him by a local woman, even though 'as an English Churchman, I have been taught to regard such things as in some measure idolatrous' (D, 8–9). Thus in the opening pages of the book a potent form of Catholic symbolism is brought forth, in which sacramental and devotional imagery is surprisingly present and efficacious, and touches Jonathan despite his scepticism.

Jonathan's struggles over the meaning of Catholic icons ready us for Stoker's sustained exploration of religious symbolism, in which the certainties of Protestant thought – in which the blood of Christ at the Eucharist is merely a sign rather than an effectual substance – are undermined. Within the first third of the novel Harker moves from his Anglican distrust of Catholicism to being revived, after his escape from Dracula, in what seems to be a Catholic infirmary in Budapest, as we see in a letter written to Mina by 'Sister Agatha' of 'the Hospital of St. Joseph and Ste. Mary' (D, 94). Here Jonathan undertakes what appears to be a Catholic or syncretic marriage with Mina, led by a 'chaplain and the Sisters' and sealed in wax by Mina's wedding-ring, in what she calls 'an outward and visible sign' of trust that directly mirrors St Augustine's definition of a sacrament ('an outward and visible sign of an inward and invisible grace'), a definition which also appears in the Catholic catechism and *The Book of Common Prayer*.

Similarly, the seven Catholic sacraments – baptism, confirmation, Eucharist, penance, anointing the sick, the taking of Holy Orders, and matrimony – appear in various forms throughout *Dracula*, with particular attention being paid to the sacrament of the Eucharist, the body and blood of Christ. The meaning of this body and blood remained, in the Victorian era, the defining issue of difference between Protestant, Catholic and Anglo-Catholic religious rituals and spiritual redemption. Central to the Anglo-Catholic 'revival' of Eucharistic devotion, as led by figures such Edward Pusey and Robert Wilberforce in the 1850s, was a conception of Christ's body as erotic, salvific and intensely physical, as manifested in the bread and wine, body and blood, of His comestible body. Such ideas were themselves a return to late medieval languages of spirituality, of feasting on the 'wonderful blood' of Christ's body;[5] they find their fullest expression in the poetry of writers such as Gerard Manley Hopkins and Christina Rossetti, but they also influence, and were influenced by, the more widespread embrace of Gothic mediaevalism of which Stoker's *Dracula* is a part.

Much of Harker's description of the castle, a building which dates back 'to medieval times' (D, 25), draws directly from the stock motifs of Gothic

literature and shows the influence of the popular and easily-recognisable
'Gothic' of writers like Matthew Lewis, Horace Walpole, Ann Radcliffe and
the direct sources of *Dracula*, like John Polidori's *The Vampyre*. Such
Gothicism represents Stoker's aesthetic choices that create a world of atmos-
pheric description, and eventually sees the men hunting Dracula defining
themselves as Crusaders, 'as old knights of the Cross' (*D*, 297). However,
this Gothicism is accompanied by a slightly different kind of mediaevalism,
replete with theological and sacramental meanings. The novel's journey to
Transylvania is a way of making a set of sustained connections between the
late Victorian plot of the novel and sacramental imagery, at the heart of
which is the ambiguous salvific power of Christ's blood, as figured in
Catholic theology. The presence of Catholicism as an 'old', haunting religion follows the novel's plot back to England and is fully articulated in
'the ruin of Whitby Abbey' (*D*, 61), which haunts the entry of Mina and
Lucy into the novel and overlooks the Count's arrival in England. The
abbey (a Benedictine foundation, built in 657, disestablished in 1538) is
described as 'a most noble ruin, of immense size, and full of beautiful and
romantic bits; there is a legend that a white lady is seen in one of the
windows' (*D*, 61); this legend probably refers to St Hilda (d. 680), abbess
of Whitby, here a local revenant overseeing the point at which Lucy will be
feasted upon by the Count.

Many critics have treated blood as if it is simply part of the novel's
depiction of sex, or, as Troy Boone writes, 'the transfer of blood stands for
sexual intercourse'.[6] However, the basic premise of *Dracula* – that there are
people who need blood to live, who drink blood to receive life – clearly
invites and demands a consideration of Eucharistic theology. The theme of
communion, or inverted communion, in the novel makes Dracula's bloody
meals 'a ghastly parody of the Eucharist'.[7] The book's overarching sacra-
mentalism and its anxieties about and hints of Catholicism demand that we
read Dracula's relationship with blood not as aberrant, but connected to the
drives and desires of all the other characters.

The protean and ultimately tragic character of Renfield, the lunatic
described by Dr Seward as being 'of sanguine temperament' (*D*, 60), is
perhaps the novel's crucible of understanding of the sacramental nature of
blood. Driven by a belief in blood as the source of life (inspired by his reading
of Scripture), Renfield vampirically seeks to eat insects, sparrows, kittens and
cats in the pursuit of immortality, what Seward diagnoses as a 'zoophagous
(life-eating)' mania – a perverted but not illogical version or inversion of the
life-giving power of the Eucharist, with its celebration of the ongoing vitality
of and eternal life-giving properties of the body and blood of Christ.

Renfield's motto, a citation of the biblical book of Deuteronomy that 'the blood is the life', appears twice in the novel; first, after a violent outburst in which Renfield licks drops of Seward's blood from the floor and then, once secured, 'he ... went with the attendants quite placidly, simply repeating over and over again, "The blood is the life! The blood is the life!"' (*D*, 132). Later, in a troubling interview with Mina and Seward, for which he prepares by eating insects and spiders, Renfield calmly and intelligently deliberates blood and elemental philosophy:

> I used to fancy that life was a positive and perpetual entity, and that by consuming a multitude of live things, no matter how low in the scale of creation, one might indefinitely prolong life. At times I held the belief so strongly that I actually tried to take human life. The doctor here will bear me out that on one occasion I tried to kill him for the purpose of strengthening my vital powers by the assimilation with my own body of his life through the medium of his blood – relying, of course, upon the Scriptural phrase, 'For the blood is the life'. Though, indeed, the vendor of a certain nostrum has vulgar-ized the truism to the very point of contempt. Isn't that true, doctor?. (*D*, 218)

Renfield is misquoting Scripture for his own purposes. In context, the quotation is: 'Only be sure that thou eat not the blood: for the blood *is* the life: and thou mayest not eat the life with the flesh' (Deuteronomy 12:23), an injunction *against* the eating of blood, which in turn forms the basis of Jewish dietary laws. Renfield's directly reverses the sentiment of the biblical passage. Furthermore, the 'nostrum' – a quack remedy or patent medicine – to which Renfield refers draws ironic parallels between his aberrant eating of blood and everyday medicinal remedies, extremely popular in the 1890s, of blood pills and blood purifying mixtures. At least two brands of such medicine, Hughes's Blood Pills and Clarke's World-Famous Blood Mixture, adapted the biblical quotation, 'The blood is the life', for their products. In an advertisement that appeared in newspapers in 1896, Hughes's claimed that

> These Pills allow full play to the vitality and vigour inherent in the human body, and thereby help to fructify and strengthen the very essence of life. For the Blood is the Life.[8]

Likewise, advertisements for Clarke's remedy, widely-advertised from the 1870s, opened with the headline: 'For the blood is the life'.[9] Like Renfield, popular medicine was misusing the biblical spirit of the prohibition of eating blood; it was understanding blood over-literally (or, in theological terms, focussing on the *accident* of physical material) without understanding its mysterious, spiritual properties and its symbolic power. These remedies were making vampires of normal people, blood-eaters thriving on a belief, taken for science, in the life-giving nature of blood.

In his diary, Renfield's doctor, Seward, writes, ambiguously, of his manic patient: 'He *is* a selfish old beggar anyhow. He thinks of the loaves and fishes even when he believes he is in a Real Presence. His manias make a startling combination' (*D*, 97). Seward's language summarises the theological difference between Catholic and Protestant conceptions of the Eucharist – the 'Real Presence' of Christ's body and blood in the bread and wine *versus* the accident, or material sign, of the bread and wine which function as tokens of Christ's body; the 'loaves and the fishes' point to Renfield, or Seward's, own theological confusion.

'Unclean! Unclean!'

The climax of the novel's description of blood is the vivid tableau of Mina Harker sucking at Dracula's open wound as a Jonathan, 'as if in a stupor, lies at her side (*D*, 262). In Dr Seward's account,

> With his left hand he held both Mrs Harker's hands, keeping them away with her arms at full tension; his right hand gripped her by the back of the neck, forcing her face down on his bosom. Her white nightdress was smeared with blood, and a thin stream trickled down the man's bare breast, which was shown by his torn-open dress. The attitude of the two had a terrible resemblance to a child forcing a kitten's nose into a saucer of milk to compel it to drink. As we burst into the room, the Count turned his face, and the hellish look that I had heard described seemed to leap into it. His eyes flamed red with devilish passion; the great nostrils of the white aquiline nose opened wide and quivered at the edges; and the white sharp teeth, behind the full lips of the blood-dripping mouth, champed together like those of a wild beast. With a wrench, which threw his victim back upon the bed as though hurled from a height, he turned and sprang at us. But by this time the Professor had gained his feet, and was holding towards him the envelope which contained the Sacred Wafer. (*D*, 262)

This dramatic and arresting moment is replete with sexual symbolism, as Mina kneels of the edge of the bed, in her stained nightdress, in an intimate bedroom scene. But this scene also calls to mind many other images, including Mina's menstruation, Jonathan's martyrdom and the Count's Christ-like giving of his blood.[10] Mina is, clearly, an unwilling participant, 'forced' to suck at the Count's breast.

Perhaps the strangest detail is Seward's simile that Dracula coerces Mina like 'a child forcing a kitten's nose into a saucer of milk'. This has been interpreted as a metaphor for fellatio, as 'an oedipal child's fantasy of a mother's castration', converting milk into blood, or 'a parody of breast feeding' marked by 'subtle inversions of gender', and indeed the reference to milk is suggestive of a connection between milk and blood, the Madonna and Christ.[11] Seward's simile of the kitten may also bring our mind back to Renfield's desire for a kitten for his own bloody purposes ('a kitten, a kitten, I only wanted a kitten', he wheedles to Dr Seward), although the image of the kitten led to milk is inductive, educative, rather than cruel: the child in Seward's simile is teaching the kitten to drink.

Gil Anidjar has suggested another kind of source for this striking tableau, one rooted not in repressed sexuality but in popular religion. He focuses on Christ's side-wound, 'an image of wounded attachment'.[12] He briefly invokes St Catherine of Siena (d. 1380) who was famous for receiving the stigmata (marks of Christ's wounds). In her mystical marriage to God, she pressed herself to Christ's bloody side-wound and kissed or drank from this wound. Like Dracula's non-phallic embrace of Mina, St Catherine's embrace by Jesus is a bloody communion, and one that might appear both gory and tasteless to Anglican readers. As Catherine's biographer Raymond of Capua (d. 1399, beatified 1899) wrote,

> And placing the right hand on Catharine's neck, he drew her to the wound of her sacred side, saying to her, 'Drink, daughter, that luscious beverage which flows from my side, it will inebriate thy soul with sweetness and will also plunge in a sea of delight thy body, which thou didst despise for love of me'. Catherine thus placed at the very fountain of life, applied her mouth to the sacred wound of the Saviour, her soul drew thence an ineffable and divine liquor; she drank long and with as much avidity as abundance; in fine, when our blessed Lord gave her notice, she detached herself from the sacred source, satiated, but still eager, because she experienced no repletion at being satiated, nor pain at still desiring. O ineffable mercy of the Lord, how delightful thou art to those who love thee! How delicious to such as taste thee! ... [C]ontemplate, in fine, that soul which derives its strength from God, which praise cannot render haughty, and which gains over the flesh a last triumph, by *drinking* what it shuddered with horror merely to see![13]

There are clear parallels, allusions even, between Stoker's account of Mina and Raymond's account of St Catherine, down to the details of the right hand guiding the woman by the neck, and the multiple ways that, in both accounts, disgust is converted to savour. On one level, Stoker is merely offering this scene as an inversion of Christ's Eucharistic body; however, after her enforced drinking from the wound, Mina draws our attention back to the circulation of blood from the Bible to her own lips, as she sobs 'Unclean! Unclean! I must touch [Jonathan] or kiss him no more' (*D*, 264), as she casts herself as the biblical leper of Leviticus: 'And the leper in whom the plague *is* ... he shall put a covering upon his upper lip, and shall cry, "Unclean, unclean"' (Leviticus 13:45).

Again we see how blood transforms – here, backwards in time to the biblical injunction, travelling first from vampirism to leprosy (itself a cypher for syphilis), and then as a barrier between Mina and Jonathan – a spectral blood that stays on her lips even as it has been rubbed off.

Stoker may well have been familiar with this image of St Catherine, for in the later nineteenth century several English-language biographies of her had appeared, including a widely-read account by the Evangelical reformer Josephine Butler.[14] The story of St Catherine kissing or drinking from Christ's side-wound is omitted in Butler's biography, which focuses on St Catherine's social and political activism. However, a brief account of St Catherine's drinking of Christ's blood was included in the biography *The History of St Catherine of Siena and Her Companions*, by Augusta Drane, an English Dominican nun.[15] The image of St Catherine, like the image of Mina drinking at Dracula's side, was thus remarkably versatile and open to interpretation in the context in which Stoker was writing.

All the characters in Stoker's novel become linked to each other through the sharing of blood, through transfusions, cuts, wounds, sucking and bleeding. Blood, as written in *Dracula*, might be read as radically relativised: from Harker's eating of the *hendl* to the experimental blood transfusions to the miraculous Eucharist, blood is presented as far less stable than either a 'racialist' or Protestant account would allow. As Larry Rickels has argued, *Dracula* 'releases the blood inside the cross' and causes us to see the centrality of blood to western culture.[16] But it also suggests that blood is at once an essential symbol and one without an essential meaning. For, as Van Helsing says, 'there are always mysteries in life' (*D*, 179), and, in *Dracula*, blood remains the most precious and mysterious of substances.

Notes

1 John Paget, *Hungary and Transylvania; with remarks on their condition*, 2 vols. (London: John Murray, 1839), vol. 2, 521.
2 This meal is interpreted as a resistance to eating meat in David Del Principe, '(M)eating Dracula: Food and Death in Stoker's novel', *Gothic Studies* 16 (2014), 24–38.
3 Judith Halberstam, 'Technologies of Monstrosity: Bram Stoker's *Dracula*', *Victorian Studies* 36 (1993), 333–52, quote on p. 333.
4 Halberstam, 'Technologies of Monstrosity', 333–34 and 337.
5 Bettina Bildhauer, *Medieval Blood* (Cardiff: University of Wales Press, 2006) and Caroline Walker Bynum, *Wonderful Blood* (Philadelphia: University of Pennsylvania Press, 2007).

6 Troy Boone, '"He Is English and Therefore Adventurous": Politics, Decadence, and *Dracula*', *Studies in the Novel* 25 (1993), 76–91, quote on p. 88.

7 John Allen Stevenson, 'A Vampire in the Mirror: The Sexuality of *Dracula*', *PMLA* 103 (1988), 139–49, quote on p. 144.

8 *Barry Dock News* (18 September 1896), 8.

9 *The Times* (8 November 1881), 10.

10 As Jesus says, 'Take ye and eat: This Is My Body' (Matthew 26:26).

11 Jean-Jacques Lecercle, 'The Kitten's Nose: *Dracula* and Witchcraft', *Essays & Studies* 54 (2001), 71–86. Ira Konigsberg, 'How Many Draculas Does It Take to Change a Lightbulb?', in Andrew Horton and Stuart McDougal, eds., *Play It Again Sam: Retakes on Remakes* (Berkeley: University of California Press, 1998), pp. 250–75, and Alexandra Warwick, 'Vampires and the Empire: Fears and Fictions of the 1890s', in Sally Ledger and Scott McCracken, eds., *Cultural Politics at the Fin de Siècle* (Cambridge: Cambridge University Press, 1995), pp. 202–20, quote on p. 212.

12 Gil Anidjar, *Blood: A Critique of Christianity* (New York: Columbia University Press, 2014), 199.

13 Here quoting from one of several Victorian translations that Stoker might have consulted: Raymond of Capua, *The Life of St Catharine of Siena*, trans. Mother Regis Hamilton (New York: P. J. Kenedy, 1862), 109–10.

14 Josephine E. Butler, *St Catharine of Siena: A Biography* (London: Horace Marshall, 1878). The 1885 and 1888 editions were best-sellers.

15 Augusta Theodosia Drane, *The History of St. Catherine of Siena and Her Companions* (London: Burns and Oates, 1880), 42. Likewise, Sarah Atkinson, 'A Citizen Saint', *Irish Monthly* 3 (1875), 18.

16 Larry Rickels, *The Vampire Lectures* (Minneapolis: University of Minnesota Press, 1999), 116.

10

CAROL SENF

Dracula and Women

Dracula: the one-word title implies that its eponymous character will dominate Stoker's novel, but even the earliest scenes point to the significance of the women in it. A key early moment is Jonathan Harker's ambivalent response when confronted by Dracula's three sisters (or wives, or lovers):

> All three had brilliant white teeth, that shone like pearls against the ruby of their voluptuous lips. There was something about them that made me uneasy, some longing and at the same time some deadly fear. I felt in my heart a wicked, burning desire that they would kiss me with those red lips. (D, 38)

This hallucinatory nightmare of conflicted desire is fairly rapidly displaced by a realist scene of domestic comedy back in Britain, when Harker's fiancée, Mina, meets her confidante Lucy Westenra for 'a capital "severe tea"' in a Robin's Hood Bay inn (D, 85). Mina's diary records, satirically, that the two demure young women might have 'shocked the "New Woman" with our appetites' (D, 85). Even so, this comic rendition of female desire has a stronger edge. Mina writes in her diary entry later as Lucy sleeps that her face is now flushed and satiated, and speculates: 'If Mr Holmwood fell in love with her seeing her only in the drawing-room, I wonder what he would say if he saw her now' (D, 85). Her thoughts continue:

> 'New Women' writers will some day start an idea that men and women should be allowed to see each other asleep before proposing or accepting. But I suppose the 'New Woman' won't condescend in future to accept; she will do the proposing herself. (D, 85)

Within a few terrible weeks, Lucy will suffer an unimaginable punishment for her active 'appetites'. Instead of a sanctified marriage to Lord Holmwood, the prospective husband is compelled to drive a stake through her body to destroy the undead vampire, the beast of uncontrollable desire, that Lucy has become. As she is dispatched, her body presents a last horrific (yet clearly orgasmic) manifestation of the alien perversity that has infected her: 'The Thing in the coffin writhed; and a hideous, blood-curdling screech came from the opened red lips. The body shook and quivered and twisted in wild contortions; the sharp white teeth champed together till the lips were cut and mouth with smeared with crimson foam' (*D*, 201).

If this is a portrait of a punitive patriarchy containing the wayward desire of middle-class women, *Dracula* is also a book that increasingly relies on the intellectual, administrative and mothering capacities of Mina Harker, in a plot where men have their masculinity continually unravelled and where victory over dark forces is seriously risked only when the brotherhood foolishly exclude Mina from their plans. *Dracula*, it is safe to say, is deeply conflicted and confused when it comes to gender.

The New Woman

In using the term 'New Woman', Mina refers to a cultural phenomenon made possible by the burgeoning women's movement in the late nineteenth century. The term had been coined by the women writers Sarah Grand and 'Ouida' (pen-name of the writer Louise Ramé) in a pair of articles called 'The New Aspect of the Woman Question' in the *North American View* in 1894, and it was soon in wide circulation.[1] This figure was never an entirely coherent construct, being characterised either as overtly sexual or inversely as a 'mannish' woman, merely impersonating male capacities, the latter figure much mocked by *Punch* in cartoons, usually dressed in frumpish clothes, wearing spectacles and often indulging in the very masculine act of smoking. This ridicule nevertheless revealed anxiety about the campaign for women's suffrage, for property rights, for equal access to education and sometimes (although rarely explicitly) for the right to sexual self-determination. In her history of the gender politics of late Victorian London, Judith Walkowitz notes how women's presence in the public sphere advanced rapidly. Married women had finally been granted property rights in 1882 and there had been a major victory for women with the repeal of laws that allowed for the arrest and forcible examination of women suspected of being 'street-walkers'.[2] These concerns were often being articulated in public discourse for the first time in the 1880s and 1890s.

Not only does 'New Woman' describe intellectuals who sought equal rights for women, but it was also a ubiquitous archetype in the 1890s, appearing in many novels by overtly feminist writers such as Olive Schreiner, Sarah Grand, Mona Caird or George Egerton.[3] The 'Woman Question' was taken up in novels of the 1890s by significant male writers like George Gissing, Henry James and Thomas Hardy, and on stage in controversial plays by Arthur Pinero and George Bernard Shaw and in the staging of

August Strindberg's *Miss Julie* (1888) or Henrik Ibsen's excoriating play on women's social restriction, *Hedda Gabler* (1891). Stoker was invoking a very current debate, and as personal manager to Ellen Terry, one of the leading actresses on the London stage, would have been very sensitive to the shifting attitudes to gender in the public sphere.

Indeed, the impact of Stoker's his work at the Lyceum might have had on his treatment of women is an important consideration. The Victorian theatre was a place of sexual nonconformity, and there were constant insinuations of sexual impropriety against theatre people in the Victorian period. Lisa Hopkins argues that the 'hysteria which so often surrounds Stoker's writing about gender could well be seen as the product of a radical insecurity on this front'.[4] Stoker was very close to Ellen Terry, who was famous for transforming herself across the range of female roles, moving 'from charming maiden to voluptuous hoyden'.[5] How much was watching Terry perform part of the transformation of Lucy Westenra from virginal daughter to anti-maternal monster? As Catherine Wynne has noted, Terry, as a working mother, was always greeted with some ambiguity, 'most famously by her own son, who describes her as possessing a double self as she transforms between E.T. (working actress) and Nelly Terry (mother)'.[6] Stoker presents this female dichotomy in *Dracula*, and explores the speed with which one might transform into the other. This seems directly connected to his fascination with the performative transformation of the gendered self in theatre.

The early reception of *Dracula* suggests that even Gothic pot-boilers were noted for registering debates about gender in the 1890s. Andrew Lang might have observed lewdly in *Longman's Magazine* that Lucy 'who became a vampire after receiving three proposals in one day must have been a minx', but *Daily Telegraph* noted a more serious connection to gender politics: 'Already the public is getting tired of romance and is once more asking for the social problems and the deeper analysis into character which were temporarily obscured by the extravagances of the New Woman'.[7]

If other reviewers focused on Dracula's 'bevy of lovely yet loathsome females', observing that the master vampire 'uses beautiful women as his agents and compasses the death of many innocent people', that was because the vampire was far more commonly associated with women than men at the time.[8] The image of the night hag or succubus offered a folkloric version of demonic women who sapped male potency, an image repeated, for instance, in Edvard Munch's series of paintings called 'Love and Pain' in 1893 – paintings more familiarly known under the name 'The Vampire'. Florence Marryat's novel *The Blood of a Vampire*, which also appeared in 1897, concerns a mixed-race beauty who slowly leeches her upstanding, European male admirers of their life-blood, her desire figured as a deadly exotic wasting disease. Stoker's early drafts for *Dracula* also show his indebtedness to Sheridan Le Fanu's 'Carmilla', where the woman vampire from Styria is an aristocrat who lives on the blood of younger female serfs. Blood is the life; it is also a lesbian desire.

In 1897, *Dracula* also spoke to the anxiety that the ambitions of the New Woman in campaigning for sexual equality risked perverting motherhood, and therefore, by extension, the very future of the Anglo-Saxon race itself. As one reviewer noted:

> The horrible part of the matter is that young children constitute so large a percentage of the vampire's victims. Mr Bram Stoker's vampire used to put babies into bags, and take them home for the supper of other vampires ... Our author further records cases in which children on Hampstead Heath were waylaid by female vampire ... who began giving them sweeties, and ended by sucking their blood.[9]

Maternity was often at the core of narratives of Western decline or what was histrionically termed the 'suicide' of the Anglo-Saxon race. In Stoker's binaristic vision of femininity, Lucy's unholy inversion of motherhood is eventually displaced by Mina Harker's return to racial purity, after her partial contamination by the Count, and her final role is to retreat from her intellectual position as the sifter of textual evidence and to serve instead as mother to a future generation of Anglo-Saxons safe (for the moment) from the invasive threat of foreign blood.

Dracula and Feminism

It was over half a century before scholars paid serious attention to Stoker's novel – in the early 1970s. Significantly, the rebirth of interest in *Dracula* coincided with Second Wave Feminism, a movement that emerged in the late 1960s and focused on women's struggle for equal rights and opportunities, but also wished to emphasise the importance of considering the cultural consequences of sexual difference. Second wave feminist literary criticism offered a critique of the representation of women in canonical literature, the eclipse of women's voices and the tendency of dominant 'patriarchal' culture to think in stark oppositions and implicit hierarchies about the politics of gender, particularly taking aim at the crude Madonna/Whore binary that typically constrained cultural representations of women.[10] *Dracula* is ripe for this kind of critique: it was not surprising that Second Wave scholarship focused on the women in the novel.

This is where the influential arguments that much of the novel's great appeal derived from its hostility toward female sexuality were first articulated. Critics like Phyllis Roth, Judith Weissman and Gail Griffin argued that Mina is finally redeemed because the book ends with her as a mother who perpetuates the ethos of the Protestant north against the corruption of the south, and that any dangerous New Womanly sexual overtones are erased. This symbolic opposition of women between the vampiric *femme fatale* and the still-dominant domestic model of the 'Angel in the House' makes *Dracula* exemplary of binaristic, patriarchal thinking.[11]

Second Wave Feminism was influential on these scholarly readings of *Dracula*, but a shift began to take place in the early 1980s. Critiques emerged that suggested that there might be what Julia Kristeva called a third 'signifying space' beyond assertions of First Wave gender equality or Second Wave gender difference.[12] This was Third Wave Feminism (later sometimes contentiously called 'Postfeminism'), a movement that was initially intertwined with radical poststructuralist theories in France.[13] These writers, like Kristeva and Luce Irigaray, rejected the gender binary itself as a social construct. 'In this third attitude, which I strongly advocate', Kristeva said, 'the very dichotomy man/woman as an opposition between two rival entities may be understood as belonging to *metaphysics*'.[14] Feminists also began an auto-critique that questioned earlier waves for ignoring questions of race, class and sexuality and for presuming unexamined white middle-class norms for feminist criticism.

Of these more 'intersectional' approaches, queer theory has been the most influential, because the liminal figure of the vampire, occupying the in-between space of life and death, intrinsically troubles sex and gender binaries. Christopher Craft's formative essay in this regard links the lurid plot of *Dracula* to gender politics, in part because the more common medicalised term for homosexuality in the 1890s was 'sexual inversion' (the pioneering case studies of men and women who desired those of the same sex were gathered together by British sexologists Havelock Ellis and J. A. Symonds under the title *Sexual Inversion* in 1897). This was a diagnosis that theorised that the male homosexual had 'inverted' supposedly 'natural' masculine and feminine traits. In *Dracula*, the scene at the graveyard where Lucy is brutally put back in her box is because she has 'inverted' the normative feminine passive position to assert an active, masculine sexuality.

The risk of merely identifying binary structures, even unstable ones, is that the specificity of *Dracula* is lost to large transhistorical abstractions or generalisations. Some of the most rewarding feminist interventions have been to situate the novel very precisely within discourses of the late Victorian period where the formations of gender and sexuality were undergoing very particular recalibration.

In medicine, for instance, behaviour considered 'aberrant' in women was often biologised or psychologised as the product of somatic disorder, an intrinsic medical weakness. Women were considered to have more sensitive nerves and delicate constitutions that could easily be thrown out of order given the inherent instabilities of their complex reproductive systems. Dangers abounded at puberty, at periodic menstruation, at motherhood, and women risked 'post-partum insanity' and mental and physical dangers at menopause unless properly managed. Eminent doctors, such as Henry Maudsley, advised against women's education in case it risked over-stimulation and consequent nervous collapse. Women were also considered more open to hypnotic suggestion because they had weaker reserves of will-power. 'A woman instinctively responds more easily than a man to influences from without, even in spite of herself', Havelock Ellis authoritatively recorded in *Man and Woman*, first issued in 1894.[15]

In many ways, Lucy's descent into vampirism is structured as a medical case. Lucy's symptoms of sleep-walking, delirium and over-sexualised reactions suggest a case of hysterical degeneracy, as outlined, say, by the famous psychologist and neurologist Jean-Martin Charcot in Paris in the 1880s, or in the relatively new disorder of the female sex, 'nymphomania'. *Dracula* was written soon after Josef Breuer and Sigmund Freud's *Studies in Hysteria* (1893), a book constructed as a series of case studies of 'disturbed' women that require the intervention of a (male) analyst to speak their own unspeakable desires, which, blocked, have produced bodily symptoms of hysteria. Between the lines of these case studies, the reader discerns the lives of constrained women, driven to distraction by the frustrations of rigid social containment. But the medical 'cure' for Lucy's case is far more violent than this: 'In *Dracula* the vampire-hunters gather around the Undead body of the transformed vampire Lucy in her tomb and perform a ceremony on her which is a fusion of medical operation (cliterodectomy?), rape and cathartic expulsion'.[16]

Contemporary approaches to menstruation through more anthropological and psychological lenses are important, too. Stoker may have known of some of this research through his brothers, three of whom were prominent doctors (Thornley Stoker certainly advised his brother on blood transfusion medicine). From Lucy's first encounter with Dracula to her final staking, she is an exemplary case study of the pathologisation of the menstruating woman and the patriarchal control and containment of female sexuality by medical discourse. Maria Parsons suggests that *Dracula* was influenced by recent developments in obstetrics and gynaecology, especially those that focused on menstruation as the primary cause of women's mental and physical ill health:

> In particular, the redevelopment of the speculum and the curette, revolution-ized gynaecological practice. Furthermore, menstrual outflow was measured

and its consistency and colour recorded in order to determine normative points of reference. This both allowed and contributed to the diagnosis and treatment of a wide ranging number of female ailments as menstrual.[17]

Lucy's pathology is highly over-determined, with symptoms of somnambulism, anaemia and hereditary heart disease. She might even also be diagnosed as a drug addict, displaying the compulsive behaviours of the opiate addict that formed an important part of how Decadence or degeneracy was represented in the 1890s. Women's dependency on opiates, Kristina Aikens has argued, can reveal how *Dracula* 'illuminates a complex relationship between middle-class women and the opiates that ... could serve as a means of patriarchal oppression or resistance to it'.[18]

In short, Lucy becomes an instance of how Victorian women could be disciplined and controlled by apparently objective medical discourse, where the normal is defined negatively by an obsessional definitional focus on the pathological or abnormal. *Dracula* therefore contributes to the kinds of discourses

> whereby the female body was analyzed, qualified and disqualified as being totally immersed in its sexuality. The body, saturated by female sexuality, was then integrated into the sphere of medical practice. Women's bodies and their sexuality were medicalized for the sake of the family and society. The medical profession acquired the power of possession and control over women through this medicalization, which rendered pathological natural female functions such as parturition and menstruation.[19]

As the other half of this feminine equation, Mina is also examined for signs of pathology by the men of the novel, particularly after she develops her deep affinity with the vampire once contaminated by the Count in the novel's most perverse marriage-bed scene. Perhaps she is less the faithful Mina that some early reviewers praised. But Mina Harker has more roles in *Dracula* than merely serving as the foil to the pathological case of Lucy Westenra. Mina is in fact at the centre of the conjuncture of technology and gender identity in the novel. *Dracula* self-consciously embraces modernity, emphasises the speed with which characters travel, the profusion of guidebooks, railway time-tables, telegrams, typewriters, microphones and phonographs. Mina the type-writer in this book, is clearly a condensation of the emergent professional 'typewriter girl' in 1890s culture. In effect, Mina *constructs* the text we read as an intelligence briefing 'from a mass of type-writing' (D, 351). Mina's skills at shorthand and typing points to the emergence of women into the professional working world who were 'an index of the increasing numbers of women teachers and office workers in the lower-middle-class sector of the labor force', tropes and devices that are associated with the New Woman.[20] The typewriter girl or the female telegraphist were the most visible cultural renditions of the entry of women into the workface in the late Victorian period, with all the attendant anxieties that produced.[21] But for all the potential liberation in this portrait of Mina as a working professional woman, the nerve centre of operations, Stoker redeploys these representations against the women's movement, David Glover argues: 'No matter how chivalrous or romantic his literary sentiments were, he seldom missed an opportunity to excoriate the presumption of sexual equality'.[22]

First published in 1897, *Dracula* has never been out of print, and its popularity seems to be growing rather than diminishing. Similarly, interest in its structural dichotomy of types of women characters continues. While the fears about vampiric sexuality have modulated somewhat, and even been embraced as a form of dissident or queered sexuality, Stoker's response to his own time always prompts us to question whether Mina and Lucy are agents of female empowerment or portents of sexual anarchy. Does Mina's familiarity with technology and her skill at communication represent Stoker's endorsement of the New Woman? Or does her appearance at *Dracula*'s conclusion with her son suggest that Stoker advocated a return to more traditional feminine roles? These ambivalences interested Stoker's contemporaries and continue to pique the curiosity of readers more than a century later.

Notes

1 See Sally Ledger, *The New Woman: Fiction and Feminism at the Fin de Siècle* (Manchester: Manchester University Press, 1997) and Elaine Showalter, *Sexual Anarchy: Gender and Culture at the Fin de Siècle* (New York: Virago Press, 1992).

2 Judith Walkowitz, *City of Dreadful Delight: Narratives of Sexual Danger in Late-Victorian London* (Chicago: University of Chicago Press, 1992).

3 Sally Ledger and Roger Luckhurst, 'New Woman', *The Fin de Siècle: A Reader in Cultural History c. 1880–1900* (Oxford: Oxford University Press, 2000), p. 75.

4 Lisa Hopkins, *Bram Stoker: A Literary Life* (Basingstoke: Palgrave, 2008), 18.

5 Catherine Wynne, *Bram Stoker, Dracula and the Victorian Gothic Stage* (New York: Palgrave Macmillan, 2013), 79.

6 Wynne, *Gothic Stage*, 98–99.

7 Lang review in *Longman's Magazine* (1901) and *Daily Telegraph* (3 June 1897), both in John Edgar Browning, ed. *Bram Stoker's Dracula: The Critical Feast, An Annotated Reference of Early Reviews and Reactions, 1897–1913* (Berkeley: Apocryphile Press, 2011), p. 32.

8 *The Argus* (Melbourne, Australia, 6 Nov. 1897) and the *San Francisco Chronicle* (17 Dec. 1899), in Browning, *Critical Feast*, pp. 84 and 104.

9 *The Hawkes Bay Herald* (23 April 1898), in Browning, *Critical Feast*, p. 91.

10 A collection of primary texts is available in Linda J. Nicholson, ed., *The Second Wave: A Reader in Feminist Theory* (London: Routledge, 1997). An early summary (and critique) of Second Wave feminist literary criticism appears in Toril Moi, *Sexual/Textual Politics* (London: Routledge, 1985).

11 Phyllis Roth, 'Suddenly Sexual Women in Bram Stoker's *Dracula*', *Literature and Psychology* 27 (1977); Judith Weissman, 'Women and Vampires: *Dracula* as a Victorian Novel', *Midwest Quarterly* 18 (1977); Gail B. Griffin, '"Your Girls That You All Love Are Mine": *Dracula* and the Victorian Male Sexual Imagination', *International Journal of Women's Studies* 3 (1980); Stephanie Demetrakopoulos, 'Feminism, Sex Role Exchanges, and Other Subliminal Fantasies in Bram Stoker's *Dracula*', *Frontiers: A Journal of Women Studies* 2 (1977).

12 Julia Kristeva, 'Women's Time' in Toril Moi, ed., *The Kristeva Reader* (Oxford: Blackwell, 1986), p. 209.

13 See key anthology Elaine Marks and Isabelle de Courtivron, eds., *New French Feminisms* (New York: Schocken Books, 1988).

14 Kristeva, 'Women's Time', in Moi, *The Kristeva Reader*, 209.

15 Havelock Ellis, *Man and Woman: A Study of Human Secondary Sexual Characters*, 6th edn. (London: A + C Black, 1930), 408.

16 Rebecca Stott, *The Fabrication of the Late-Victorian Femme Fatale: The Kiss of Death* (London: Macmillan, 1992), 49.

17 See Maria Parsons, 'Vamping the Woman: Menstrual Pathologies in Bram Stoker's *Dracula*', *The Irish Journal of Gothic and Horror Studies* 1 (2006), https://irishgothichorror.wordpress.com/.

18 Kristina Aikens, 'Battling Addictions in *Dracula*', *Gothic Studies* 11, no. 2 (2009), 41. See also Susan Zieger, *Inventing the Addict: Drugs, Race and Sexuality in Nineteenth-Century British and American Literature* (Amherst: University of Massachusetts Press, 2008), 42.

19 Marie Mulvey-Roberts, '*Dracula* and the Doctors: Bad Blood, Menstrual Taboo and the New Woman', in William Hughes and Andrew Smith, eds., *Bram Stoker: History, Psychoanalysis and the Gothic* (New York: St Martin's Press, 1998), p. 85.

20 David Glover, *Vampires, Mummies and Liberals: Bram Stoker and the Politics of Popular Fiction* (Durham, NC: Duke University Press, 1996), 96.

21 Katherine Mullin, *Working Girls: Fiction, Sexuality and Modernity* (Oxford: Oxford University Press, 2016).

22 Glover, *Vampires, Mummies and Liberals*, 106.

PART III

New Directions

11

XAVIER ALDANA REYES

Dracula Queered

What is *Dracula*'s investment, consciously or unconsciously, in the sexual politics of representation? Is *Dracula* about raising the spectre of promiscuity in the transformation of Lucy and Mina into vampires, which the plot then works to contain? What does the circulation of blood symbolise in Lucy's transfusion scene? Does the mixing of blood throughout the novel invoke the horrors of miscegenation, the threat to 'cultural and racial difference' represented by the vampire bite?[1]

Such readings propose that the novel negotiates taboos strongly connected to heterosexual fantasies. But Richard Dyer has traced the similarities between the vampire and the homosexual, and noted that both subjects are characterised by 'the necessity of secrecy, the persistence of a forbidden passion, and the fear of discovery'.[2] However, any simple correspondence should be challenged, and in this chapter I want to distinguish between *gay*, a specific sexual identity, and *queer*, a political label that expresses difference in sexual desire, a more open and non-specific non-heteronormative form of desire and identity. This approach will make it possible to explore *Dracula* as more than just a text to be read as symptomatic of hidden sexual secrets and questions whether the vampire can ever be read as a stable metaphor.

This chapter begins by taking into consideration the vampire's metaphoric associations with the homosexual but then moves on to try to find the more radical queer potential at its heart. At stake is the vampire's embrace of an explicit sexuality, which alters clean-cut metaphoric appropriations of the Count and his progeny as simple homosexual proxies. This gives the potential for *Dracula* to provide for new models that criticise the stable identities of both straight *and* gay, heteronormative *and* homonormative. The vampire, and Dracula in particular, may act as an oppositional force that can embody the political impetus of queer theory.

Sexual Repression and the Vampiric Metaphor

The first part of *Dracula*, in which Jonathan Harker meets the Count and the three 'weird sisters' (*D*, 48) who will eventually vampirise him, has been fertile ground for critical interventions seeking to highlight the text's homo-eroticism. Dracula interrupts and condemns the seduction of Harker by making it clear that 'This man belongs to me!' (*D*, 39). But his reaction, when challenged, is similarly telling. Lest the intervention be read as any-thing but an expression of romantic interest, one of the women, with 'ribald coquetry', accuses the Count of having 'never loved; you never love!' (*D*, 40). He defends himself from this charge by emphasising that he 'too can love' (*D*, 40). Consequently, the vampirism in the novel has been read as a powerful metaphor for a homosexual desire that cannot manifest openly in a society that condemns it.

The most significant early critic to tease out and explore the implications of such a psychosexual reading through the symbolism of the kiss of the vampire was Christopher Craft. His essay appeared in 1984, six years after the publication of the English translation of Michel Foucault's influential *Introduction to the History of Sexuality*, which spoke of the invention of homosexuality as a Victorian medical pathology, and a year before Eve Kosofsky Sedgwick's book-length study of homosociality in literature, *Between Men*, often seen as the fore-runner of Queer Theory.[3] Craft under-stands the novel's construction of monstrosity as analogous with sexual desire, so that vampirism can both 'express ... and distort ... an originally sexual energy' and, by doing this, lay bare the real anxiety in the narrative 'that Dracula will seduce, penetrate, drain another male'.[4]

Through a species of gender inversion in which women, usually connected with a passive sexual appetite, become active after they have been vampirised, Craft reads the moment of biting as one of metaphorical penetration. In this light, the vampiric kiss of the three sisters can be taken as an extension of Dracula's original one: his children do his bidding and sublimate the one desire the novel cannot represent, 'the actual penetration of a male', which has to be fulfilled through a series of 'heterosexual displacements'.[5] Signifi-cantly, for Craft, these moments are disavowed, for at no point does the novel directly represent Harker, or any other male in the narrative, in the act of being bitten. Biting is implied and appears only on the brink of taking place. This has the effect, Craft argues, of 'repeat[ing] the threat of a more libidinous embrace between Dracula and Harker': it reifies the threat of penetration as an inherent source of male anxiety and fuses fear and desire.[6] Craft also provides the possible socio-historical impulse behind his desire, drawing parallels to accounts of same-sex eroticism as 'inversion' at the time, such as that of the poet and critic John Addington Symonds, who understood this desire as the improper correlation of sexual organs and sexual instinct. The period in which *Dracula* was published coincides, in fact, with the 'first sustained discourse about . . . male homoerotic love' as sexual inversion.[7]

Craft extends this socio-historical reading to account for the punishment of the sexually active woman (the fanged and penetrative Lucy in *Dracula*) who, in her rejection of the quiescent role she has been allocated by patriarchal, heterosexual norms (incarnated by Van Helsing and the Crew of Light), effectively embodies lesbian desire understood as another form of sexual inversion. Further proof of this inversion is Lucy's preying on children, which reverses the nurturing maternal role of woman and, in one episode, parodies breast-feeding, as the child 'she clutche[s] strenuously to her breast' is actually being fed upon (*D*, 197). Lucy's vampirism necessitates her punitive destruction. The expunging of evil is connected to sexual repression in a sleight of hand that sees in Lucy's staking a forceful penetration. As Craft argues:

> This enthusiastic correction of Lucy's monstrosity provides the Crew of Light with a double reassurance: it effectively exorcises the threat of a mobile and hungering feminine sexuality and it counters the homoeroticism latent in the vampire threat by reinscribing (upon Lucy's chest) the line dividing the male who penetrates and the woman who receives. By disciplining Lucy and restoring each gender to its 'proper' function, Van Helsing's pacification program compensates for the threat of gender indefinition implicit in the vampiric kiss.[8]

Lucy's 'post-penetrative' peace, therefore, appears as an indication that the 'dangerous signifier' she had become has been neutralised, and the heteronormative order restored. In another displacement, Lucy experiences what should have been Dracula's correction because 'Stoker simply could not represent so explicitly a violent phallic interchange between the Crew of Light and Dracula'.[9] The book ends with the Count hurriedly dispatched by the slice of a knife rather than the thrust of a stake.

The displacement of homoerotic desire onto the feminine in *Dracula* makes this transgressive desire *bisexual*. According to Margaret Howes, this bisexuality could be understood as an explanation for a man's desire for other men: everyone is bisexual, but their place in the scale of masculinity or femininity, which is biologically determined, decides their ultimate 'sexual appetite'.[10] In *Dracula*, this forbidden and sinful desire is repressed and eventually sublimated through vampirism, as this condition allows for a mixture of both feminine and masculine attributes in women. Dracula becomes Harker's monstrous and unsatisfied desire, and the novel's turn to vampiric women is a re-direction of Harker's horror of falling prey to the Count. This, in turn, belies a deeper fear of emasculation through the feminisation entailed by an acceptance of desire for another male. Much as it does in Craft's argument, the vampire is inherently connected to sin, but stands as the only real mediator of repressed sexual desire.

These interpretations show how much meaning may be uncovered by approaches that emphasise *Dracula*'s incapacity to say what it really wants to say. Contemporaneous discourses of 'repressed sexuality' affected the writing and yet also offer us the key to a reading of certain images and actions as sexual displacements. The vampires are symptoms insofar as they are a result of the time and writer who produced them and reflect prevalent contemporaneous sexual discourses.

However, these examples also lay bare the dangers inherent in psychosexual, socio-political readings: namely, that entire episodes and motifs, alongside the impetus and structure of the novel, must be reduced to its capacity to channel sexual anxiety, and measures only the degree to which vampirism succeeds at being a metaphor. While comparing the process of biting Harker's neck with penetration might be easy to defend, given the erotic interactions between characters in the weird sisters' episode considered above, the comparison between staking and sexual intercourse seems little more than a strained analogy, and is more problematic than helpful. Ken Gelder suggests this key scene is 'overcoded', which suggests it is not easily reducible.[11] If we follow this line of thinking, *Dracula* cannot be read as *anything but* an exercise in the displacement of repressed desire, since this is what the novel really would like to express, but cannot.

Yet questions arise. Why would Stoker have such an interest in writing about sex yet deliberately go through the effort of encoding the text with a number of analogies that render it 'other' than what it appears to be at a surface level, that is, a novel about creatures that come back from the dead to drink the blood of the living? And what precisely is gained from 'outing' Stoker, reading *Dracula* as a novel written from the closet that explores the horror of compulsory heterosexuality?[12] What does this ignore? The novel is evidently very interested in pursuing the horror behind the figure of the vampire, as well as the very real danger of contagion and/or death that follows from being bitten. More pragmatically, the staking of Lucy can be read less as symbolic sexual punishment than as narrative necessity: her transformation gives the reader a glimpse into what could happen to Mina, and introduces the techniques required to exterminate vampires: it is not all sexual dread.

Whether we favour the repressed meaning approach (Stoker was unaware of the highly sexualised discourse in his writing) or the deliberate approach (Stoker was aware of what he was doing and purposely buried meaning within the text), the result is that vampires may only ever be understood as allegorical, always standing in for something else. This has a number of limitations. To interpret specific repressed sexual meanings in *Dracula* buries more fluid conceptions of sexuality, both in the 1890s and for later readers. Even more problematically, reading to uncover repressed sexuality runs the risk of continuing repression because it carries on marking non-heteronormative desire in *Dracula* as transgressive and 'unnatural'. Oddly, modern readers who eroticise the vampire in order to separate themselves from the Victorian mind-set might further contribute to the 'Victorian myth of repression'.[13] These readings short-circuit any empathy readers may establish with sexual alterity and associate difference with transgression, punishment and murder, even when other narrative explanations might be available. There is a difference between suggesting that vampires are erotic and explaining vampirism as a metaphoric *negotiation* of sexuality. The former endows the vampire with ancillary meaning and allows for a playful re-appropriation and enjoyment of his/her difference. The latter merely reduces the vampire to a subsidiary, imperfect code.

It is precisely in maintaining the vampire's mobility as a liberating metaphor that a queer reading strategy emerges. If the vampire 'cannot see herself in the mirror', Sue-Ellen Case observes, we can take this to mean that these figures remain 'outside that door into the Symbolic' (Jacques Lacan's name for the heterosexual, normative law).[14] To put it differently, the vampire is a category, regardless of any specific ascription to a gendered form of desire, that is *queer* beyond any fixity of sexual identity, straight or gay. *Dracula* and other vampire fictions certainly engage in the exclusionary terms that structure non-heteronormative sexuality in patriarchal societies, but they are also texts that offer the chance to imagine creatively a form of life otherwise unthinkable.

The dilemma continues to be that in *Dracula*, as in many other texts, vampires remain a source of evil to be exterminated. Enjoyment of their alterity is premised on an embrace of perverse sexuality. As Case observes, as the vampire moves towards a clearer sense of sexual identity, the explicitly lesbian vampire who is both a vampire *and* a lesbian, it may be that 'her attraction' dangerously lies in 'her proscription'.[15]

The overtly lesbian (or gay) permutation of the vampire poses other problems. What happens to the reservoir of sexual latency of the vampire once it stops working as a metaphor? If vampires are openly homosexual, or even polysexual, as in the TV series *True Blood* (2008–14), where they have become assimilated into the general culture, we might want to start questioning whether their role as sexual metaphors is weakened in the process, or else must be understood in new ways. It may be that these new sexualised vampires, who have sex *and* bite, have political value because they can be used to explore the sexual discourses behind sexual discrimination.[16] I want to suggest that vampires after *Dracula* are less direct metaphors than direct critiques of the cultural structures of sexual oppression still at work in contemporary society.

Dracula and After: Sexual Vampires and Oppositional Queerness

Judith Halberstam has influentially warned of the danger of essentialism in focusing on the monster as a code for homosexuality. Reducing the vampire to 'one interpretive model' only reproduces the model critical attempts claim to have discovered, which means that 'an analysis of the vampire as perverse sexuality runs the risk of merely stabilizing the identity of perversity, its relation to a particular set of traits'.[17] In contrast, Halberstam reads *Dracula* as capable of embracing various forms of difference that include gender, class, race and sexuality. *Dracula* represents the production of sexuality itself, and thus avoids being an essentialist narrative of any given or pre-scribed form of sexuality. Rather, the vampire is all sexualities rolled into one and becomes the mechanism by which the monster comes to represent sexuality in the first place.

However, Halberstam still warns that this tactic of avoiding forms of universal otherness can end up in a similar position to that of reading for repression. The very form of the novel makes it clear that *Dracula*'s monstrosity is 'a completely controlled production of a group of professionals – doctors, psychiatrists, lawyers'. Writing is a form of power and the subjectivities that it stabilises are very much connected to 'the establishment of a kind of middle-class hegemony'.[18] To think of Dracula as an engine of monstrosity aims to replace sexual essentialism with a more all-encompassing concept, but this is still a symptomatic interpretation. Count Dracula remains, in Halberstam's reading, the dark other of the fin de siècle. Dracula and his horde continue to be 'the other side of a national identity that, in the 1890s, coincided with a hegemonic ideal of bourgeois Victorian womanhood'.[19] Is there any way in which we can articulate the potential queerness in Stoker's novel without relying on readings that continue to regard it as pathological?

The obvious and most pessimistic answer is no – not without uprooting the text from its late-Victorian context. *Dracula* demands to be read as a novel that presents difference as aberrant because the vampires are them-selves portrayed as dangerous exiles from humanity. To stake them is to cure a corrupting pathology and restore the normal. Dracula's links to an aristo-cratic past and his dying lineage, the contrast between the archaic world he embodies and Mina's techno-informational England, emphasise that the

Count is a stalwart of a world left behind. Dracula does not encapsulate the modern and the progressive. Homosexuality is a bedfellow of vampirism in *Dracula* because they both embody what is beyond the law, even if the law deciding so is ultimately revealed to be the Christian, patriarchal and conservative moral code of Van Helsing and the Crew of Light. To suggest that vampirism may be an enjoyable subject position in the novel, given that it is abjected as vile and harmful, would be an experiment in perversion itself.

But let's entertain the idea of this perverse reading, one that deliberately goes against the grain and celebrates the Count as a liberating and empowering figure. This is what queer reading means, according to Sedgwick: to read for 'the open mesh of possibilities, gaps, overlaps, dissonances and resonances, lapses and excesses of meaning when the constituent elements … aren't made … to signify monolithically'.[20] What would it mean to queer *Dracula*?

At a primary level, as pure fantasy projection, Dracula is alluring. Despite the many negative associations his undead state provokes, and his eventual destruction, the gloomy aspects of his figure are complicated by other qualities. He is a strong and powerful character who has magical powers and exerts control over others. He is truly polymorphic: beyond his transformations into wolf and bat, he is also capable of coming across as a 'quiet, business-like gentleman' and, some characters expect, 'a good specimen of manhood' (D, 209). The fact that he is at the margins of the action, always in the shadows, means that he can be more eagerly imagined. His harem of women, the admission that he too can love, and his admonition that Harker is 'mine' can be taken as indicators of his fluid, unrestrained and mobile sexuality. In a way, the Count can reproduce, or at least turn others into his children, a characteristic that allows him to transcend his biological limitations. Although vampirism is portrayed negatively in the novel, this perception relies on our identification with the normative view of the Van Helsing's Crew of Light, steeped in a repressive and conservative status quo. Dracula – and vampires generally – can function as oppositional queer figures that challenge assimilation by heteronormative culture but also the concomitant dangers of homonormativity.

The rise of the sympathetic vampire, especially after Stephanie Meyer's successful *Twilight* novels (2005–8), has led to a more general embrace of monstrosity, not just as acceptable but even as aspirational. The vampire's otherness is a marker of originality and of a reclaimed difference that has permeated popular culture.[21] One need only think of pop superstar Lady Gaga, renowned for her eccentricity, naming her fans 'little monsters'. Vampires are now re-envisioned as an update of the rebellious teenage lover. Their supernatural powers make them desirable and comparable to the superhero, who has dominated Hollywood cinema in the twenty-first century. Even that most abject of monsters, the zombie, may now be pitied and loved back to a human state, as in Isaac Marion's *Warm Bodies* (2010). Gay and queer vampires have followed suit, appearing predominantly in visual media in either supporting roles, as in TV shows *The Vampire Diaries* (2009–) or *True Blood*, or even as main cast members, as in *The Lair* (2007–9).

There is, of course, a long tradition of queer vampires in Gothic fiction, especially following Anne Rice's *Interview with the Vampire* (1977), and an even more considerable number of erotic gay vampire novels. The new queer vampires have openly dissident sexualities, but are more visible and entirely part of mainstream culture. Homoerotic representations of vampires in this context (vampires that express and consummate male-to-male, female-to-female or bisexual desire), may be seen as not just providing for a parallel, imagined world in which such desires are 'normal', but also as forms of 'interrogat[ion] and restructur[ation]' of the relationships thereby established.[22] Although some gay and queer vampire narratives perpetuate the fantasy that non-heteronormative desire needs to exist in an imagined world, others challenge the privilege of genital sex as a marker of gay or queer desire or identity, and propose intimacy as an alternative.[23]

Yet recent developments in vampiric representation also suggest a need to be aware of the role of the queer vampire within a neoliberal context that has, to some extent, co-opted and turned formerly oppositional sexual identities into marketable lifestyles. Anne Rice's vampires, after all, cannot have sex and their sexual politics are confused and conservative.[24] They force us, among others things, to begin asking of vampires (and perhaps the Gothic in general) what exactly makes them queer at a time 'where same-sex desire is increasingly viewed as "normal" and even sanctioned by the institution of marriage'.[25] *Dracula* may prove an alternative to models of queer identity weakened through assimilation. Making the monster monstrous again might be a way of re-politicising vampires.

The Count's potential as oppositional figure resonates with the work of queer critics who have registered a dissatisfaction with queer liberalism in contemporary culture and Queer Studies. For David Eng, the process of integration of gays and lesbians into heteronormative structures, through same-sex marriage or the right to adoption, has little more than appeased those who should remain ever vigilant and refuse to adapt or mould to a dominant social order. Simultaneously, the surrender of a 'mass-mediated queer consumer lifestyle', which is now actively sold beyond specialist publications, has deflected attention from the more pressing matter of the still-marginalised nature of queer identity.[26] The LGBTQA community finds itself embedded within such rigid structures of economical hierarchy that, as

Lisa Duggan notes, even the dominant national lesbian and gay civil rights organisations are 'no longer representative of a broad-based progressive movement' associated with the early years after the Stonewall riots in 1969 that founded the gay liberation movement.[27] This is precisely the reason why a confrontational 'no future' attitude is necessary for some: the child, as an image of a 'reproductive futurism' – the driving force of hetero-centrism – must be abandoned in favour of the 'sterile, narcissistic enjoy-ments' diametrically opposed to the form of social organisation championed by heteronormative assimilation.[28] In this radical view, an oppositional queer politics becomes the real ideological alternative to homonormativity.

Read against this backdrop, a perverse recuperation of Dracula as a beacon of that radical negation seems attractive. If vampires are only allowed to be themselves when their transgressive veneer, their abject other-ness, has been removed (the bite defanged), then the truly queer vampire will be the one that returns us to the disgusting, the objectionable and the shocking. Dracula, as he is presented in the novel, embodies this extreme alterity and so can be brought back from the dead for theoretical purposes. Among other perversities, the type of reproduction he promises simultan-eously reproduces his ontological status: future vampires will seek, like him, to drink the blood from the living and will stand in direct opposition to life (and its promise of a future). Dracula is also the most sexually fluid of vampires, speaking his desire for Harker, yet potentially harbouring other desires for the women he preys upon. Naturally, this re-thinking of the Count is useful only insofar as it stands grounded in a denial of a regularis-ing, normative system seeking to destroy its difference via the expulsion of what it perceives to be pernicious and dangerous. It offers an identity model, but, as I have been arguing, Dracula is both a vampire and a potentially queer subject. Mixing the two risks a collapse of a very real identity category into a fictional one. Caution is therefore necessary.

While Dracula may still be productively 'queered', such an endeavour might be run passed actual queer subjects. Further work in this area would benefit from the kind of sociological studies of 'fans' that assess the reception of the novel by self-identifying queer subjects. I have taken for granted that a degree of attraction towards the power Dracula holds would be appealing, but this reading might essentialise the myriad reactions that the Count arouses. *Dracula*'s classic status and its academic and critical currency means that the novel is widely read and studied. This does not necessarily translate into identificatory pleasure. A study of female fan empathy in 2005, which drew on responses from members (or ex-members) of The London Vampire Group, The Vampyre Society, the Anne Rice Vampire Lestat Fan Club and others, showed that, while women often cross-identify with male vampire figures, *Dracula* the novel, and especially the Count, were unanimously disliked.[29] The reasons given for this dislike touched on the frustration of not being able to sympathise with a character who appears to have been constructed to be despised. This dissatisfaction did not, crucially, extend to later adaptations of the novel that have sought to make the Count more humane and that even to turn him into a romantic hero, such as Francis Ford Coppola's *Bram Stoker's Dracula* (1992). This could speak to the fans' own preference for the male vampire as a heterosexual figure. It is also worth noting that the same fans showed a passion for Anne Rice's male vampires, who often establish relationships with other men, yet have remained problematic for queer theorists.[30]

Although I am wary of the many pitfalls of drawing clear-cut conclusions from only one study, the representative nature of the answers are suggestive, especially since there is no indication that any of the female interviewees identified as queer. The reticence towards Count Dracula speaks to the general embrace of monstrosity as a positive category that has allowed readers to experience difference with pride. Maybe we should not be focusing on the possible abstract, theoretical return to *Dracula* for the benefit of intellectuals, and instead celebrate the novel's already tangible legacy in a plethora of new texts which parade openly gay and queer vampires. While *Dracula* can provide material for further work seeking to recover a politically aware and confrontational form of queerness through monstrous representation, some of *Dracula*'s post-Stonewall children seem to be enjoying their new-found homonormative freedom.

Notes

1 John Allen Stevenson, 'A Vampire in the Mirror: The Sexuality of *Dracula*', *PMLA* 103, no. 2 (1988), 139.
2 Richard Dyer, 'Children of the Night: Vampirism as Homosexuality, Homosexuality as Vampirism', in Susannah Radstone, ed., *Sweet Dreams: Sexuality and Gender in Popular Fiction* (London: Lawrence and Wishart, 1988), pp. 47–72, quote on p. 64. See also John D'Addario, 'We're All Suckers for Dracula: Bram Stoker and the Homoeroticism of Vampires', *The Advocate* (24 October 1989), 40–42.
3 Michel Foucault, *The History of Sexuality: Introduction* (London: Allen Lane, 1978); Eve Kosofsky Sedgwick, *Between Men: English Literature and Male Homosocial Desire* (New York: Columbia University Press, 1985).
4 Christopher Craft, '"Kiss Me with Those Red Lips": Gender and Inversion in Bram Stoker's *Dracula*', *Representations* 8 (1984), 107–33, 107, 110.
5 Craft, '"Kiss Me"', 110.
6 Craft, '"Kiss Me"', 110.
7 Craft, '"Kiss Me"', 112.

8 Craft, '"Kiss Me"', 122–23.

9 Craft, '"Kiss Me"', 124.

10 Marjorie Howes, 'The Mediation of the Feminine: Bisexuality, Homoerotic Desire, and Self-Expression in Bram Stoker's *Dracula*', *Texas Studies in Literature and Language*, 30, no. 1 (1988), 104–19, quote on p. 106.

11 Ken Gelder, *Reading the Vampire* (Abingdon and New York: Routledge, 1996), 76–79.

12 Barry McRea, 'Heterosexual Horror: *Dracula*, the Closet, and the Marriage-Plot', *Novel: A Forum on Fiction* 43, no. 2 (2010), 251–70.

13 Robert Mighall, 'Sex, History and the Vampire', in Williams Hughes and Andrew Smith, eds., *Bram Stoker: History, Psychoanalysis and the Gothic* (Basingstoke: Palgrave, 1998), pp. 62–77, quote on p. 75.

14 Sue-Ellen Case, 'Tracking the Vampire', in Katie Conboy, Nadia Medina and Sarah Stanbury, eds., *Writing on the Body: Female Embodiment and Feminist Theory* (New York: Columbia University Press, 1997), pp. 380–400, quote on p. 388.

15 Case, 'Tracking the Vampire', 395.

16 Xavier Aldana Reyes, '"Who Ordered the Hamburger with AIDS?" Haematophilic Semiotics in *Tru(e) Blood*', *Gothic Studies* 15, no. 1 (2013), 55–65.

17 Judith Halberstam, *Skin Shows: Gothic Horror and the Technology of Monsters* (Durham, NC: Duke University Press, 1995), 88.

18 Halberstam, *Skin Shows*, 91.

19 Halberstam, *Skin Shows*, 89.

20 Eve Kosofsky Sedgwick, 'Queer and Now', in *Tendencies* (Durham, NC: Duke University Press, 1993), p. 8.

21 Susannah Clements, *The Vampire Defanged: How the Embodiment of Evil Became a Romantic Hero* (Grand Rapids, MI: Brazos Press, 2011).

22 Andrew Schopp, 'Cruising the Alternatives: Homoeroticism and the Contemporary Vampire', *The Journal of Popular Culture* 30, no. 4 (1997), 231–43, quote on p. 238.

23 For examples, see Schopp, 'Cruising the Alternatives', 237–41.

24 George E. Haggerty, 'Anne Rice and the Queering of Culture', *Novel: A Forum of Fiction* 32, no. 1 (1998): 5–18, quote on p. 16.

25 E. L. McCallum, 'The "Queer Limits" in the Modern Gothic', in Jerrold E. Hogle, ed., *The Cambridge Companion to Modern Gothic*, (Cambridge: Cambridge University Press, 2014), pp. 71–86, quote on p. 71.

26 David L. Eng, *The Feeling of Kinship: Queer Liberalism and the Racialization of Intimacy* (Durham, NC: Duke University Press, 2010), 3.

27 Lisa Duggan, *The Twilight of Equality: Neoliberalism, Cultural Politics, and the Attack on Democracy* (Boston, MA: Beacon Press, 2003), 45.

28 Lee Edelman, *No Future: Queer Theory and the Death Drive* (Durham, NC: Duke University Press, 2004), 2, 13.

29 Milly Williamson, *The Lure of the Vampire: Gender, Fiction and Fandom from Bram Stoker to Buffy* (London: Wallflower, 2005), 59–61.

30 See Schopp, 'Cruising the Alternatives'.

12

MARK BLACKLOCK

Dracula and New Horror Theory

In the 1990s, Gothic criticism took a 'spectral' turn in the wake of Jacques Derrida's shift from ontology to 'hauntology' in his lectures, *Spectres of Marx*. This pun was meant entirely seriously: to be, according to Derrida, is to be *haunted*.[1] In the twenty-first century, there has been a very different series of philosophical reflections that have attempted to use horror fiction as a kind of resource for inquiries into the state of human being and its limits, a movement variously called 'speculative realism' or 'object-oriented ontology'. These approaches, self-consciously developed on the margins of orthodox philosophy and outside conventional academic Gothic criticism, have been controversial.[2] If they often reference horror fiction, they do so rather instrumentally and think of these texts as good to think with. This chapter investigates what these approaches might illuminate about *Dracula*.

Nihil Unbound?

In his 1933 essay 'The Last Messiah', the Norwegian philosopher Peter Wessel Zapffe diagnosed the human species as suffering from a surfeit of consciousness. Comparing over-evolved human intelligence to the outsized antlers of deer, Zapffe described the advent of the 'cosmic panic' caused by this excessive awareness:

> One night in long bygone times, man awoke and saw himself.
>
> He saw that he was naked under cosmos, homeless in his own body. All things dissolved before his testing thought, wonder above wonder, horror above horror unfolded in his mind.[3]

Zapffe's thought ended up in an anti-natalist position: the argument that it is better never to have been born. His existential pessimism and notion of humanity as a 'captive' in a universe that offers no sanctuary has enjoyed new life as a reference point for both writers of horror fiction and theorists who have been drawn to generic writing for its ability to express such philosophical notions in cultural form. It echoes with the pessimistic philosophy of weird fiction writer H. P. Lovecraft in the 1920s and 1930s, a writer who pursued a vision of a cruelly indifferent universe. The questions of what happens when human thought acknowledges the contingent position of the human within the cosmos, and how that might be addressed, has become a motive force behind this kind of philosophy. Using this framework interestingly readjusts the focus on *Dracula*. The Count becomes less an alluring figure of transgressive desire, an endlessly mobile allegorical figure, and is instead taken as a dark, inhuman power that evades subjective capture.

One of the key thinkers in the emergence of this new philosophy has been Bruno Latour. Eschewing the central position of the human in the philosophical universe of Enlightenment thought since Kant, Latour argued instead for a 'non-modern' constitution, which allowed agency to the non-human, objectal world that had always been bracketed off or ignored by anthropocentric philosophy. This approach recognises the hybrid constructions that are neither purely human nor purely inhuman, but criss-cross between systems of both human and non-human origin.[4] In this re-balancing of subjects and objects, Latour wants to displace the absolute domination of human subjects over non-human objects in modernity. This explains why this move has been called *object-oriented* ontology. And might not the liminal figure of the vampire be a perfect exemplum of this new in/human, subject/object hybrid?

While Latour sees a welcoming opening up of connections and networks in this reframing, a distinctly less positive tendency can be discerned in the work of Graham Harman, who formulated his 'weird realism' by critiquing the remaining metaphysical traces in Latour, and has since argued that philosophers should turn to the work of H. P. Lovecraft. For Harman, Lovecraft's horror fiction constitutes a body of inquiry that exposes the horrific weirdness of non-human objects in a way that fundamentally challenges phenomenological philosophy necessarily centred on subjects.[5]

This tendency was fully brought together with the Gothic in the journal *Collapse*, a key forum for such theoretical fusions.[6] In an issue called *Concept Horror*, Robin McKay asked in the editorial: 'If the overriding affect connected with what we "know" – but still do not really know – about the universe and our place in it, would be one of horror, then, inversely, how might the existing literature of horror inform a reading of these tendencies of contemporary thought?'[7] The essays that followed tacked between philosophers of this new dispensation and influential horror fiction writers like Thomas Ligotti and China Miéville.

The nature of this inquiry is distilled in philosophical terms in Ray Brassier's question in his book *Nihil Unbound*: 'How does thought think the death of thinking?'[8] Can we read *Dracula* as a philosophical parable that engages this speculative question? Does Stoker's novel provide resources for the negotiations of that which is beyond thought? Read with such inquiries at the front of our minds, *Dracula* reveals itself as determinedly engaged with the limits of thought, knowledge and being in surprising ways. What is offered here are two detailed readings of *Dracula* that illustrate how this new horror theory might yield new insights.

The Darkening Garden

Speculative Realism has certainly made a mark in literary critical, cultural and philosophical discussions. Let's start, however, with a complementary exploration of horror from within genre criticism. John Clute has published extensively on genre fiction and is editor of encyclopaedias of science fiction, fantasy and horror, genres he collects under the more inclusive Russian term *fantastika*.[9] Similar to the philosophers, Clute operates outside conventional academic argument, a mode he often explicitly resists. Clute's *The Darkening Garden: A Short Lexicon of Horror* (2006) is an analysis of the structural organisation of horror texts. His system, expressed in idiosyncratic mini-essays, proposes an analysis of horror that coheres with central tenets of the philosophical turn described above. A stroll around *The Darkening Garden*, then, provides an opportunity for defining the mode in which *Dracula* operates.

A useful place to start is with Clute's essay on the 'Bound Fantastic'. Here we find a key distinction in Clute's scheme between the 'bound' and the 'free fantastic': bound or free from attachment to the planet earth. Science fiction, he suggests, is a form of the fantastic that describes freedom from the planet earth, while horror reveals that we are inexorably bound to it. Horror is 'Enlightenment's dark, mocking twin' that 'exposes the lie that we own the world to which we are bound'.[10] For Clute, horror is the most extreme and materialistic of the fantastic modes, 'a process of uncovering the true nature of the prison, which is seen to be inescapable' (311–12).

Clute offers a prescriptive, four-part, developmental model of the horror plot: Sighting, Thickening, Revel and Aftermath, categories he relates to Spring, Summer, Autumn and Winter respectively. Although this is not mentioned, this schema is an echo of Northrop Frye's 'Theory of Myths' proposed in his influential *Anatomy of Criticism* in 1957. Frye paired distinct modes with the seasons: Comedy with Spring, Romance with Summer, Tragedy with Autumn and Irony and Satire with Winter. Frye's stated aim was 'to give a rational account of some of the structural principles of Western literature in the context of its Classical and Christian heritage', structural principles which he read as operating between the poles of 'undisplaced myth' and 'the low mimetic', drawing heavily on mythical sources to describe the archetypes he read across canonical literature from a certain distance: 'In the criticism of literature, too, we often have to "stand back" from the poem to see its archetypal organization'.[11]

Located at the borders of the romantic quest, where it shades into irony, Clute's version of horror would seem to represent a small subset in terms of Frye's model. Where Frye's system aims at a universal theory, Clute offers the caveat that his rules, while prescriptive, are so in order to be bent and tested: 'The models or moves suggested here are inherently open ... to modulations, contradictions, ... mirror reversals, spoofing' (314).

Let's work through Clute's four phases of horror. First comes Sighting, 'a glimpse of terror to come; it is uncanny to experience ... and it tells us that something worse than what we just sighted is in the offing' (331–32). The Sighting is presentiment of full revelation, but based on an experience that constitutes for the character a form of cognitive dissonance. This is carried forward by Thickening, a narrative slowing through an excess of detail: 'life is inherently *impeded*: there seems no exit from the suffocating tangle of plot; the atmosphere of things literally thickens; it is hard to breathe; in the end there has been a progressive *unmapping* of the paths within the world' (337). We might read this as equivalent in literary critical terms to Ian Watts's notion of 'delayed decoding', which Watt reads in Conrad's *Heart of Darkness* (1899), a work that provides Clute with his key example through its iconic recognition of 'the horror, the horror'.[12] Indeed, *Heart of Darkness* might be exemplary of the Thickening phase, a sticky, slow and claustrophobic journey up-river. The Thickening also, in Clute's scheme, develops that first Sighting or glimpse: 'the phenomenal world is increasingly revealed as a rind that, once peeled, exposes the vacancies within the false consciousness of "normal" life, and the imposture of the history of the world' (337).

Next comes the Revel: 'a formal event bound in time and place, an event in which the field of the world is reversed: good becomes evil; parody becomes jurisprudence; the jester is king; Hyde lives; autumn is the growing season'. Its revelation 'is most devastating when the truth it delivers is revealed to be some form of Vastation, some defining expression of the malice of the world' (324). The concept of Vastation is captured in the opening lines of H. P. Lovecraft's 'The Call of Cthulhu': 'The most merciful thing in the world, I think, is the inability of the human mind to correlate all its contents. We live on a placid island of ignorance in the midst of black seas of infinity'.[13] Vastation is the desolation resulting should such correlation occur.

Finally comes Aftermath, a deathly stillness: 'the central sense conveyed by Aftermath, after all, is that there is nothing to be done, that there is no cure to hand, no more story to tell' (279). The Aftermath offers no consolation: the monster may have been vanquished but the story-tellers are faced with the unconcealed truth of the world and how it will continue. They have entered the Heart of Darkness: there is no consolation in horror.

Dracula as a Darkening Garden

How does Clute's model open up Stoker's *Dracula*? Using the motifs Clute identifies as central to each phase, we can identify clear structural corres-pondences with Stoker's novel. The Sighting can be readily identified: Clute writes that 'a Sighting is often first experienced ... in a Mirror' (332). In his journal, Jonathan Harker writes:

> I had hung my shaving glass by the window, and was just beginning to shave. Suddenly I felt a hand on my shoulder, and heard the Count's voice saying to me, 'Good morning'. I started, for it amazed me that I had not seen him, since the reflection of the glass covered the whole room behind me. In starting I had cut myself slightly, but did not notice it at the moment. Having answered the Count's salutation, I turned to the glass again to see how I had been mistaken. This time there could be no error, for the man was close to me, and I could see him over my shoulder. But there was no reflection of him in the mirror! The whole room behind me was displayed, but there was no sign of a man in it, except myself. (*D*, 27)

This Sighting is the moment at which the terror of what is to come in the narrative is first glimpsed: that the Count is in some way a supernatural being, his absence in a mirror mocking the laws of physics and nature. Harker experiences this mirror encounter first as 'an increase [of] that vague feeling of uneasiness which I always have when the Count is near' (*D*, 27), before a trickle of blood provokes a more definite presentiment of future ill: 'When the Count saw my face, his eyes blazed with a sort of demoniac fury, and he suddenly made a grab at my throat' (*D*, 28). We should note also the specificity of this Sighting: a glimpse of absence, of a void where there should be something.

This is the first glimpse, or Sighting; actually, though, Harker's journal rehearses in miniature all the stages of the four-stage model of *The Darkening Garden*. Within this initial section of the novel Harker experi-ences Thickening, in his repeated attempts to escape the rooms in which he is contained in the castle, encountering locked doors, stolen papers and clothes, forged letters, confusion and the gradual slip from unease towards more substantive affect: 'Then the horror overcame me' (*D*, 40). In this section, Thickening transmutes rapidly into Revel, as Harker discovers the

Count's lair and witnesses his nocturnal metamorphoses. Aftermath is Harker's wrecked body and fevered brain, the man found barely alive in the convent hospital after his horrific ordeal. Even worse, using the logic of doomed repetition, the novel moves to England with the Count and the whole sequence of ghastly revelation is rewound – the wax cylinder played once more – and the phases begin again. As Clute argues, '[o]nce a Sighting has been made, there is no Return' (332), and so it is with the novel, as Jonathan Harker's work in Romania prepares the ground for Dracula's departure to England, and for Harker's Vastation to be staged at the centre of the empire.

The fact that the reader encounters Dracula's arrival in England with a more advanced awareness than that possessed by the characters in the novel means that we experience a key feature of Thickening as identified by Clute: déjà vu. 'The past inhabits our present, doubles the stories being told. Recursiveness slows the course of story' (338). The documentary structure of *Dracula* thickens and repeats the stories being told, as the same events are related from different perspectives: in Mina's journal, in the *Dailygraph* report of the arrival of the Demeter, in the ship's log. These echoes are felt again in the repeated nocturnal disturbances befalling Lucy over consecutive nights in Whitby, as Mina waits in vain for news of Jonathan and similar events occur with minor variations, a narrative mirroring of Jonathan's own journal. The Count's metamorphoses into bats and canines are similarly repeated. Clute writes that if anything is discovered in the Thickening phase, it is falsity, a rind of lies. And so the inexplicable behaviour of Renfield contributes nothing to the characters' understanding of events. Lucy's condition improves and dramatically worsens, despite repeated blood transfusions. Even the arrival in the narrative of Van Helsing at first introduces only further confusion and an ambiguous turn of phrase: 'I have for myself thoughts at the present. Later I shall unfold to you'. (*D*, 112)

The repetition of narrative occurs also at the intertextual level. Writer and reader both are bound, as Clute says, by 'prior stories ... the accumulated mass of precedent and conversation contained in everything already written and read' (338). This generic familiarity serves to thicken the narrative with the reader's foreknowledge of vampire stories from the first wave of the Gothic, the echoes of *The Mysteries of Udolpho* or *The Rime of the Ancient Mariner*.

Clute argues that the Thickening phase introduces an awareness of the historical conditions allegorised in the narrative, in a way that corresponds with literary critical readings that identify *Dracula* as representative of the imperial Other: 'we recognize, in the life of the monster, an exposure of history itself: ... the lubricious otherness of the breeds without the law who sue to join the golf club' (338). This is what Stephen Arata identifies as the 'anxiety of reverse colonization' in *Dracula*, only expressed in rather more demotic language.[14]

The transition between Thickening and Revel in *Dracula* would seem to be marked by the appropriate marshalling of information, as the narrative information is fixed in the sharing of Mina's and Jonathan's diaries and the transcription of Dr Seward's. Each of these transmissions of information thickens the narrative much as bureaucratic form-filling thickens a day's work: there does indeed seem to be 'no exit from the suffocating tangle of plot' (338). Yet it moves the characters forwards from blindness and into the realisation of what they truly face in the Revel phase: 'the action of the real world announcing itself. It is "Reason" awakening itself from sleep' (324).

And so we find Van Helsing able to reflect upon this passage, a movement towards the terrible knowledge of what the Count really is: 'There are such beings as vampires; some of us have evidence that they exist. Even had we not the proof of our own unhappy experience, the teachings and the records of the past give proof enough for sane peoples' (D, 220). From that moment onwards, the Revel unfolds rapidly. Renfield is destroyed and comes to final realisation: 'I must not deceive myself; it was no dream, but all a grim reality' (D, 258). The Count circumvents defences to prey on Mina:

> Then he spoke to me mockingly: 'And so you, like the others, would play your brains against mine. You would help these men to hunt and frustrate me in my designs! You know now, and they know in part already, and will know in full before long, what it is to cross my path'. (D, 267)

What follows is a race around the Count's London sites in an attempt to purify them, a carnivalesque narrative dance, that leads eventually back to Transylvania.

However, the Aftermath is finally where Stoker reveals himself as a Victorian Gothic romancer, rather than as a nihilistic modern horror writer. There is Christian redemption in *Dracula*, both in Morris's dying words – 'The Curse has passed away!' (D, 350) – and in Harker's final note about his son: 'This boy will someday know what a brave and gallant woman his mother is' (D, 351). 'To flash-freeze the future is the final gift of Horror' (280), but such optimism, no matter how brief, has no very little purchase in it, Clute argues. Forty years after Stoker turns from the nihilistic potential of his own fiction and reaches for a restoration of consolatory order, Zappfe will say, as a true Modernist, that Man:

> as he stands before imminent death, grasps its nature also, and the cosmic import of the step to come. His creative imagination constructs new, fearful

prospects behind the curtain of death, and he sees that even there is no sanctuary found. And now he can discern the outline of his biologicocosmic terms: He is the universe's helpless captive, kept to fall into nameless possibilities.[15]

The redemptive logic of *Dracula*'s conclusion thus leaves it on the threshold of modern secular horror, glimpsing a hint of the void yet ultimately disavowing it. In *Dracula* we might have found the crux that separates Gothic romance from modern horror.

In the Dust of *Dracula*

Thinkers identified with Speculative Realism tend more overtly to use horror fiction as an instrument to think with rather than read as such: it is not literary criticism. The example I will use here is Eugene Thacker's *In the Dust of This Planet*, a book that has enjoyed surprising popular cultural visibility. Not only has it influenced the weird cosmic philosophy on display in the first series of the TV series *True Detective* (2014), the distinctive black and white cover of the book has also been seen stencilled on the back of a leather jacket worn by American rapper Jay-Z. Speculative Realism really is the new rock and roll.

Eugene Thacker structures his arguments concerning Horror in signature baroque fashion, but his argument is stated clearly: 'that *"horror" is a non-philosophical attempt to think about the world-without-us philosophically*'.[16] This is another clear instance of object-oriented ontology: the horror that results in the overthrow of subjective, anthropocentric views. Thacker works in the branch of Speculative Realism that follows Ray Brassier's *Nihil Unbound*, a book that considers nihilism as a 'speculative opportunity'.[17] Indeed, Thacker reviewed Brassier's book, writing that nihilism 'is interesting precisely because it poses the question of a fundamental incommensurability between thinking and living, between subject and world'.[18]

In the Dust of This Planet eccentrically revives medieval demonology to read Gothic and horror fiction representations of the demons. Paying attention to the persistence of the figure of the demon in 'our technologically advanced, scientifically hegemonic, and religiously conservative post millennium world' suggests to Thacker that they are moments of negotiation between the human and the non-human (22). Thacker's analysis identifies three distinct demonic types. In the first, the anthropological, the demon is a metaphor for the relation of the human to malevolent force, be it religious, psychological or social. In the second, the mythological, the demon works allegorically to describe the human encounter with the non-human. And in the third, the ontological, the demon functions as a 'stand-in for the abstract, indifferent, non-being of the world … a way of talking about the perspective of the non-human' (31).

Count Dracula, early identified as demonic by Jonathan Harker, and frequently referred to as 'unhuman' (D, 284) and 'not human' (D, 213), is an over-determined figure who might be grasped as an embodiment of each of these forms of demon. There are any number of literary critical readings of the novel that mine Thacker's first category, discerning the anthropological nature of the demon as represented in the text: *Dracula* as an avatar of the imperial Other, the Freudian father-figure or the fin-de-siècle anxiety over evolutionary degeneration. Dracula works as an emblem of that which was feared within the late-nineteenth century discourse of the subject and society.

But Dracula is also a mythological demon. In the parable of the Gerasene demons, cast out by Christ into a herd of swine, the demon famously declares: 'My name is Legion, for we are many' (Mark 5: 1–20). This allows Thacker to identify the multiplicity of the demoniac, its irreducibility into the singular, its acts of possession and contagion:

> The mythological interpretation of the demon takes place less by the use of metaphor, and more by the use of allegory, in which the very story of our ability or inability to comprehend the world and cosmos is encapsulated in the ritual acts of invasion, possession, metamorphosis, and exorcism. (27)

Thacker reads these ritual acts as demonstrating the mobile limits of human comprehension. Again, *Dracula* yields rich reward. The Count is an invading force, both in terms of national and human boundaries. He possesses humans and non-humans according to need, morphing into the form of a bat, a dog, a wolf and, indeed, into mists, fogs and hazes. His victims are ritually exorcised, of course: Lucy in her coffin, and Dracula himself, in the closing pages of the novel.

Van Helsing's summary account of the monster that his group faces describes the vampire as a demon that assumes such multiple forms:

> This vampire which is amongst us is of himself so strong in person as twenty men, he is of cunning more than mortal, for his cunning be the growth of ages, he have still the aids of necromancy, which is, as his etymology imply, the divination by the dead, and all the dead that he can come nigh to are for him at command, he is brute, and more than brute, he is devil in callous, and the heart of him is not, he can, within his range, direct the elements, the storm, the fog, the thunder, he can command all the meaner things, the rat, and the owl, and the bat, the moth, and the fox, and the wolf, he can grow and become small, and he can at times vanish and come unknown. (D, 220–21)

This series of metamorphoses in which Dracula's ontological status is made explicit indicate a particularly compelling mode in which *Dracula* might be read as an expression of 'a concept of the demonic that is fully immanent, and yet never fully present'. Thacker writes: 'This kind of demon is at once pure force and flow, but, not being a discrete thing in itself, it is also pure nothingness' (35–36). The forms that most consistently represent the world-without-us in this ambiguous state are 'a whole bestiary of impossible life forms – mists, ooze, blobs, slime, clouds and muck' (9).

Mists and clouds most draw our attention as we read *Dracula*, who both transforms himself into mists and controls the climate throughout the novel. His arrival in Whitby is wreathed in such phenomena: 'The horizon is lost in a gray mist. All is vastness; the clouds are piled up like giant rocks, and there is a "brool" over the sea that sounds like some presage of doom' (*D*, 71). The metaphoric sense of clouds as boding ill omen are stressed – no silver-linings here – and the etymological partnership of the English word 'cloud' with the mucky 'clod' align these forms more closely to the earth than to the heavens. When the storm bringing the ship finally breaks, 'the whole aspect of nature at once became convulsed' (*D*, 74). These are no fluffy nimbi, floating airily in a blue sky:

> white, wet clouds, which swept by in ghostly fashion, so dank and damp and cold that it needed but little effort of imagination to think that the spirits of those lost at sea were touching their living brethren with the clammy hands of death, and many a one shuddered at the wreaths of sea-mist swept by. (*D*, 74)

Again, when the Count comes for Mina, he once again assumes this form of a dank cloud. Mina describes:

> a thin streak of white mist, that crept with almost imperceptible slowness across the grass towards the house, seemed to have a sentience and a vitality of its own ... The mist was spreading, and was now close up to the house, so that I could see it lying thick against the wall, as though it were stealing up to the windows. (*D*, 240)

As Mina witnesses the mist seeping through the cracks of her door and congealing into the Count's corporeal form, thought of the interstitial nature of the mist comes to her unbidden: 'Things began to whirl through my brain just as the cloudy column was now whirling in the room, and through it all came the scriptural words "a pillar of cloud by day and of fire by night"' (*D*, 241). Within moments, conscious thought itself is over-run as the monstrous Count precipitates from the haze: 'The last conscious effort which imagination made was to show me a livid white face bending over me out of the mist' (*D*, 241).

For Thacker, the essential qualities of mists and ooze are that they are neither entirely natural nor supernatural, not entirely present nor entirely absent: 'the ethereal nature of mists means that while they may appear solid and to have distinct forms, they are also immaterial, and can readily become formless' (53). Such metaphors are the means by which the hidden world metaphorically and counter-intuitively manifests itself: 'where the hiddenness of the world presents itself in its paradoxical way (revealing itself – as hidden)' (53). Such revelation creeps, slides and congeals, before dissipating again: Dracula is formless, everywhere and nowhere.

Dracula is also prone to forms that are between dust and miasma, as when 'a whole myriad of little specks seems to come blowing in through the broken window, and wheeling and circling round like the pillar of dust that travellers describe when there is a simoon in the desert' (D, 134–35). This is a description that alerts us to the mythography of djinns and dust devils, that demons have long taken such forms that confuse the boundary between the external and the internal, granular matter that enters the body through any orifice, spreading disease, or specks that appear before the eyes, products of a disturbed mind or vision. At his death, the Count materially dissipates one final time: 'It was like a miracle, but before our very eyes, and almost in the drawing of a breath, the whole body crumbled into dust and passed from our sight' (D, 350). Like *Dracula* himself, Thacker too concludes in dust: 'If historical mysticism is, in the last instance, theological, then mysticism today, a mysticism of the unhuman, would have to be, in the last instance, climatological. It is a kind of mysticism that can only be expressed in the dust of this planet' (150).

Here a number of my arguments dovetail. First, there is Zapffe's notion of man as captive on earth, and its echo in Clute's argument that horror binds man to the planet. Second, recall the interrogation of the non-human aspects of nature, the object-oriented ontology, that underpins Speculative Realism. The Count's power is located as having a mystical though natural source: 'With this one, all the forces of nature that are occult and deep and strong must have worked together in some wonderous way', explains Van Helsing:

> The very place, where he have been alive, Undead for all these centuries, is full of strangeness of the geologic and chemical world. There are deep caverns and fissures that reach none know whither. There have been volcanoes, some of whose openings still send out waters of strange properties, and gases that kill or make to vivify. (D, 296–97)

As Thacker observes, highlighting the ambiguity of our relationship with our non-thinking environment, 'Demons possess not only humans and animals, but also the very landscape' (36).

Van Helsing, the medium for the gradual revelation of the immensity of the non-human, is an expert in the negations of being beyond the limits of thought. In a telling detail, shortly after succumbing to hysterical laughter at the bleakness of their situation following Lucy's funeral, he reveals that his wife suffers from dementia: 'and me, with my poor wife dead to me, but alive by Church's law, though no wits, all gone, even I, who am faithful husband to this now-no-wife'. (*D*, 164) Van Helsing's very mode of speech, an exercise in dialectical ambiguity, voices the shortcomings of precise methods in the face of the non-human.

The definitive utterance on that which lies beyond thought, its excesses and limits as might be exposed through the horror genre, is appropriately enough pronounced by Mina, whose own mind is made porous through infection. 'Omne ignotum pro magnifico' (*D*, 294) – all that is unknown is magnificent – a summary statement, perhaps, of this object-oriented, non-human reading of *Dracula*.

Conclusion

Here are just two readings of *Dracula* informed by emergent horror theory. Cognate studies offer more chances for what we might call 'Draculation'. Graham Harman's *Weird Realism* might also allow us to read the object-orientation of the text with an eye to what cannot be reduced to phenomenological concerns. Eugene Thacker has recently published two further volumes in his *Horror of Philosophy* series, with typically baroque titles: *Starry Speculative Corpse* and *Tentacles Longer Than the Night*. These promise new avenues for reading monstrosity philosophically.[19]

Some scientists have argued that since the year 2000 we have entered a whole new geological epoch, marking humanity's distinct and irreversible effect on the global environment. From the Holocene we have passed to the Anthropocene. Many figures associated with ecological criticism tend to reach for horror and weird fiction to track this catastrophic transformation.[20] Of course they do: how else can we hope to defeat the Legion undead who stalk our thickening dreams in impending clouds of unknowing than by turning to the grimoires and manuals of demonology offered us by our own time?

Notes

1 Jacques Derrida, *Spectres of Marx: The State of the Debt, The Work of Mourning and the New International*, trans. P. Kamuf (London: Routledge, 1993).
2 The most rigorous and informed account is Steven Shaviro, *The Universe of Things: On Speculative Realism* (Minneapolis: University of Minnesota Press, 2014).

3 Peter Wessel Zapffe, 'The Last Messiah', trans. by Gisle R. Tangenes, *Philosophy Now* 45 (2004), 35–39, quote on p. 35.

4 Bruno Latour, *We Have Never Been Modern*, trans. C. Porter (Cambridge, MA: Harvard University Press, 1993).

5 Graham Harman, *Weird Realism* (Winchester, UK: Zero Books 2012).

6 The full text of *Collapse: Concept Horror* 4 (2008) is available online: archive .org/stream/CollapseVol.IvConceptHorror/CollapseIV_djvu.txt.

7 Robin McKay, 'Editorial Introduction', *Collapse: Concept Horror* 4 (2008), 3–28, quote on p. 4.

8 Ray Brassier, *Nihil Unbound* (Basingstoke: Palgrave McMillan, 2007) 223.

9 John Clute, 'Fantastika' entry in his online *The Encyclopedia of Science Fiction*, sf-encyclopedia.com/entry/fantastika.

10 John Clute, 'The Darkening Garden' (2006), in the essay collection, *Stay* (Basildon: Beccon Publications, 2014), 311. All further references in the text.

11 Northrop Frye, *Anatomy of Criticism: Four Essays* (Princeton, NJ: Princeton University Press, 1957), 133, 140.

12 Ian Watt, *Conrad in the Nineteenth Century* (Berkeley and Los Angeles: University of California Press, 1979), 175.

13 H. P. Lovecraft, 'The Call of Cthulhu', in Roger Luckhurst, ed., *Classic Horror Stories* (Oxford: Oxford University Press, 2013), p. 24.

14 Stephen D. Arata, 'The Occidental Tourist: *Dracula* and the Anxiety of Reverse Colonization', *Victorian Studies* 33 (1990), 621–45, quote on p. 623.

15 Clute, 'The Darkening Garden', 280; Zapffe, 'The Last Messiah', 35.

16 Eugene Thacker, *In the Dust of this Planet: Horror of Philosophy, Volume 1* (Winchester: Zero Books, 2011), 9. All further references in the text.

17 Brassier, *Nihil Unbound*, xi.

18 Eugene Thacker, '*Nihil Unbound: Enlightenment and Extinction* (review)', *Leonardo* 42 (2009), 459–60, quote on p. 459.

19 Graham Harman, *Weird Realism* (Winchester: Zero Books, 2012). Thacker's *Horror of Philosophy*, vols. 2 and 3 both appeared from Zero Books in 2015.

20 Stephen Morton, *Dark Ecology: For a Logic of Future Coexistence* (New York: Columbia University Press, 2016). See also 'Global Weirding', a special issue of the journal *Paradoxa* 28 (2016).

13

KEN GELDER

Transnational Draculas

In Elizabeth Kostova's bestselling debut novel *The Historian* (2005), a young woman accompanies her father on a prolonged search for Dracula's tomb, travelling to Amsterdam, Istanbul, Paris, Athens, Slovenia and a host of other European locations: everywhere, it seems, except Transylvania. Each section of *The Historian* is prefaced with a quote from Stoker's novel, which drives the quest to find out where the vampire is now hiding. *The Historian* entirely depends on *Dracula* for its narrative, themes and atmosphere, demonstrating its sheer familiarity with that novel and its eponymous anti-hero. But it also wants to show that Dracula has exceeded Stoker's novel, outlasting and out-pacing it. Of course, Dracula himself has precisely this ambition as he plans his migration from Transylvania to London to become – as he famously tells Jonathan Harker – 'a stranger in a strange land' (*D*, 23). In 1908, ten years after Stoker's novel, the sociologist Georg Simmel published an essay titled 'The Stranger' (*Der Fremde*), identifying this migrating figure as quintessentially modern. The stranger, as he puts it, is not 'the wanderer who comes today and goes tomorrow, but rather . . . the man who comes today and stays tomorrow'.[1]

This projection into the future of someone who arrives and does not leave gives us a good sense of where Dracula is heading after Stoker's novel. This chapter will track the vampire's arrival in three quite different places: the American South, Japan and Sweden. It wants to suggest, as a general observation, that the vampire does indeed turn out to be a stranger in a strange land who is nevertheless also already recognisable, even familiar. The vampire, to draw on Simmel's stranger again, 'does not belong' even as it makes itself at home; it 'indicates that one who is close by is remote' and 'that one who is remote is near'.[2]

America

When did vampires migrate to America? In Stephanie Meyer's popular *Twilight* novels (2005–8), vampires are the 'cold ones' who arrive in the

New World early on and soon outnumber the Quileutes, a Native American community from the northwest coast of the United States. Meyer's account of these vampire conquistadors unfolds in *Eclipse* (2007) and is presented as if it is an established part of Quileute legend – with vampires cast as colonial invaders who bring modernity (and death) to indigenous populations, remaining in perpetual conflict with them right to the present day: since they never go away. In Seth Grahame-Smith's *Abraham Lincoln, Vampire Hunter* (2010), vampires migrate to the American South in the late sixteenth century (well before the time of *Dracula*) and go on to become slave traders and plantation owners. Lincoln is horrified by vampires – and by slavery – and as he gains political influence he gathers together a sort of Crew of Light that includes a senator named William Seward to fight against them. In New Orleans he meets the writer Edgar Allan Poe, who is obsessed with vampires. Poe tells Lincoln that vampires, persecuted in Europe, fled to America to enjoy its 'freedoms': 'They loved its lawlessness. Its vastness. They loved its remote villages and its ports brimming with the newly arrived. But more than anything, Lincoln, they loved its *slaves*'.[3]

In the 2012 film adaptation of Grahame-Smith's novel, directed by Timur Bekmambetov, Lincoln defeats the slave-trading Confederate vampires in the Civil War, personally killing a powerful vampire plantation owner called Adam in a climactic fight on board a train. In the novel, however, slave revolts play a larger role in overcoming the vampires. Lincoln loses some of his family to vampires but at least, the novel concludes, he 'had driven the worst of them out of America'.[4] One particularly troublesome vampire remains, however: John Wilkes Booth.

The Lacanian critic Slavoj Zizek has noted that Bekmambetov's film is 'ridiculous' in one obvious sense and revelatory in another, offering a sort of delirious 'hallucination' that literally demonises the slave trade and Southern secessionism in mid-nineteenth century America.[5] In fact, this particular hallucination has a longer history in vampire fiction, going back at least as far as Anne Rice's vampire Lestat novels, early examples of 'plantation gothic'.[6] This description certainly applies to the early part of the narrative where a young man, Louis, recalls his life as a French Catholic slaveholder in 1791, the owner of an indigo plantation in Louisiana called Pointe du Lac, not far from New Orleans. The slavery system was already deeply unstable by this time: in the year Louis begins his story, around one hundred thousand slaves had risen up against their owners on the French-owned colony of Saint Domingue, burning down sugar plantations and hundreds of coffee and indigo plantations. The slave revolt in Saint Domingue 'aroused the most intense alarm amongst the possessing classes on both sides of the Atlantic'.[7] In *Interview with the Vampire*, Louis's brother Paul urges his family to leave, to 'sell all our property in Louisiana, everything we owned, and use the money to do God's work in France'.[8] In fact, indigo plantations – like Louis's – were struggling financially by the 1790s; one of the effects of the slave rebellion in sugar-producing Saint Domingue was a rise in the number of sugar plantations on the mainland. A neighbouring French plantation in *Interview with the Vampire*, owned by the Frenieres, produces sugar. For the vampire Louis, the South is deliriously attracted to this slave-produced substance: 'This refined sugar', he says, 'is a poison. It was like the essence of life in New Orleans, so sweet that it can be fatal, so richly enticing that all other values are forgotten' (41). In this plantation gothic novel, sugar is a bit like blood, bringing both life and death; the South is addicted to it.

It turns out that the vampire Lestat 'wanted Point du Lac' (15) for himself; like Dracula, he aims to acquire property that, in this case, is tied to trans-Atlantic slave trading. When he turns Louis into a vampire, Louis realises that he, too, is a kind of slave: 'That's how vampires increase', he says, 'through slavery. How else?' (84). Later on, Louis leaves New Orleans for Paris, returning to Europe to try to discover the origins of vampires – but without success. The links to Paris in *Interview with the Vampire* are significant: that city 'keeps alive the particular colonial foundations of New Orleans' by situating it in the framework of the 'circum-Atlantic and the third coast – that is to say Gulf Coast – territory of French and Spanish colonialism and the slave trade'.[9] New Orleans is cast as a city full of new arrivals, 'migrants of all kinds', including slaves and slave traders – and vampires. There are so many strangers here that vampires themselves go unnoticed; or rather, like immigrant African slaves ('yet unhomogenised and fantastical'), they stand out and blend in at the same time. Louis returns to New Orleans at the end of the novel, disillusioned with vampires in Europe: as if New Orleans is now his proper home. 'I might never leave New Orleans', he finally tells Lestat – although his future in the post-slavery American South now seems almost without purpose (336).

The Mississippi-born novelist Charlaine Harris begins the first of her Sookie Stackhouse novels, *Dead Until Dark* (2001), by both acknowledging and distancing herself from Rice's influence. Rice's cosmopolitan New Orleans mixes together racialised immigrant groups of people from Europe and Africa, including vampires: some are assimilated, some not. Harris's novels, on the other hand, are more localised, set in a small provincial town in northern Louisiana called Bon Temps (not far from the actual town of Shreveport). Bon Temps makes very little space for racial difference: speaking about the hotel she works in, for example, Sookie comments, 'Blacks didn't come into Merlotte's much'.[10] But the question of assimilation – who stands out, who blends in – is now much more significant.

When the vampire Bill Compton arrives in town, some local characters are drawn to him (Sookie especially), and some are repelled. Compton is a kind of contradiction, a vampire-stranger but also, it turns out, a *local*: which means his arrival is also a return. A Confederate soldier in the Civil War, he had defended Louisiana's right to secede from the Union and remain a slave-owning state. Compton's family is from the Old South, arriving and settling in Louisiana just a few years before the Stackhouses. 'My folks were here', he says, 'when Bon Temps was just a hole in the road at the edge of the frontier' (46). Both the Comptons and the Stackhouses were slave owners; Compton in fact returns to Bon Temps to claim his inheritance. Sookie does the same thing after her grandmother is murdered: 'It was my house now', she proudly announces: 'The house and the twenty acres surrounding it were mine, as were the mineral rights' (133). No wonder Sookie and Bill Compton are drawn to each other. They both take possession of antebellum southern properties, thus placing themselves at the beginning and the end of white settler domination in the American South. Compton's aspiration to 'mainstream' should be understood in precisely these terms, as a landowner and Confederate in a secessionist southern state who now wants to be accepted by Americans at large.

The emphasis on assimilation (or mainstreaming) in Harris's Sookie Stackhouse novels links them to what is often called *post-racialism*, the view that expressions of racial difference are now beside the point, overtaken by a larger national/communal imperative to be 'American'. Although he was the first black U.S. president, Barack Obama gave significant expression to this post-racial aspiration in his often-cited 2004 address to the Democratic National Convention: 'There is not a Black America and a White America and Latino and Asian America. There's the United States of America'.[11] This speech was given just a few months after Alan Ball's television adaptation of Harris's novels, the *True Blood* series, began on HBO. In Harris's novels, a minor black American character called Lafayette is killed early on, but *True Blood* keeps him alive as a major character who energises the narrative. Harris's novels had also presented a fun-loving white woman called Tara Thornton, a friend of Sookie's who appears only occasionally. But *True Blood* turns this figure into one of its key protagonists, a volatile, disaffected black American. These and other changes to the way racial identities are understood distinguish the *True Blood* series from Harris's novels and pose a fascinating challenge to their benign, post-racial vision.

When Tara introduces herself in *True Blood*, she notes that she is 'named after a plantation'. *Tara* is in fact the name of the antebellum mansion in Margaret Mitchell's epic Civil War novel, *Gone with the Wind* (1936), owned and doggedly defended by Mitchell's feisty white Southern heroine,

Scarlett O'Hara ('No one was going to take Tara away from her … She would hold Tara, if she had to break the back of every person on it').[12] In *True Blood*, on the other hand, Tara doesn't own any property at all, having walked out of her alcoholic mother's makeshift house. Later on, the vampire Franklin kidnaps her, takes her to the secessionist King of Mississippi's antebellum mansion, ties her to the bed and systematically rapes and abuses her. When she finally escapes, running across the property in her white nightdress, she looks just like a runaway slave. In season two of *True Blood*, Tara meets a troubled black American man called Benedict and falls in love. But a rich white woman holds them both under her spell, forcing Benedict to commit a number of crimes on her behalf. Finally released from her cruel influence, Benedict approaches Andy Bellefleur, the town's redneck police officer, to confess. He is clutching a knife, although it seems more like a gesture of disarmament than a threat. But Sookie's brother Jason – who has recently undergone some paramilitary training and wants to be a police deputy – thinks that Benedict is about to attack Andy. He draws his gun and shoots the black American man in the back, killing him.

This scene is never mentioned in commentaries on *True Blood*, but it must surely resonate with American audiences who know only too well that fatal shootings of black American men by white police officers are commonplace, not least in the American South. The 2014 race protests in Ferguson, Missouri, coincided with the last season of *True Blood* and followed the fatal shooting by police of a black American man, Michael Brown. The "hands up, don't shoot" slogan became a defining feature of these protests, coming in the wake of the Black Lives Matter campaign that followed the fatal shooting of George Zimmerman in February 2012 by a white neighbourhood watch volunteer in Sanford, Florida. The shooting of Benedict in *True Blood* addresses the grim fact that white police officers in America shoot and kill a disproportionately high number of black American men. The event itself complicates the fantasy framework of white vampires in the American South seeking either to secede (like the King of Mississippi) or assimilate (like Bill Compton). This is certainly a clear and urgent challenge to the view that the United States is in some kind of post-racial predicament.

When Tara herself is finally turned into a vampire, she is horrified to realise she is now the thing she most despises – the very thing that had enslaved her in her previous life. Put to work in Pam's vampire nightclub, she is reprimanded when she tries to assert herself: 'So I'm basically your slave', she tells her employer, recognising that (as Tara puts it) 'The more things change, the more they fucking stay the same'. Tara is eventually killed towards the end of *True Blood*; the series refuses to assimilate this representative of enslavement, black American abjection and racial difference. She is conspicuously absent in the closing scene of the series where the remaining cast sit happily around a table in the sunlight, eating and talking peacefully together in a glowing 'post-racial' gesture of community that is strangely haunted by those characters who are no longer there.

Japan

For Nina Auerbach in *Our Vampires, Ourselves* (1995), vampires are defined primarily by their capacity to assimilate, to adapt to their surroundings: 'they blend into the changing cultures they inhabit'. But they are not indiscriminate in terms of the destinations they choose for themselves. 'Vampires', she perceptively suggests, 'go where the power is'.[13] For Auerbach, the United States is thus the most appropriate destination for an ambitious modern vampire. But in fact, vampires have migrated to a range of different places around the world, not just America. This section will look briefly at vampires in Japan, turning its attention to two so-called 'light novels', Hideyuki Kikuchi's *Vampire Hunter D* (1983) and the well-known anime film director Mamoru Oshii's *Blood: The Last Vampire: Night of the Beasts* (2000). Both novels are tied to proliferating series across different media in Japan and the Anglophone world. There are around thirty *Vampire Hunter D* novels so far, as well as spin-off series and prequels; there are also animated films, audio dramas, video games, manga adaptations by Saiko Takaki (beginning in 2007) and so on. *Vampire Hunter D: Bloodlust* (2000) – globally distributed by the Los Angeles-based Urban Vision Entertainment – is also credited as the first Japanese anime film to be originally recorded in English, with a cast of British and American actors providing the voices.

These are texts that take the vampire to Japan and then send this figure back out into the Anglophone world. Oshii's novel is transnationally networked in a similar way, a partial adaptation of Hiroyuki Kitakubo's high-quality English language anime film, *Blood: The Last Vampire* (2000), which was shown in Canada and Australia some time before premiering in Japan – and which was in turn adapted as a Hong Kong-British-French live action film by the French director Chris Nahon in 2009. A long-running spin-off anime television series called *Blood+*, directed by Junichi Fujisaku, premiered in 2005 – followed by *Blood C* (from 2011) and *Blood C: The Last Dark* (from 2012). English dubs of these series were distributed in the United States, Australia and elsewhere, and manga adaptions of these series have also been released in English. These two novels are just a small part of a much larger assemblage of vampire narratives in transnationalised contemporary Japanese media.

Kikuchi's *Vampire Hunter D* is a sort of pastiche, a prolonged tribute to the memory of Dracula – distant in terms of place here, but also in terms of time, since the novel is set a long way into the future: the year 12090. It is dedicated to local manga artist Osamu Kishimoto, and also to 'the entire cast and crew of *Horror of Dracula*', a British horror film from 1958 directed by Terence Fisher and starring Christopher Lee as Dracula. Names in *Vampire Hunter D* are displaced or modified citations: the powerful predatory vampire here is Count Magnus Lee, and his daughter is Lamica (after Lamia, the mythological woman in John Keats's 1819 poem). Events take place around a village named Ransylva somewhere on a remote 'frontier', giving an eastern calibration to the western genre – folding 'the samurai and the cowboy' together, to produce a local subgenre that has been referred to as 'Zen Gothic'.[14] D himself is a 'dhampir', a figure derived from Balkan folklore that is part-vampire, part human; he is solitary, strikingly beautiful man with great fighting skills. Hired by a young woman to protect her family, D finally kills Count Lee by using a 'trick' taught to him by 'the Sacred Ancestor'.[15] It is implied that the Sacred Ancestor is Dracula himself, although the novel cannot quite bring itself to speak his name: 'the great vampire, king of kings, Dra–' (100). Dracula functions as a distant point of origin in *Vampire Hunter D*, but he is also a generative force, shown to stimulate and influence events far into the future at the edges of a place that is now barely recognisable as 'Japan'. He literally plays out the role of a 'stranger' in the modern (distant future) world, as someone who is indeed, to recall Simmel's remarks above, both 'near' and 'remote'. In *Vampire Hunter D*, Dracula somehow arrives in Japan, remains there, and orchestrates everything that follows in a series of novels and other media-based narratives that show no sign of coming to an end. This is why Stoker's novel is understood here as 'sacred'. On the other hand, *Vampire Hunter D* creates a landscape that is literally *marginal* to Japan, a distant 'frontier' space that is cast as a sort of weird anomaly. It is as if Dracula arrives in Japan in order to produce a massive cultural displacement: one that sees the residues of western vampire narratives (Stoker's *Dracula*, Fisher's *Horror of Dracula*) inhabit the very edges of the Far East.

Mamoru Oshii's *Blood: The Last Vampire* is much more directly engaged with contemporary Japan, opening in Tokyo in 1969 where students are protesting against the Vietnam War. Rei Miwa is involved in the protests, but as he runs from the police he sees a young girl dressed in a blue school uniform kill a large beast with a Japanese sword. Two men in a dark car arrive and quickly whisk her away. Rei's life at home is defined by violence and abuse; when they hear of his involvement in the student riots, his parents forbid him to leave their house. Not long afterwards, a strange man appears in his bedroom ('I just knocked and came in'), introducing himself as a detective called Hijime Gotouda. Students are being killed, he tells Rei, their bodies disappearing. Later on, he launches into long account of the various means of disposing of corpses, and of 'things that come back from the grave' around the world: 'The Slavs had the *vampyr*', he observes; 'The Russians had the *uppyr*. The Greeks had the *vrykolakas*'.[16] Gotouda turns out to be an agent from the Vatican, an 'inquisitor' who is tracking vampires as they migrate from country to country. He is searching in particular for a girl called Saya Otonashi, a vampire-human hybrid (rather like D in Kikuchi's novel) who Gotouda thinks is working for a secret Jewish organisation who are also hunting vampires around the world.

Saya is enrolled as a 'transfer student' at Rei's school, but she has the reputation of being 'unapproachable'. She speaks Japanese but she is also 'fluent in English'. Rei says at one point, 'Some might think she's a returnee who's been living overseas' (100). In his commentary on the anime film of *Blood: The Last Vampire*, Neal Baker writes that Saya 'remains a cipher of indeterminate provenance': although she does speak in English, she 'talks to herself in Japanese' and 'signifies "Japanese" through her high school uniform and samurai sword'.[17] In Kitakubo's film – set a couple of years before the novel, in late 1966 – the high school itself is adjacent to the Yokota US air base (an actual air base to the west of Tokyo) and B-52 bombers are flying off to Vietnam. Baker regards the film as 'a critique of the [post-World War Two] US-Japan security alliance', although he later thinks the film is 'ambivalent' about this alliance and its various risks and benefits.[18]

Saya's task in the film seems to be to keep the vampires that haunt the US airbase from leaving Japan and causing havoc elsewhere: in Vietnam itself, for example, which was occupied by Japan during Second World War. For Christopher Bolton, Saya thus responds to 'the fear of renewed Japanese intervention abroad'; as she pulls a vampire away from one of the departing B-52 bombers, she thus shuts down 'the threat that the monster will escape Japan's shores on America's back' – although she also ensures the bombers are free to go about their deadly work unhindered.[19] This is certainly an interesting reorientation of Auerbach's notion that vampires – and in this case, part-vampires – 'go where the power is'. Saya may be helpful in restraining Japan's imperial ambitions, but both the anime film and the novel raise the question: is she Japanese, or is this essentially an intervention from *outside* Japan? Baker notes that the film eventually reveals an old photograph of Saya from somewhere in Europe, dated 1892. This is just a few years before the publication of Stoker's novel, of course, but as Baker notes, it is also 'a period when foreign elements were rapidly introduced to traditional Japanese life'.[20] Rei and the other students at school think that

Saya's connection to a secret global Jewish organisation is reflected through her own strange (or stranger) identity. 'She must be a Japanese Jew!' someone exclaims. 'Do we even know that she's Japanese?' someone else remarks; 'She looks foreign' (104). Saya is indeed an indeterminate figure, simultaneously 'near' and 'remote': a stranger in a strange land. She is familiar in some respects (even 'traditionally' Japanese, with her samurai sword), but strikingly different in others: enough to make her stand out, as a distinctive figure. The novel ends thirty years into the future – in the late 1990s – with Rei now married, settled and working, taking on a normalised role in contemporary Japanese society. Saya, on the other hand, remains eternally the age of a teenage schoolgirl, 'a violently beautiful predatory monster' who may or may not be working in Japan's best interests (293).

Sweden

In John Ajvide Lindqvist's novel *Let the Right One In* (2004), a vampire child Eli and her guardian Håkan (who may also be a vampire) arrive in Blackeberg, a suburb in the outer north west of Stockholm, Sweden. The year is 1981 and Blackeberg is a relatively new place, a satellite suburb tied not to the past (like the various European cities visited in Kostova's *The Historian*) but to the present, the *contemporary*. Soon, it is densely populated, full of apartment blocks. 'Only one thing was missing', the novel tells us – 'A past':

> Where the three-storeyed apartment buildings now stood there had only been forest before.
>
> You were beyond the grasp of the mysteries of the place; there wasn't even a church. Nine thousand inhabitants and no church ... [That] tells you something of how free they were from the ghosts of history and of terror.[21]

The novel means this literally: what troubles this suburb is not 'the ghosts of history' at all, but encounters that are specifically to do with Sweden's position in the modern world. Vampires arrive in Blackeberg at the same time, the novel tells us, that 'a Soviet submarine runs aground outside of Karlskrona' (95), a Swedish naval base. The reference here is to a Soviet submarine, which did indeed surface on the Swedish coast in October 1981 and inflamed a local sense of an 'immediate Soviet threat' that led to increased military spending in Sweden and the establishment of tighter controls over its borders.[22] 'Sweden', as the novel puts it, 'would become a changed nation. A *violated* nation. That was the word that was continually used: violated' (95).

Eli and Håkan move into an apartment next door to a boy named Oskar Eriksson, who lives with his divorced mother. Oskar is bullied at school, his nose bleeds easily and he is incontinent; an abject figure, he withdraws into a vivid and sometimes murderous fantasy life. When he meets Eli – who seems around the same age as him, twelve years old – he begins to take an interest in his new neighbours. His mother complains about their noisy arguments: 'I just have to say ... about these new people ... what neighbours. Did you hear them?' (85) Oskar, however, is more forgiving and more curious, listening to the new arrivals through a bedroom wall that is covered with wallpaper 'depicting a forest meadow': 'On the other side, on the other side of the forest, there was Eli' (83). This is the closest this novel gets to Transylvania ('beyond the forest').

Tomas Alfredson's 2008 film adaptation of *Let the Right One In* draws on Freud's famous rejection of the Christian imperative to love thy neighbour. 'Not merely is this stranger in general unworthy of my love', Freud writes, 'I must honestly confess that he has more claim to my hostility and even my hatred'.[23] 'The Vampire Next Door' is the subtitle of an important 1997 essay about modern vampires by Jules Zanger, which complains that vampires have now lost their 'metaphysical' and 'religious' features to become, 'in our concerned awareness for multiculturalism, merely ethnic, a victim of heredity, like being Sicilian or Jewish'. 'This new, demystified vampire', he writes, 'might as well be our next door neighbour, as Dracula, by origin, appearance, caste, and speech, could never pretend to be'.[24] But Dracula, as he arrives in London, is already the stranger who wants to be neighbourly, which is one reason why he provokes so much hostility amongst Londoners. In any case, the 'merely ethnic' is a signifier that applies as much to Dracula as it does to Eli in *Let the Right One In* – and it only adds to the strangeness of the stranger/neighbour/vampire as a migrating figure, welcomed in one way and hated in another.

The title of Lindqvist's novel is a command, an imperative: one must only let 'the right one' into one's home, one's country. The question of issuing an invitation to a stranger becomes central to the novel. When Eli appears outside Oskar's bedroom window (rather like J. M. Barrie's Peter Pan, with whom she has much in common), she tells him: 'Say that I can come in' (182). Later on, Oskar is invited in to Eli's apartment. 'Say that I can come in', he says, repeating Eli's earlier request. 'You can come in', she replies (295). Later on, as Eli grasps the significance of the need to be invited in, he decides to test Eli as she waits outside his door. 'Oskar', she says, 'you have to invite me in'. But he wants to see what happens when he doesn't, so she steps into his apartment and in a few moments blood begins to flow out of her eyes, her mouth and her skin. 'You can come in, you can', Oskar tells her in a panic, 'you are welcome, you are ... allowed to be here!' (375–76). Earlier in the novel, Håkan ritualistically murders a boy and drains his blood to feed Eli. At the same time, police arrest five Lebanese men in the largest drug seizure ever recorded in Sweden: another reference to an actual event from October 1981. The two events are then tied together in the novel through local gossip and suspicion:

> There were speculations that the ritual murderer was also a foreigner. It seemed plausible enough, weren't blood rituals common in those Arab countries? . . . You heard about that. Brutal people. Iran. Iraq. The Lebanese.

> But on Monday the police released a composite sketch of the suspect . . . A normal Swede. With a ghost-like appearance, a vacant gaze. Everyone was in agreement about that, yes, this is what a murderer looked like . . . Every man in the western suburbs who resembled the phantom picture was subjected to long, scrutinising looks. These men went home and looked at themselves in the mirror, [and] saw no resemblance whatsoever. (94)

This interesting passage distinguishes locals from 'foreigners', then undoes that distinction, and then distinguishes locals from other locals: or rather, it ends by distinguishing locals from *vampires*, which bring something 'foreign' with them even when they move in next door. Håkan, it is worth noting, is in fact Swedish, an ex-schoolteacher from Karlstad. But Eli is more obviously a kind of immigrant, not local or perhaps not *quite* local: Tomas Alfredson has noted that he cast the actor Lina Leandersson as Eli in his film because she was born in Sweden but is also of Iranian descent, suggesting 'the vampire's foreignness'.[25] The difference between the foreign and the local are confused here, of course.

In Lindqvist's novel, however, Eli's foreignness is differently configured. Oskar recalls a Jewish woman who had visited his school and shown the students photographs of concentration camps during the Holocaust. 'Eli was looking a little bit like the people in those pictures', he thinks (131). Later on, police hear Håkan calling out Eli's name and – recalling Christ's last words on the cross ('*Eli, Eli, lama sabachthani?*') – wonder if he was calling out to God (162). The Hebrew connotations of Eli's name give us a contemporary impression of Stoker's representation of Dracula as a fin-de-siècle version of the 'Wandering Jew' and an embodiment of anti-Semitic stereotypes of the eastern European Jew as a threat to national economies in the West. This figure seemed, from a Western European perspective in particular, both 'near' and 'remote', a version of Simmel's stranger: 'For the emancipated Jewries of Western Europe, the invasion of Jewish Eastern Europe was . . . uncanny . . . not because the Eastern European Jew was entirely alien but because he was just a shade too familiar'.[26]

But in *Let the Right One In*, Eli's Jewish connotations are downplayed; she is, we could say, both a 'shade too familiar' and just a shade too 'alien' or foreign. In any case, she poses no threat to the national economy of Sweden. Unlike Dracula, who buys property in London and accumulates wealth from across Europe, Eli and Håkan are itinerant renters and seem impoverished. On the other hand, they kill and feed on a number of locals, including a young boy, a helpful man who thinks Eli is 'malnourished', and a woman, Virginia, who has trouble committing to long term relationships (*'Let a person in'*, she thinks, *'and he hurts you'* (239)).

Eli in *Let the Right One In* is rather like Saya in *Blood: The Last Vampire*, an indeterminate figure, someone who – just like the stranger – makes herself at home but 'does not belong'. She is also *sexually* indeterminate, although she dresses as a girl. Oskar thinks she is a girl early on, but she tells him: 'I'm nothing. Not a child. Not old. Not a boy. Not a girl. Nothing' (185). The first half of the novel uses the pronoun 'she' to describe her; then it switches to the male pronoun 'he'. Her guardian, Håkan, is in love with Eli and is presented in the novel as a homosexual paedophile, on the run from police after locals burned down his house. He disfigures himself with acid when he is about to be discovered after trying to drain someone's blood; later, Eli kills and feeds on him, but he rises from the dead and seeks Eli out, tying the young vampire down in an attempt to sodomise him. Anne Billson has suggested that 'sexuality is conspicuous by its absence in *Let the Right One In*'.[27] But this is certainly not true of the novel, where Eli's growing intimacy with Oskar means that the latter will eventually take Håkan's place. Håkan was Eli's guardian and lover, but he had also 'entered into Eli's service' (234): rather like Tara with Pam in *True Blood*, or Louis with Lestat in *Interview with the Vampire*. When they travel, they travel together, inseparable.

Vampire narratives since *Dracula* have invariably cast the arrival of the stranger/vampire as a viral threat to a nation's sense of wellbeing. As *Let the Right One In* knows very well, vampire narratives can therefore directly address a nation's anxieties about the arrival of foreigners, immigrants, asylum seekers and so on. It tells us that Sweden feels 'violated' when its borders are breached, as if something violently sexual has happened. Oskar feels 'infected' when Eli kisses him, and recognises, to his horror, that 'I'm going to become a ... vampire' (397): a transformation we don't see, incidentally, in Alfredson's film adaptation. Later on, before he kisses him again, Eli says to Oskar: 'Would you want to ... become like me?' (484). The novel turns locals into stranger/vampires, even as it confuses the differences between them. It presents the vampire's kiss as a 'violation', but it is also massively liberating and invigorating: 'For a few seconds, Oskar saw through Eli's eyes. And what he saw was ... himself. Only much better, more handsome, stronger than what he thought of himself. Seen with love'

(485). This is the dual effect of the arrival of the immigrant, who is both welcomed (invited in) and vilified and hated (regarded as an assault on local and national identities); he opens borders and secures them at the same time.

In June 2016, Sweden limited the possibility of asylum seekers – from the Middle East especially – gaining residence permits. As the *New York Times* commented, 'one of the most welcoming countries for refugees … [has now] introduced tough new restrictions on asylum seekers, including rules that would limit the number of people granted permanent residency and make it more difficult for parents to reunite with their children'.[28] At the end of *Let the Right One In*, Eli has rescued Oskar and they have bonded, with Oskar (like Håkan before him) 'infected' by this strange vampire figure. He leaves his home, his mother and Blackeberg and boards a train on the Stockholm-Karlstad line, with an 'old-fashioned' trunk beside him with Eli hiding inside. This is in one sense an act of people smuggling. Karlstad is where Håkan came from; it is west of Stockholm, on the way to the North Sea. We remember that Dracula travels west in Stoker's novel as he makes his way to London to become 'a stranger in a stranger land'. 'Is someone meeting you at the other end?' the conductor asks Oskar: but no one will meet them, and it will be evening when the train arrives at its destination. *Let the Right One In* takes 'permanent residency' apart, investing instead in migration – and in the hope that one might be welcomed when one arrives, and invited in: that one might be 'the right one'. There is, of course, no suggestion that Oskar and Eli are actually going to leave Sweden, even as they travel west. But this is consistent with the predicament of the stranger in the modern world, as 'the man who comes today and stays tomorrow'.

Notes

1 Georg Simmel, 'The Stranger' (1908), in Donald N. Levine, ed., *On Individuality and Social Forms* (Chicago: University of Chicago Press, 1971), p. 143.
2 Georg Simmel, 'The Stranger', 143.
3 Seth Graham-Smith, *Abraham Lincoln, Vampire Hunter* (New York: Grand Central Publishing, 2010), 203.
4 Graham-Smith, *Abraham Lincoln*, 307.
5 Slavoj Zizek, *Trouble in Paradise: Communism after the End of History* (London: Allen Lane, 2014), 63–64.
6 Jason S. Friedman, '"Ah Am Witness to its Authenticity": Gothic Style in Post-modern Southern Writing', in Lauren M. E. Goodlad and Michael Bibby, eds., *Goth: Undead Subculture* (Durham, NC: Duke University Press, 2007), p. 192.
7 Robin Blackburn, *The Overthrow of Colonial Slavery, 1776–1848* (London: Verso, 1988), 155.
8 Anne Rice, *Interview with a Vampire* (New York: Ballantine, 196), 41.

9 Barbara Eckstein, *Sustaining New Orleans: Literature, Local Memory, and the Fate of a City* (New York: Routledge, 2006), 150–51.

10 Charlaine Harris, *Dead Until Dark* (New York: Ace Books, 2001), 151. All further references in the text.

11 See, for example, Sarah Nilsen and Sarah E. Turner, *The Colorblind Screen: Television in Post-Racial America* (New York: New York University Press, 2014), 1.

12 Margaret Mitchell, *Gone with the Wind* (New York: Pocket Books, 2008), 603.

13 Nina Auerbach, *Our Vampires, Ourselves* (Chicago: University of Chicago Press, 1995) 6.

14 Wayne Stein and John Edgar Browning, 'The Western Eastern: De-Coding Hybridity and CyberZen Gothic in Vampire Hunter D', in Andrew Hock Soon Ng, ed., *Asian Gothic: Essays on Literature, Film and Anime* (Jefferson, NC: McFarland, 2008), pp. 218–20.

15 Hideyuki Kikuchi, *Vampire Hunter D*, trans. Kevin Leahy (Milwaukie: Dark Horse Books, 2005), 233. All further references in the text.

16 Mamoru Oshii, *Blood: The Last Vampire: Night of the Beasts*, trans. Camellia Nieh (Milwaukie: Dark Horse Books, 2000), 119. All further references in the text.

17 Neal Baker, 'The US-Japan Security Alliance and Blood: *The Last Vampire*', *Journal of the Fantastic in the Arts* 13, no. 2 (2002), 143.

18 Baker, 'The US-Japan Security Alliance and Blood', 143, 148.

19 Christopher Bolton, 'The Quick and the Undead: Visual and Political Dynamics in Blood: *The Last Vampire*', in French Lunning, ed., *Mechademia 2: Networks of Desire*, (Minneapolis: University of Minnesota Press, 2007), 139.

20 Baker, 'The US-Japan Security Alliance and Blood', 148.

21 John Ajvide Lindqvist, *Let the Right One In*, trans. Ebba Segerberg (Melbourne: Text Publishing, 2007), 2. All further references in the text.

22 Ola Tunander, *The Secret War Against Sweden: US and British Submarine Deception in the 1980s* (London: Frank Cass, 2004), 287.

23 Sigmund Freud, *Civilisation and Its Discontents*, trans. James Strachey (New York: W. W. Norton, 1962), 57.

24 Jules Zanger, 'Metaphor into Metonymy: The Vampire Next Door', in Joan Gordon and Veronica Hollinger, eds, *Blood Read: The Vampire as Metaphor in Contemporary Culture* (Philadelphia: University of Pennsylvania Press, 1997), p. 19.

25 Carol Siegel, 'Let a New Gender In? American Responses to Contemporary Scandinavian Gothicism', in Charles Crow, ed. *A Companion to American Gothic* (Oxford: Wiley Blackwell, 2013), p. 555.

26 Olga Litvak, 'The Jewish *fin-de- siècle*', in Michael Saler, ed. *The Fin-de-Siècle World* (London: Routledge, 2015), p. 561.

27 Anne Billson, *Devil's Advocates: Let the Right One In* (Leighton Buzzard: Auteur, 2011), 70.

28 Dan Bilefsky, 'Sweden Toughens Rules for Refugees Seeking Asylum', *New York Times*, 21 June 2016.

PART IV

Adaptations

14

CATHERINE WYNNE

Dracula on Stage

Dracula made a one-off stage appearance on 18 May 1897 shortly before it was published as a novel. Stoker staged a reading of the novel at London's Royal Lyceum Theatre, where he had worked as the actor-manager Henry Irving's business manager since December 1878, in order to protect its dramatic copyright.[1] Appropriately enough, the Lyceum was the home of the 'vampire trap', a technical stage innovation, first used in John Robinson Planché's *The Vampire; or the Bride of the Isles* at the Lyceum (then known as the Royal Opera House) in 1820. The trap allowed the vampire to appear and disappear as if by supernatural agency. Surely this was a good sign? Five months after the novel publication of *Dracula*, Charles Lindley Wood, the Second Viscount Halifax and a collector of ghost stories, wrote to Bram Stoker to congratulate him on his novel and suggested that Stoker dramatise *Dracula*. Halifax even proposed that Irving should play Dracula. The leading actor of late Victorian Britain, Irving relished plays with occult content from melodrama to Shakespeare.

Despite this first reading and Halifax's later recommendation, the first successful dramatisation of *Dracula*, adapted by an actor Hamilton Deane, premiered at the Grand Theatre in Derby, England, in 1924. Staged twelve years after Stoker's death, this version *Dracula* became a box office hit. So the Count on stage emerged from the British Midlands to triumph on the London and American stages only in the late 1920s.

Melodrama was the dominant theatrical genre in the nineteenth century, yet the mode permeated far beyond theatre and pervaded the wider culture. Melodrama has been read as a way for Victorian society to find an ethical system in a post-sacred world: 'conventionally moral and humanitarian in its point of view ... concluding its fable happily with virtue rewarded after many trials and vice punished'.[2] Stoker similarly presents a melodrama in *Dracula* in which modernity is under siege from evil, rebarbative forces. Its vampire villain was a version of the 'Fated Man' of melodrama, capable of transformation into other life forms and into dust. *Dracula* – visually elaborate and high voltage – was influenced by the nineteenth-century stage, making it both stagey and, as adaptors discovered, stageable.

Stoker had a long working life in the theatre. An unpaid theatre critic for Dublin's *Evening Mail* in the 1870s, he reviewed Irving's *Hamlet* in November 1876. The actor subsequently invited Stoker to a select reading of 'The Dream of Eugene Aram', a melodramatic poem about a murderer. Stoker records being 'spellbound' by the 'magnetism' of Irving's genius and collapsed in 'hysterics'.[3] In December 1878 Stoker joined the Lyceum Company with the ambition of using the opportunity to develop a writing career. However, Harry Ludlam notes that Stoker's 'behind the scenes work was staggering'.[4] In a letter in 1899, the American theatre critic William Winter thanks Stoker for the copy of *Dracula* that he had sent and commends its author for sustaining his writing, despite his 'prodigious burden of executive work'.[5]

The Lyceum, however, taught Stoker about production: 'I was very much struck by the care in doing things. Now I began to understand why everything was as it was'.[6] Significantly, the Lyceum's elaborate effects honed the imagination of a writer equipped with a Gothic predisposition. In an early short story, 'The Chain of Destiny' (1875), a woman is threatened by a vision of a supernatural monster in her bedroom window until her lover shatters the glass. The story prefigures the effects of the stage on the imagination of the audience as the woman is transfixed by the image, much as Irving's audience were mesmerised by Lyceum illusions. The painter Helen Allingham, for instance, describes being 'stupefied' by the effect of *Faust*, in which Irving played the supernatural tempter Mephistopheles.[7] A contemporary actor confirms that Irving was a 'masterly exponent of the imagination, mystery and witchcraft of the theatre'.[8] H. A. Saintsbury recalled how on entering the Lyceum 'the spirit gripped you; it had enveloped you before you took your seat; gas-lit candles in their wine-coloured shades glowed softly' and the music 'insinuated itself upon you'.[9] The Count is a product of Stoker's Gothic imagination, the Lyceum's cult of the supernatural and the nineteenth century's immersion in melodramatic excess.

Dracula's effects are theatrical. Harker, for instance, looks out of his castle imprisonment to see the Count emerge from a window and 'crawl down the castle wall over the dreadful abyss, *face down*, with his cloak spreading out around him like great wings' (D, 35). Harker cannot 'believe [his] eyes', conceiving it in terms that are reminiscent of theatrical devices as 'some trick of moonlight, some weird effects of shadow', but it is not a 'delusion' as Dracula scales downwards 'just as a lizard moves along a wall' (D, 35). Deane understood the theatricality of this scene.

His 1924 adaptation opens with a prologue in which Dracula is seen emerging from a 'vast ruined castle' to crawl down the wall 'face downwards'. In lines that are taken directly from the novel the prologue describes how he descends 'with his cloak spreading out around him like great wings'. In the actor's note, Deane instructs that the 'Inverness' cape 'must be heavily wired, so that when face downwards it assumes the shape of a Bat's Wings'.[10]

With the stage set of Whitby Abbey and St Mary's Churchyard, Stoker cultivates the novel's menacing atmosphere. The sleepwalking Lucy ventures to her favourite churchyard seat and Mina, in pursuit, sees her figure emerging and disappearing as clouds pass across the moon. In an essay on theatrical lighting, Stoker explains how Irving developed stage lighting to enhance atmosphere. Irving 'noticed that nature seldom throws broad effect with an equality of light. There are shadows, here and there, or places where ... light is unevenly distributed. This makes great variety of effect' which he attempted to reproduce because the 'audience always notices effect, though the notice is not always conscious; it is influenced without knowing the reason'.[11] As if illuminated by limelight, frequently used on stage at the Lyceum to focus attention on the central figure, Lucy's white-clad form can be seen through the 'spells of shadow' and over it, Mina observes, there 'was undoubtedly something, long and black' with a 'white face and red, gleaming eyes' (D, 87). Later in Mina's bedroom, Dracula materialises out of the mist, like the vampire on stage emerging from his trap.

Stoker commenced his research for *Dracula* in the spring of 1890. Christopher Frayling observes in Stoker's working notes that the book's structure 'looks suspiciously like the "synopsis of scenery" page in a Lyceum programme – four acts, each with seven scenes, many supplied with ready-made curtain lines'.[12] Stoker had to submit his script to the Examiner of Plays, as it was a legal requirement that all plays intended for performance had to be examined. On 9 May 1897 George Redford wrote to Stoker to confirm that the adaptation fulfilled the legal requirement of copyright law and provided Stoker with a 'Provisional License' as he was satisfied that there was 'nothing unlicenseable in the piece'. Redford's concluding comment is significant: 'After all the book's the thing'.[13] It is evident that *Dracula* as a novel, rather than as a play, was the priority at this point. Despite its sexual content, Redford did not censor it.

Dracula; or the Undead is in manuscript form in the British Library and consists of five acts and forty-five scenes. Much of Stoker's script is a cut and paste job from the proof copy of the novel which was published shortly after the Lyceum performance. Stage directions and emendations are supplied in

Stoker's handwriting, although his notes diminish as the script progresses. The most heavily annotated section of the script is the Prologue, which consists of eight scenes. Stoker attempted to organise the opening pages of the novel by condensing them into a monologue by Harker at the castle door:

> Well this is a pretty state of things! After a drive through solid darkness with an unknown man whose face I have not seen and who has in his hand the strength of twenty men … I wondered why the people in the hotel at Bistritz were so frightened. And why the old lady hung the crucifix round my neck.[14]

This speech seems to derive almost directly from Victorian melodramatic exposition.

In the scene of the three vampire women's attack on Harker, Stoker is explicit about the encounter:

> FIRST WOMAN – Go on! You are the first, and we shall follow; yours is the right to begin.
> SECOND WOMAN – He is young and strong; there are kisses for us all.
>
> *Count suddenly appears before them and lifting the woman who is just fastening her lips on Harker's throat, by the neck hurls her away.*
>
> DRAC – How dare you touch him, any of you? How dare you cast eyes on him when I had forbidden it? Back, I tell you all! This man belongs to me. Beware how you meddle with him, or you'll have to deal with me.
> THIRD WOMAN – You yourself never loved; you never love. (13)

Dracula confirms, however, that he too 'can love' (13) and when the first woman asks if there is nothing for them, he throws them a sack in which is heard the 'wail' of a child. Then the '*Count lifts up Harker who has fainted and carries him off* (13). Despite the erotic and homoerotic feel of this scene, the censor left it unchanged. The manuscript ends with the dying Quincey proclaiming that the mark on Mina's forehead, made by Van Helsing's holy wafer, has disappeared. Her purity is restored.

The playbill announcing the performance on 18 May was posted to the Lyceum door half an hour before its commencement. The reading would have taken at least four hours. The cast was drawn from the Lyceum Company; the most famous member of Stoker's production was Edith Craig, Ellen Terry's daughter. Legend has it that Irving made negative comments on the dramatic reading of *Dracula*. When Irving was asked for his opinion, he allegedly replied that it was 'Dreadful!'[15] *Dracula*'s potential for the stage, and for the Lyceum in particular, was thus ignored.

The dramatic reading of *Dracula* coincided with the Lyceum's change of fortune; in December the previous year, Irving broke his leg on the second night of *Richard III* and could not perform for several months. The plays that came after *Madame Sans-Gêne* were disastrous. Irving made poor choices – disregarding *Dracula* was probably his worst commercial one – and the theatre suffered from what a contemporary describes as a 'dearth of material'.[16] That Irving was in search of iconic characters is confirmed by Stoker's friend, Hall Caine. Caine, the bestselling writer to whom Stoker dedicated *Dracula*, remarks in his autobiography that in conjunction with Stoker and Irving he drafted ideas for plays with figures such as 'the Wandering Jew', the 'Flying Dutchman' and the 'Demon Lover', but his 'efforts' did not satisfy Irving.[17] All of these supernatural entities are akin to the vampire.

Deane appreciated *Dracula's* potential for the stage. The actor had been a member of the Henry Irving Vacation Company in 1899 – formed by the minor actors of the Lyceum who went on tour when the main company was not performing in London or in the provinces.[18] By the early 1920s Deane had his own successful provincial company. Securing the permission of Stoker's widow, Florence, Deane decided to adapt *Dracula*. Like Stoker, he had to submit his play to the Lord Chamberlain's office in order to get it licensed for performance. Now housed in the British Library, the play under discussion here is the original typescript copy from 1924, which was licensed for performance on 15 May.[19]

Deane's production notes for *Dracula* instruct that at the rise of the curtain there should be three minutes of 'specially orchestrated Hungarian music in which the sound of sleigh bells is recurrent'.[20] He centred the action of the play on Harker's London home and its immediate environs. Lucy is already dead when it opens despite blood transfusions from Seward, Morris and Godalming. Dracula is staying with the Harkers and their home lies between the dilapidated Carfax, Dracula's recently purchased abode, and Seward's asylum. The play opens in Harker's drawing-room as Seward and Harker discuss Mina's strange illness. Dracula first appears in the dark drawing-room before the maid who has just switched off the lights. He is

> a tall thin man in evening clothes, with a heavy black cloak flung round him, accentuating the intense pallor of his face. He stands surrounded with a slight haze, looking down at her with an evil smile. She gives a slight scream and reaches for the switch, as she does so he disappears. Next second the lights are full on and there is no one there. She covers her face with her hands – then stares straight in front of her. (3)

What becomes clear later in the play is that during this encounter Dracula has hypnotised her so he can use her to facilitate his attacks on Mina.

Dracula, as Seward describes to Van Helsing, is a 'courtly, cultured man with a manner that belongs to another period – I nearly said another world' (5). With his urbane count, Deane deviates from Stoker's conception of the vampire. Stoker's Dracula is a repulsive figure with profuse eyebrows, 'cruel-looking mouth' (23) and sharp teeth and nails. The novel's vampire is largely an absent presence, haunting the characters' thoughts; in the play Dracula is eerily present (6). In her consultation with Van Helsing, the 'chalkily white' Mina recounts how her illness dates from a 'terrible dream in which mist enveloped her room' and out of it appeared 'a livid white face bending over me' (7). Alone with Seward, Van Helsing in dialogue that comes directly from the novel, discusses the limitations of science: 'you do not let your eyes see nor your ears hear – and that which is outside of your daily life, is not of account to you' (10). Later, when alone in the library, he is speaking to himself into the mirror of the over mantel when he is accosted by the vampire who, of course, has no reflection in the mirror:

VAN HELSING: (*turns suddenly – dropping pipe and tobacco.*) The Devil!
DRACULA: Oh, come – not as bad as that. (12)

In order to confirm his theory that Dracula is a vampire, Van Helsing leaves Mina lying on the sofa in the library as bait to lure the Count. However, the Examiner of Plays censored the description of the attack. Throughout the play red lines are drawn through the censored material and hand written changes are inserted in red ink. In the original typescript, a hand appears and switches off the light: 'nothing can be seen except a white hand treated lightly with phosphorus, slowly withdrawing from the switch. The instant the hand disappears the figure of Count Dracula rises from behind the Chesterfield – and without looking round he bends over towards the throat of the girl on the couch – She gives a piercing indrawn scream' (15–16). This is replaced by a shorter direction that entirely removes the description of the attack: 'Dracula enters ... crosses towards her saying as he does so "At last Madame I have the pleasure of seeing you alone". He stands at the head of the couch smiling towards her'(16). Then Van Helsing and his team burst into the library. Dracula disappears and re-emerges through the library's folding doors in the guise of a genial house guest: 'And how is the patient now? Better – I hope?' (16).

In Act 2 Renfield warns Mina to leave her home. Protected by a garlic garland, Mina is left alone in her bedroom with her maid, who under the influence of Dracula, removes the garlic and opens the window to allow the vampire to attack. Again the censor intervened. In the original version, there is a 'crash' and the 'whole window falls in, and the head and shoulders of a gray wolf is seen against the bright moonlight – remains a second, then withdraws – and a steady stream of smoke, rushes through the broken pane. Mina gives a piercing scream, and falls in a dead faint' (12). The curtain drops and then rises to show Dracula 'bending towards the figure on the floor' (7). The censor removed the wolf and only a pane of glass is broken and, 'through the aperture thus made creeps in a stream of smoke, whilst *outside* the window she sees the face of Dracula as the curtain falls' (12).

In Act 3 the dangerously ill Mina describes in the original typescript how the vampire

> placed his reeking lips on my throat. I have a vague memory of something very sweet all round me and I seemed sinking into deep green water, and then everything went black. How long this horrible thing lasted I don't know – but it seemed ages before I came to, and saw his awful, sneering mouth – and as I looked – it was dripping with fresh blood. (7)

In the authorised version, this is all removed. Mina just sees Dracula's face and faints. Renfield, seeking sanctuary in the house, is pursued by Dracula who murders him. Dracula, however, is cornered by the group of men but disappears before they can catch him.

In the epilogue the group of men enter the coach house at Carfax to eradicate Dracula in his earth box. In the original script there is a graphic description of the annihilation: 'Harker first – then Morris and Godalming plunge their knives into the heart – blood from the sponges at haft of knives, wells up on the white shirt front – the face gives a convulsive twist and shudder' (13). The censor required that the audience should not see the staking of the vampire, so instead the group circle the box and all that is seen is a movement of Harker's arm. Then Seward 'draws the cloak over the features – and the men stand up' as Mina enters with a lantern (reminiscent of Holman Hunt's famous painting *The Light of the World* (1853–54) in which Christ with a lantern knocks at a door overgrown with weeds).

MINA – Well?
HARKER (goes to her – puts his right arm round her) Count Dracula is at rest
V. H. 'In Manus tuas Domine' (he 'crosses' himself)

Like the conclusion of a conventional melodrama, Christianity is restored, virtue rewarded and evil exorcised, as the vampire is put to a holy rest.

Whilst retaining much of the original story in terms of the nature of the vampire and the methods used to repel him, as well as much of the dialogue from the novel, Deane transformed the story into a domestic melodrama. In the novel, Dracula's attack is an attack on England; in Deane's version, Dracula's attack is on a home where an unwelcome guest sups blood, not wine. Deane devised the black cloak for Dracula that became the character's trademark on stage and screen. He played Van Helsing, his wife, Dora Mary Patrick was Mina and Edmund Blake played the vampire. Ludlam notes that Blake's 'prominent gold tooth' gave the character a 'portentous touch'.[21] After tremendous success in the provinces, Deane, initially hesitant about negative reaction in London, finally brought the play to London's Little Theatre in February 1927 with Raymond Huntley assuming the role of Dracula. Though the *Times* commented that the 'style of speech' was 'dreadfully stilted', the production was effective and its use of alarming noises, including the 'baying of hounds off stage', demonstrated a 'sure sense of the theatre'.[22]

Deane's *Dracula* was a commercial phenomenon in London, transferring to the Duke of York's Theatre and then to the Prince of Wales Theatre. When patrons fainted, Deane saw the potential for publicity. He employed a 'good, plain, brisk and efficient' nurse from Queen Alexandra Hospital, who, at key moments, 'walked slowly and quietly down the aisles'. The stunt worked as she attended to an 'average of seven patients a night'.[23] The success of the play drew the attention of an American theatrical producer, Horace Liveright. Deciding that the play required changes to suit an American audience, he employed a scriptwriter, John L. Balderston, to work with Deane to revise it. *Dracula* opened at the Fulton Theatre in New York in October 1927 with an unknown Hungarian actor, Bela Lugosi, in the title role. Dracula would make him famous once the Deane-Balderston script became the basis for the famous 1932 Universal Studios film (see Chapter 15).

The Deane-Balderston adaptation is a tighter script with a reduced character list. The central female figure is Lucy Seward, Dr Seward's daughter, who is engaged to the young solicitor, Jonathan Harker. The play opens in the library of Seward's sanatorium, which is decorated in a medieval style with the requisite divan for the supine heroine. A tense atmosphere is created during Seward's opening discussions with Harker regarding his daughter's health by the howling of dogs and Renfield's maniacal laugh offstage. Renfield's constant escapes from his incarceration heighten tension throughout the play. The Count visits from his neighbouring Carfax estate and Seward ponders his interest in Lucy: 'He seems genuinely interested in Lucy. If he were a young man I'd think –'[24] Indeed, the attraction between the vampire and his victim is evident as Lucy succumbs to the Count's charms and distances herself from her fiancé.

As in Deane's 1924 play, Van Helsing discourses on the limitations of modern science: 'The strength of the vampire is that people will not believe in him' (27). Similarly, the doctor sets up the female as a trap to lure the vampire into revealing his identity. Modern technology enabled Dracula to plan his attack. In a non-stop flight from Transylvania, Dracula left after sunset and arrived just before dawn. As in the 1924 Deane play, Van Helsing is surprised by Dracula in the library but shows him his medicine to cure Lucy. Rather than garlic, this play uses wolfsbane – a poisonous plant alleged to have properties that ward off werewolves. It enrages the Count. Dracula also hypnotises the maid to remove the wolfsbane so he can attack Lucy. Dracula's attempt to murder Renfield fails but, similar to Deane's play, he disappears from the library as Harker and Seward try to trap him. They regroup in the vault where they destroy Dracula in his coffin. The violent staking of the vampire in his sleep is mitigated by the vampire's 'look of peace' (74) and Renfield's proclamation: 'Thank God, we're free!' (74). The play ends on a note of heightened tension as Van Helsing makes a curtain speech warning the audience: 'When you get home tonight and the lights have been turned out and you are afraid to look behind the curtains and you dread to see a face appear in the window ... why, just pull yourself together and remember that after all *there are such things*' (74).

Like its British predecessor, the play was an immense success. A reviewer, Joseph T. Shipley, notes in the *New Leader*, that although it was 'hokum' it nonetheless cast a 'wicked spell' on the audience: '[a]re we here ... victim of those vague upshooting alarms and superstitions, that justify the saying "scratch a civilized man you reach a barbarian"; so that the play is probing some deep emotional basis, older and more vital than our science, that forbids us wholly to disbelieve'.[25] The review focuses on its impact: 'Hold himself aloof as he may, the scientific observer must at least admit that the rest of the audience at "Dracula" are as spellbound as though they were "savages under the skin"'.[26] Long before he had written *Dracula*, Stoker was attuned to the effect of melodrama on the audience. In a review of a spectacular scene at the Theatre Royal in Dublin in 1872, Stoker observes that it was only 'necessary to watch the faces of an audience' to show the success of a scene.[27] It would, however, take the 1924 and 1927 plays to reveal the impact that his creation had on theatre audiences.

Exactly fifty years after its New York premiere, Deane and Balderston's *Dracula* made a Broadway revival at the Martin Beck Theatre. With Frank Langella in the title role, the play became a love story. Langella, a suave and handsome vampire, was described by the critic Walter Goodman as 'more Byronesque than Lugosilike'.[28] For John Simon, Langella had the 'right amount of eroticism' and 'even more autoeroticism'.[29] The set and costumes, produced from drawings by Edward Gorey, drew critical acclaim. A child prodigy, Gorey claimed to have read *Dracula* between the ages of five and seven.[30] The Gorey set was 'towering gray' with 'monochromatic costumes ranging from white to gray to black with just a titillating droplet of red'.[31] Famous for his Gothic pen and ink miniature novels, Gorey's work was reproduced in a magnified form on stage. Images of bats were everywhere: 'bat-winged *putti* over Lucy's canopied bed; bats all round her father's Dr Seward's sanatorium library'.[32] Gorey's sinister set design infused a tired play with new life and he won a Tony Award for Best Costume Design.

The novel's theatrical afterlife has not been limited to revivals of the 1924 and 1927 plays. In 1927 Florence Stoker commissioned Charles Morrell to produce an adaptation and the play premiered at the Royal Court Theatre in Warrington, England, but it was not a success. Concurrent with the Deane-Balderston revival on Broadway was *The Passion of Dracula* at Cherry Lane Theatre. In 1984 Christopher Bond's *Dracula* was produced in London with Daniel Day Lewis as the Count. In 1993 Hull Truck Theatre, England, produced *Dracula* by John Godber and Jane Thornton. In 1985 a critically acclaimed adaptation by the poet Liz Lochhead was produced for the Royal Lyceum Theatre, Edinburgh.

In what Lochhead describes as a 'free' adaptation, Lucy and Mina, are 'refigured as sisters, in their garden by the sea' in Whitby, whilst next door in London to that 'that weird house Carfax' is the 'madhouse'.[33] Unlike the passive maids of the 1924 and 1927 plays, Lochhead's vocal maid highlights issues of sexuality and class. Lochhead releases the repressed sexuality of Stoker's novel. Lucy is sexually aware whilst Mina is inhibited. Lucy beckons Dracula as her 'love' and his attack parodies the marriage night as he wraps a bridal veil around her naked form and stains veil and bed with the blood from her neck.[34] The asylum, rendered surreal, takes a more central role and Renfield's mad ravings suggest that Dracula is as much a psychological entity as a physical one. At the end of the play, both Jonathan and Mina are forced to reflect on their attraction to vampires.

Lochhead also pays tribute to Stoker's sense of the theatre in the play by quoting from the novel for some of her stage directions. For the vampire women's attack on Harker Lochhead uses the description in Stoker's text:

JONATHAN *is lying back in thrall.* VAMPIRE BRIDE 3 (LUCY) *advances and bends over him now, this is more straight out of Bram Stoker and can't be beat for atmosphere or stage direction – 'until he can feel the movement of her breath upon him … sweet, honey-sweet, sending the same tingling through the nerves as her voice, but with a bitter underlying the sweet, a bitter offensiveness as one smells in blood'.*[35]

Lochhead also quotes from Stoker for the assault on Mina as Dracula gashes his chest and *'forces her to his wound, "like a child forcing a kitten into a saucer of milk to compel it to drink"'* – Bram Stoker again.[36]

Langella set the tone for an alluring vampire in the 1970s and the book and films of Stephanie Meyer's *Twilight* saga has cemented the vampire's glamour. Theresa Heskins's 2015 adaptation of *Dracula* provided a sexualised Dracula but deployed innovative staging techniques to reinvigorate the story. Unlike Deane who reduced the novel's geographical scope, Heskins's *Dracula* was set in Transylvania, Whitby and London. Following the arc of the novel, she sharpened its dialogue, and removes Morris and Godalming. The production used sound design, the Foley technique, in which sound effects were created with 'materials which emulate[d] the sound of the real world – from a pair of leather gloves becoming a flapping bat to a plastic bag mimicking a crackling fire'. The purpose was to 'heighten tension', create a 'creepy world of the imagination' and 'keep the character of Dracula constantly present in the minds of an audience'.[37] Dracula was played by two actors – an older Dracula by Jack Klaff and a younger Dracula by Jonathan Charles. The play opens with three Foley areas devoted to different characters – Mina with a typewriter, Seward with a phonograph and a young Dracula with pen and paper. The play's focus on technology is a tribute to the original novel. Mina's opening words are: 'Begin with facts'[38] and Seward puts a cylinder into his phonograph on which is heard Harker's voice describing his journey to Castle Dracula:

> *The voice conjures Jonathan Harker himself, boarding a train on a chilly platform ...*
>
> FOLEY *A train whistles ... pistons ...*
> FOLEY *The typing becomes the sound of a train ...* (4)

Like the original novel, the script moves back and forth between the various accounts. For the scene of the vampire women's seduction of Jonathan, the women emerge spinning and twisting on 'aerial silks' before attacking their prey. The *Observer* review described how 'the creatures dangle and spin upside down from the rafters, unfurling like leaves. They are both bats and brides. As they lower themselves towards the stage, their black ribbon-ropes spread out to engulf the solitary man beneath'.[39]

Seward is Lucy's fiancé but she 'did the proposing' herself (24) – an allusion to the conversation in Stoker's novel that Lucy and Mina have in Robin Hood's Bay about the possibility that the New Woman will initiate proposals in the future. Dracula's attack on Lucy is presented as '*infinitely tender*' (39) but her staking is violent. In the closing scenes at Castle Dracula an '*impossibly youthful*' (76) Dracula comes to Mina letting her '*sink her teeth into his throat as red petals drift down*' (77). Just then

Seward approaches with his stake but, in a conflation of sex and violence, Dracula extends an arm out to choke him. Similar to Lochhead's play, the attraction to the vampire is strong as Mina cries 'No!' (77) as Harker plunges his knife into Dracula. However, liberated from her thralldom she questions was Dracula 'ever more than a dream' (78). The vampire infiltrates the psyche and releases desire. The production, as the *Observer* review outlines, was 'black with a few splashes of scarlet' and the sound 'electrifying' with live effects which were 'created by actors who perch at the top of the highly raked stalls, spectrally illuminated ... You barely glimpse wine being poured into a glass but you hear it glugging joyously in'.[40] Like the Broadway revival of *Dracula* with its Gorey Gothic, effects and design refresh the story.

In 1898 Stoker returned to Halifax for advice on staging his novel. In a letter dated 1 July (Stoker's part of the correspondence is missing), Halifax writes that although he is 'quite unable to make any suggestions' he hoped to see 'Count Dracula on the boards of the Lyceum' and begs Stoker not to 'give up the idea of that play' which had the potential to be a 'great' success.[41] 'As a man of the theatre', Philip Horne observes in the *Telegraph*, 'Stoker had a pretty good instinct for making our flesh creep'.[42] However, Stoker was unable to convert his knowledge into producing a viable adaptation of *Dracula*. Nonetheless, Stoker's story has inspired and continues to inspire playwrights and, enabled by the 'inventiveness' of adaptors and the modern stage, it has become the success that Halifax predicted over a century ago. Out of the ashes of Irving's Lyceum, Dracula emerges, re-invigorated and renewed.

Notes

1 See Charles Lindley Wood, Viscount Halifax, *Lord Halifax's Ghost Book* (London: Geoffrey Bles, 1936). See Letter to Bram Stoker (23 October 1897). Correspondence and Literary Manuscripts of Bram Stoker, Brotherton, Special Collections, University of Leeds.

2 Frank Rahill, *The World of Melodrama* (University Park and London: Pennsylvania State University Press, 1967), xiv.

3 Bram Stoker, *Personal Reminiscences of Henry Irving*, 2 vols. (London: Heinemann, 1906), vol. 1, xx.

4 Harry Ludlam, *A Biography of Bram Stoker: Creator of Dracula* (London: W. Foulsham, 1952), 52.

5 William Winter, Letter to Bram Stoker (1 November 1899). Stoker Manuscripts.

6 Stoker, *Personal Reminiscences*, vol. 1, 53.

7 Helen Allingham, Letter to Bram Stoker (8 May 1894). Stoker Manuscripts.

8 Marie Bancroft and Squire Bancroft, *The Bancrofts: Recollections of Sixty Years* (London: John Murray, 1909), 327.

9 H. A. Saintsbury, 'Irving as Stage Manager', in H. A. Saintsbury and Cecil Palmer, eds., *We Saw Him Act: A Symposium on the Art of Sir Henry Irving* (London: Hurst and Blackett, 1939), p. 396.

10 Hamilton Deane, *Dracula: An Adaptation of Bram Stoker's Famous Novel*, 1924. The Lord Chamberlain's Plays, British Library London, LCP 1924/16, 1. All quotations from this play come from original manuscript copy.

11 Bram Stoker, 'Irving and Stage Lighting', in Catherine Wynne, ed., *Bram Stoker and the Stage: Reviews, Reminiscences, Essays and Fiction*, 2 vols. (London: Pickering and Chatto, 2012), vol. 2, p. 214.

12 Christopher Frayling, *Vampyres: From Lord Byron to Count Dracula*, rev. edn. (London: Faber, 1992), 300.

13 George Redford, Letter to Bram Stoker (9 May 1897), Stoker Manuscripts.

14 *Bram Stoker, Dracula; or the Undead*, 1897. The Lord Chamberlain's Plays, British Library, London, Add MS 53630. All further references to this play will be given in the text.

15 Ludlam, *Biography*, 114.

16 Percy Fitzgerald, *Sir Henry Irving: A Biography* (Philadelphia: G. W. Jacobs, 1906), 258.

17 Hall Caine, *My Story* (London: Heinemann, 1908), 349–50.

18 Ludlam, *Biography*, 152.

19 This has been published as Hamilton Deane and John L. Balderston, *Dracula* (New York: Samuel French, 1977). David J. Skal also published a version of the Deane play that combined the British Library manuscript with an acting version used by Deane's company in 1930. Hamilton Deane and John Balderston, *Dracula: The Ultimate Illustrated Edition of the World-Famous Vampire Play*, ed. David J. Skal (New York: St. Martin's Press, 1993).

20 Deane and Balderston, *Dracula*, 1. All further references to this play will be given in the text.

21 Ludlam, 156.

22 'Little Theatre. "Dracula"', *The Times* (15 February 1927), 10.

23 Ludlam, 162.

24 Deane and John L. Balderston, *Dracula*, p. 1.

25 Joseph T. Shipley, 'Amusements: The Week on Stage', *New Leader* (12 November 1927), 421.

26 Shipley, 'Amusements', 421.

27 Wynne, *Bram Stoker and the Stage*, vol. 1, 9.

28 Walter Goodman, 'On Stage: Theatrical Stunts', *New Leader* (21 November 1977), 23.

29 John Simon, 'Theatre Chronicle', *Hudson Review* 31, no. 1 (1978).

30 Jane Merrill Filstrup, 'An Interview with Edward St. John Gorey at the Gotham Book Market', in Karen Wilkin ed., *Ascending Peculiarity: Edward Gorey on Edward Gorey* (New York: Harcourt, 2001), pp. 72–85.

31 Goodman, 'On Stage', 22.

32 Simon, 'Theatre Chronicle', 151.

33 Liz Lochhead, *Dracula* (London: Nick Hern), 2009.

34 Lochhead, *Dracula*, 47.

35 Lochhead, *Dracula*, 33.

36 Lochhead, *Dracula*, 73.

37 Theresa Heskins (Director), *Dracula* by Bram Stoker adapted by Theresa Heskins (Programme). New Vic Theatre, Newcastle-Under-Lyme, Staffordshire, 2015.

38 Bram Stoker's *Dracula*, adapted and directed by Theresa Heskins – Rehearsal Draft – February 2015. New Vic Theatre, Newcastle-Under-Lyme, Staffordshire, 2015.

39 Susannah Clapp, 'Dracula Review – Sparseness, Boldness and Electrifying Sound Design', *The Observer* (15 March 2015).

40 Clapp, 'Dracula Review'.

41 Lord Halifax, Letter to Bram Stoker (1 July 1898). Stoker Manuscripts.

42 Philip Horne, 'Great Adaptations of *Dracula*', *The Telegraph* (27 November 2006).

15

ALISON PEIRSE

Dracula on Film 1931–1959

Dracula is a novel obsessed with the technological forms of the period: the telegraph, the phonograph, the Kodak camera, newspapers and mass media. What happens when the entire story becomes enfolded within a techno-logical form? This chapter explores *Dracula* (Tod Browning, 1931), *Son of Dracula* (Robert Siodmak, 1943) and *Dracula* (Terence Fisher, 1958) in order to examine how cinema represents the Count and how his character changes with each cinematic resurrection. How is visual storytelling employed to tell a story that has already been explored as a novel, at least two European silent films and three stage plays?

This exploration is guided by the principles of character formation in playwriting and screenwriting. In *Screen Language*, Cherry Potter argues that characterisation and story are interdependent. For Potter, character-isation is the visual and verbal information that demonstrates to the audi-ence 'who a character is and what he or she wants and needs' and that it is the protagonist's wants and needs 'which determine the backbone or structure of the story'.[1] Here, Dracula is a character required to respond to the demands of the medium-specific form: in cinematic adaptations, who is he? Is he the protagonist or antagonist? What does he want and need? How do his desires impact upon the forward progression of the narrative? How are his desires articulated visually? Finally, reflecting on these three examples, how do the characteristics of the vampire change across three decades?

Dracula (1931)

Motion pictures are still in their infancy. For a while it began to look as though they had grown up, when bang! They instantly become infantile again. Little children have two passionate urges – one, to make mud pies and snowmen, and the other to go 'boo!' and frighten their playmates.

> Grown up infants like to do the same things – they wish to create
> 'monsters' to frighten people.
>
> *Rob Wagner's Script* (20 February 1932)[2]

Károly Lajthay's lost Hungarian film *Drakula halála/Dracula's Death* (1921) is currently considered the first cinematic adaptation of Stoker's novel.[3] The more famous, later adaptation is *Nosferatu: eine Symphonie des Grauens/Nosferatu: A Symphony of Horror* (F. W. Murnau, 1922). Five years after *Nosferatu*, Hollywood began its transition to sound. The process took three and a half years; *Dracula* appeared three months before the end of the transition, as the first 'talkie' horror film, and inaugurating the American horror boom of the 1930s.[4]

The film begins with Renfield, repurposed here as an estate agent travelling to Transylvania to finalise the sale of Carfax Abbey. Renfield's preliminary journey is of little interest; it is not until five minutes into the film that the horror begins. We are suddenly dropped into the dungeon of Castle Dracula. German cinematographer Karl Freund is unleashed from the static staging of Renfield's prologue and is given freedom to explore. The camera position is intimate and personal, our experience unmediated by any character. The camera comes to rest at a group of coffins. A bony, white hand reaches out, and a bride of Dracula sits up. The audience is moved away from her, pulled forward mercilessly, against its will. A man stands alone in the deepest, darkest corner of the dungeon. He wears a black cape. His black hair is slicked back. His pale skin casts a luminescent glow. Silently, he gazes at us. At first he's in medium long shot, but we keep moving closer, and now he's in medium close up, still staring, both appalled and thrilled at our intrusion. The spell is broken with a cut to the three brides appearing. A wolf howls and slowly, stiff-backed, Dracula (Bela Lugosi) ascends the stone steps and leave the dungeon.

This scene lacks all narrative motivation. We are not following the experience of Renfield. Instead, this is a purely visual, cinematic experience. We are provided with a dungeon, coffins, three pale women and a pale man dressed in black. Without a word of dialogue, we know that this is Dracula. The gothic set design invokes fear, while the roaming camera evokes dread, moving ever closer to glowering Dracula, as if hypnotised. Moreover, as we look at him, however unwillingly, his own look back into the camera lens is significant. Tom Brown has pointed out that 'direct address is often a marker of a character's particular power within the fiction'.[5] Here, Dracula's gaze into the camera lens signals his power and knowledge, unafraid to challenge us. In this sequence the audience lacks all control, and we are drawn to the darkness, despite knowing the consequences. Roy Huss argues that Browning's *Dracula* is a missed opportunity, 'shackled by the producer's decision to capitalise upon the success of John Balderston and Hamilton Deane's stage adaptation of Bram Stoker's classic novel, rather than to exploit the greater cinematic suggestiveness of the novel itself'.[6] Much of the film is very slow, drawing-room, stage bound dialogue, framed in the proverbial proscenium arch. However the opening moments begin to open up the cinematic possibilities of Dracula on screen.

Dracula's power is visually reinforced when Renfield arrives at the castle. The estate agent is dwarfed by his surroundings: a huge, expressionistic entrance hall, with glowing white pillars, an arch window lit in chiaroscuro. The magnificent winding staircase tumbles away into blackness. Dracula appears at the head of the stairs, holding a single candle, and as he descends Renfield walks across the hall towards him. In a very long, slow shot, he matches the vampire's pace, step for step, giving the scene a nightmarish, somnambulant quality. In medium close up, Dracula smiles ghoulishly and slowly intones, 'I am Dracula'. He opens his arms expansively, then as gracefully as a cat, he begins to ascend once more, expecting Renfield to follow. The light from the windows casts shadowed bars across Renfield: the audience now know that Renfield is imprisoned, even if he hasn't realised it yet. The release of knowledge is important here. The dungeon sequence and Lugosi's welcome conspire to provide the audience with more information than Renfield himself possesses. We know that Dracula is a vampire, and we can hazard more than a guess at what will befall Renfield. This creates suspense and a horrible, yet delicious anticipation. We will now watch the deadly corruption of this young man as he tumbles into the vampiric abyss.

The vampire film is fascinated with its own origins at the same time it rejects many of them; every vampire film creates its own mythologies. Ken Gelder suggests that it is a peculiar genre as it is required to respond to a set of archaic laws or expectations about vampires, in relation to their weaknesses, their modus operandi, and so on.[7] What have we learnt about *this* version of Dracula from these initial sequences? Initial inspection reveals a great deal of fidelity to Stoker's novel. The vampire lives in a grand and deserted castle in Transylvania, without servants, and sleeps in a coffin. If we delve more deeply into character design and motivation, it is worth thinking in more depth about the protagonist figure and how this is distinct between novel and film. Two weeks prior to filming, the script had significant 'unresolved problems' including 'the lack of a hero', and this lack remains an unresolved problem in the finished film.[8] In the novel, Harker begins as protagonist but fades away after escaping from Castle Dracula. Back in England, Alan Holmwood, Quincey Morris and Dr Seward compete for Lucy Westenra. Lucy becomes ill and dies, then Mina, Harker's fiancé, grows ill. An ensemble cast – Harker, Professor Van Helsing, Holmwood, Morris and Seward – pursue Dracula. The ensemble is a major issue for adaptation into other mediums. While the novel can handle the Crew of Light, collective heroism poses a problem for 'stage and film fictions more used to dealing with a single heroic protagonist'.[9] This film is unable to present a convincing and conventional hero. Renfield quickly becomes Dracula's pet, and Harker is without consequence.

We tend to think of Dracula as the protagonist. Although he is rarely on screen in the second act, it is the repercussions of his actions with which the other characters must grapple. In his treatise on the nature of storytelling, John Yorke explains the fundamental importance of desire to character. He explains 'if a character doesn't want something, they're passive. And if they're passive, they're effectively dead'.[10] So if Dracula is the 'pivotal' character he 'must not merely desire something. He must want it so badly that he will destroy or be destroyed in the effort to attain his goal'.[11] Dracula's desires indeed propel the film; it is his wants and needs that overwhelmingly consume the thoughts and actions of every other character, and they lead, without a doubt, to repeated life or death situations.

If Dracula is the protagonist, then this film is a tragedy. Classically, a tragedy contains the noble hero, the tragic flaw, the inevitable fall. Count Dracula is our noble protagonist, living in a castle, with seemingly untold power and wealth. Dracula's flaw is built into his essence: he is undead. But this is merely the story set up: the inciting event comes with Renfield's arrival and the confirmation of Dracula's relocation. In England he meets Lucy and Mina, and it is here that his desires will spiral out of control. It is his murder and vampirism of Lucy and his pursuit of Mina that leads to his 'catastrophic fall'. In line with this approach, it makes sense to view Van Helsing – who does not appear until almost halfway through the film – as the antagonist. The film concludes with Van Helsing and Harker attempting to rescue Mina from the Abbey. This is not a high stakes endeavour: hypnotised Mina is doing very little at this point beyond wandering around in a white slip, while Dracula has scurried back to his coffin. The final moments are also visually anti-climactic, composed of lengthy static long shots and long periods of silence, revealing a director unable to transcend neither his theatrical source texts nor his allegiance to silent cinema. Van Helsing kneels over Dracula's coffin, places a stake inside and raises the hammer in his other hand. Mina then clasps her chest, showing she has recovered, and Dracula's death is implied offscreen. Although supernaturally powerful, Dracula is undone by his unquenchable thirst for the blood of a young woman. And yet it is the consumption of blood that has given him such power and wealth. His flaw is irreconcilable, and he dies for it. It's counter-intuitive to think of

Dracula as a tragic hero, brought down by his desire for two English women, but it accords with Universal's marketing of the film: the poster tagline was *The Story of the Strangest Passion the World has Ever Known*! Viewing the film in this way alleviates some of the structural and characterisation problems of a weak screenplay based on a flawed stage play, adapted from an epistolary novel that is often criticised for its lack of literary merit.

Upon release, the film was a huge success. At early screenings, it did very well at the Rialto in Washington in February 1931, the local press breathlessly reporting on the 'strange, eerie, melancholy, shivery' film.[12] The film industry took note and the famous cycle of horror films began. Kyle Edwards points out that '*Dracula* introduced conventions and practices that would guide the development, production and marketing of Universal's subsequent horror films', yet I would argue there is more to the film than this statement suggests.[13] The commercial success and rapturous response the film received revealed something incredibly important: that audiences are fascinated by dark characters. There is a good reason for this popularity, one that Universal and other studios were quick to capitalise upon. Macbeth and Lady Macbeth are bad, but 'the reason they have so fascinated mankind ... since Shakespeare first created them is because, through Shakespeare's empathy with them, we not only understand their badness, we recognise it in ourselves'.[14] When the Count is the dominant character, the tone and experience of the text shifts considerably. This film is the not only the first sound horror film, but the first to allow the audience to fully experience the wants and needs of the vampire. We are welcomed into his lair, we watch him trap his victims, we witness Lucy and Mina willingly succumb. For the first time, we are given a visual and auditory space to identify with the dark recesses of a vampire's soul.

Interregnum

Universal, unhorrified by its own horrors and wise to a good box office thing, again has revived its deathless Dracula series.

New York Times (6 November 1943)[15]

Three *Dracula* films were made in 1931. In addition to Browning's film, there was a silent version and a Spanish version, *Drácula* (George Melford, 1931). Following Browning's success, the vampire proliferated throughout the 1930s but Universal did not return to Dracula until *Dracula's Daughter* (Lambert Hillyer, 1936). This was enthusiastically received by the *New York Times*, which explained 'Miss Dracula is a chip off the old block', referencing the black cape, bloodless victims and 'those two telltale marks on the throat'.[16] Despite the plaudits, though, horror was on the wane from the middle of the decade. Universal horror producer Carl Laemmle was ousted from the studio and their commitment to making big budget horror films ended. In July 1934 the United States' censorship body the Production Code Administration began to enforce the Production Code where previously the code had been largely self-regulatory. Meanwhile, the British Board of Film Censorship introduced the 'H' certificate (H for Horrific), and only passed two horror films in 1936. The comments on *Dracula's Daughter* judged that it 'would require the resources of half a dozen more languages to adequately express its beastliness. I consider it absolutely unfit for exhibition as a film'.[17]

Many critics consider the 1940s 'a dismal decade' for horror film, a 'commonly remembered for tired sequels to respected originals'.[18] There were two key strains of horror during this period. Producer Val Lewton made a number of female-centred films at RKO, including *Cat People* (Jacques Tourneur, 1942), which are best described as a 'low budget female gothic and monster movie amalgam'.[19] However, Dracula did not lurk at RKO; he remained tethered to Universal and appeared in the second wave of the studio's productions, the 'tired sequels' including *Son of Dracula* (Robert Siodmak, 1943), *House of Dracula* (Erle C. Kenton, 1945) and *House of Frankenstein* (Erle C. Kenton, 1944). It is worth referencing the strong female focus of RKO as we can see how this approach impacted upon Universal's 1940s productions. *Son of Dracula* has a contemporary setting, 'Dark Oaks', a plantation home in the Deep South. Dark Oaks is home to Kay Caldwell (Louise Allbritton), who has lured Count Alucard (Lon Chaney Jr) from Central Europe to stay with her in America. Alucard arrives, marries Kay – much to the dismay of her fiancé Frank – and carries out his vampiric activities. The twist in the tale comes when Alucard's nemesis, Professor Lazlo, realises that Kay does not care about Alucard. She has used him to achieve her dream of immortality. She instructs Frank to kill Alucard, then plans to turn Frank into a vampire as well, so they can be together for all time. The studio pushed the female angle, making much of the two feminine leads, Louise Allbritton and Evelyn Ankers, describing Allbritton as 'the new temptress of terror'.[20]

The strength of this film is the focus on the female protagonist Kay, and her sister, Clare. Yet the vampire is the film's greatest weakness. Chaney Jr is hopelessly miscast as the Count. He is neither repulsive nor seductive, and is entirely unbelievable. As one history of Universal horror film suggests, Chaney's 'lumberjack physique and Midwestern bearing' was entirely unsuited to the role.[21] It is just not Chaney Jr's performance; the script does not care for the vampire either. Although Lugosi's Dracula was predominantly in the beginning and end of the film, his presence motivated and dictated all plot and character function. In *Son of Dracula*, it is Kay who motivates the story, rejecting Frank, marrying Alucard and becoming a vampire. Her scheming and undead plotting form the central desires of the story. In his article on the crossovers between horror and film noir in the 1940s, Dain Goding even goes as far as to characterise Kay as 'the spider woman', 'the most recognisable and oft-imitated stereotype of film noir – the notorious femme fatale'.[22] Alucard is merely a pawn and lacks any narrative agency. The fact he never realises this further weakens his character. The film concludes as Kay begs Frank to kill Alucard. Frank burns Alucard's coffin, then destroys Kay's. The nominal hero is left mourning his lost love. Nobody mourns (or really notices) Alucard's demise. We have here another tragic protagonist and inevitable vampiric demise, yet the film is made much more interesting due to the strong female lead and the rather impotent, ignorant male vampire caught up in her complex, duplicitous plot. This fascinating shift in the representation of Dracula is reflective of the increased focus on female cinemagoers and the growing popularity of film noir and the woman's film in the 1940s.

Dracula (1958)

Dracula is one thing to read, quite another thing to see. The earlier film versions (the last, with Bela Lugosi as Count Dracula, was made in Hollywood in 1930), were merely foolish. The present film is foolish and extremely ugly too.

The Observer (25 May 1958)[23]

The second wave of Universal productions concluded by the late 1940s, and until the early 1950s, only Old Mother Riley and Abbott and Costello fraternised with the vampire. For most of the 1950s, Dracula remained a rare visual experience with a few exceptions: *Drakula İstanbul'da* (Mehmet Muhtar, 1953), *The Return of Dracula* (Paul Landres, 1958) and *Blood of Dracula* (Herbert L. Stock, 1957). However, it was not until 1957 that the beginnings of a significant shift in the cinematic representations of the vampire began to take place. In May 1957, British production company Hammer Films released *The Curse of Frankenstein*, a film that *Observer* reviewer C. A. Lejeune ranked as 'among the half-dozen most repulsive films I have encountered'.[24] Emboldened by this strong response (not to mention the excellent box office), six months later Hammer began filming *Dracula*.

The film begins with a close up of a forbidding stone eagle, the title of the film splashed across the screen in bright red dripping letters, accompanied by a foreboding, crashing score. Sangster's name appears on screen and the camera tracks around the eagle, revealing a stone crypt. The audience are now inside, staring at a coffin marked 'Dracula'. The camera speeds fluidly towards the coffin, but when we reach it, we do not stop. The camera wheels closer and closer until the edges of the coffin are lost beyond the frame. The nameplate rolls ever closer to us, now in close up, now filling the whole screen. Then we stop. Bright red blood spurts onto the nameplate. It drips down, thickly, and obscures the vampire's name. A fade to black concludes the prologue.

There is a certain harmony here with the introduction to Lugosi's Dracula in Browning's 1931 film. Although we do not actually meet the vampire himself, we are given the other same reference points at the same early point: the dank, underground lair, the coffin, the inestimable terror of being taken ever closer to a monster against our will. It is another example of excellent visual storytelling. In his treatise on film direction, David Mamet argues 'you always want to tell the story in cuts ... through a juxtaposition of images that is basically uninflected'.[25] Good filmmaking is not about a reliance on imagination (where all action takes place offscreen) or on verbal acuity. This sequence is a series of images: a stone eagle, a crypt, a coffin, blood that introduces us to the story world. It has no dialogue and, like Browning's dungeon prologue, does not require character point of view. The confident framing, the editing, production and sound design explains clearly to the audience what kind of film this is, and what to expect. Where this differs from Browning's film is the pursuit of visual style: Browning's film only has the most intermittent of filmic moments, while Fisher's film is an exercise in cinematic storytelling throughout.

Sangster's script then begins in earnest with a nod to the epistolary novel, as Jonathan Harker reads from his diary in voiceover. He is travelling from Klausenberg to Castle Dracula, ostensibly to become Dracula's new librarian. Harker enters the grand baronial hall and finds a note from Dracula, apologising for his absence. Another dissolve indicates time passing, and a beautiful, bosomy young woman in a flowing pink gown appears, begging him to help her escape. But she runs away and as Harker turns, his eyes open wide. Dracula (Christopher Lee) is at the top of the grand staircase, hidden in shadow. He walks swiftly and confidently down the stairs and into the frame of the camera. As he moves into close up, he smiles a little to the audience. His skin is tanned, his black hair greying at the temples, his teeth are bright white. His starched white collar covers his neck, while his black cape flows down his back. He is self-possessed and courteous, and speaks in a clear, upper class English accent as he briskly welcomes Harker, who is taken to his bedroom.

The introduction of the Count is a pivotal moment in *Dracula* adaptations. Hutchings argues, 'it is the moment when a sense of an adaptation's specificity, its relationship with and its difference from prior versions of the tale can be signalled most clearly'.[26] This film handles the process of adaptation and storytelling very differently from previous versions. First, there is a strong sense that the script has been produced by a *screen*writer, rather than an actor or someone with a background in theatre. Sangster, while certainly not the most original or radical of writers, was nonetheless attuned to the visual and verbal possibilities of the medium. Here, the introduction offers many visual clues for the audience. Dracula is not the white haired old man of the novel, the pestilent beast in *Nosferatu*, or the creaking, otherworldly foreign Count embodied by Lugosi. This confident, charming, relatively young man is engaging, enticing even. Barry Forshaw even describes Lee's Count as 'an elegant, dangerously attractive and cultivated figure with immense erotic appeal'.[27] We are drawn in, just as Lucy and Mina will be, despite already knowing what kind of a monster he truly is. With each adaptation of Dracula, a new mask can be tried on, one that reflects technological and social possibilities of the period. The principle of the vampire – to drink blood, to kill or transform humans into vampires – remains the same. The fun is in the fashioning of this mask anew: in *this* film, how the vampire looks, how he moves, who he is, how he operates. Audience pleasure comes from exploring the mask, teasing at its edges, while knowing the essential horror that lurks below the surface.

A long-held piece of wisdom regarding scene structure is 'go in late, get out early', frequently attributed to the famous script writer William Goldman. This means to start the scene as close to the moment of conflict as possible, and to leave before the conflict is resolved. Sangster's simple scene construction reflects this. The prologue, the diary, Harker's entry to the castle, the bride, the introduction to the Count, and the bedroom scene are all short and precise, and take place within the first nine minutes of the film. They are far shorter than in previous adaptations, focussing quickly on the dramatic question of the scene, and creating a strong narrative momentum.

This principle extends to the structure of the film as a whole, which has been condensed and radically simplified. By setting the entire story in one place, the journeying between England and Transylvania is moot. The Holmwood residence and the castle are the two main locations and characters are able to travel between them in a short space of time. Supporting characters are cut out, combined or simplified. Van Helsing is the clear protagonist, Dracula the antagonist, Lucy and Mina are female victims and Arthur is the confused man at the centre of the two vampirised women. As a result, the plot moves quicker than Browning's film. The first turning point is at nine minutes when, Harker's bedroom, Dracula sees a photograph of Lucy Holmwood, Harker's fiancée. Her sepia picture is lingered upon in close up. Dracula murmurs 'charming, charming', then subtly bites the inside of his cheek, twice. The vampire takes his leave and Harker reveals in his diary that he is a vampire hunter, here to destroy Dracula. Act One concludes at a brief twenty-two minutes as Harker stakes the vampire bride, then is caught by Dracula. Harker is set up as the initial protagonist then destroyed. This reveals not only the power and cunning of the Count, but also the escalating stakes of the story: who will stop the Count now?

The beginning of Act Two quickly establishes the real protagonist. Van Helsing appears, on the trail of his missing friend. He discovers the castle, the staked woman and Harker, now a vampire. Van Helsing approaches his friend's coffin, a stake and hammer in his hand, the fade to black signalling what is to happen in the darkness. This is a crucial moment for character development. Lajos Egri argues that a good pivotal 'character *must have something very vital at stake*' (excuse the pun).[28] Van Helsing now has two reasons to pursue Dracula. The first is the most noble, and longstanding: he wishes to destroy the vampire and end his reign of terror. The second is revenge, one of the most primal and universal impulses. He must now avenge loyal Harker, a good man forced to endure death twice, once by Dracula, and again, at the point of his best friend's stake. At the same time, the plot point set up with the photograph of Lucy produces motivation for Dracula. Harker kills his bride, and Dracula pursues Lucy as her replacement. The Count has suffered loss, and Harker's friends will suffer punishment as retribution.

The majority of Act Two explores the repercussions of Dracula's attacks on Lucy and how Van Helsing responds to them. We watch her death, her return, and her predilection for feeding on children. The second act concludes in the family crypt with Van Helsing staking Lucy; her brother Arthur watches in sobbing disbelief. Act Three is where Dracula, has yet again, made a mistake by turning his attention to Mina (Arthur's wife here) so soon after Lucy, with Van Helsing already on his trail. Dracula kidnaps Mina and buries her in the castle grounds, then runs into baronial hall. Arthur stops to dig his wife up, leaving Van Helsing free to face his adversary in a thrilling fight. Egri suggests the 'antagonist is necessarily as strong and, in time, as ruthless as the pivotal character. A fight is interesting only if the fighters are evenly matched'.[29] The quality of matching is evident in the final altercation, violent and extremely physical, actors and camera alike darting and whirling around the room. Dracula throws a burning candlestick at the vampire hunter, then lunges at him, strangling him. He overpowers him with ease, and pushes him onto his back and to the floor. The attractive Count is no longer polished and refined. His eyes are bright red, his hair is in disarray, his face a mask of rage – and desire. Van Helsing pretends to pass out, then as the Count leans in to his neck to administer a vampire kiss, Van Helsing throws him off, sweating, and faces him once more. Van Helsing's strength is not only his knowledge but also his ability to recall it and apply it in situations at moments of high stress. He notices the grand red curtains, draped ceiling to floor, and hurls himself onto the huge dining table. He runs the length of it and launches himself at the curtains, his weight dragging them to the floor. The room floods with morning light.

Dracula is now trapped by his own weaknesses, his 'allergy' to daylight. He falls to the floor, howling, as his feet crumble in the strong sunlight. With a second, kinetic bound, Van Helsing is on the table once more. He grabs two candlesticks, jumps down in front of the wounded vampire, and holds the sticks in the shape of a cross. Dracula's hand collapses; he falls onto his back, his face a pile of grey ash. His great cape sinks inwards, sighing, as his body disintegrates below the cut cloth. The final two shots of the film conclude the romantic subplot and the protagonist's endeavour: outside the castle, Mina recovers in Arthur's arms, while Van Helsing gazes out of the stained glass window. The credits roll.

Conclusion

When creating a character, the audience 'want to know why man is as he is, why his character is constantly changing, and why it must change whether he wishes it or no'.[30] Yet this is a script-writing principle that does not apply in the *Dracula* films. The overarching desires of vampire and hunter do not really change over the course of the story. In the Hammer film, they are worked through in a three act structure, that explores the combat between Dracula and vampire hunters. The first act is the story of Harker in which Dracula triumphs, in the second we experience Lucy's story, in which both Dracula and Van Helsing triumph – Dracula vampirises Lucy as he planned, but Van Helsing stakes her and releases her. In the final act, featuring Mina, Van Helsing rightfully triumphs as the protagonist. Van Helsing's desire to destroy Dracula, and Dracula's desire to endure are unaltered. Rather, Jimmy Sangster's screenplay is an exploration of desires put into opposition with one another.

But why is the story still satisfying if Dracula does not change? This is the nature of the horror film, a genre that Marc Blake and Sarah Bailey describe as 'an upgraded fairy tale'.[31] Indeed, it is the nature of the monster to be relentless, to continue on its path, come what may. In each film explored, the common thread is that Dracula's bloodlust (always twinned with romantic or erotic cravings) is his downfall, his fatal flaw is his yearning for the beautiful young woman that will lead to his destruction, whether that is the ethereal young Mina in 1931, treacherous Kay in 1943, or the married and sexually experienced Mina of 1958, who quivers in anticipation of his nightly visit. While the nature of the vampire may remain the same across the decades, his role changes greatly. The confused script and lack of understanding of sound film direction in 1931 casts Dracula as a tragic protagonist. The seismic shifts in American culture and society in the 1940s recast 'Count Alucard' as a mere subsidiary plot device. The inconsistency of character role is resolved in the 1950s with Hammer. Dracula is finally cast as the powerful cinematic monster he was destined to become. After staring out of the window, Van Helsing runs his hand through his hair and thoughtfully walks away. He is perhaps ruminating on the success of Sangster's writing and Fisher's direction, the Count satisfactorily characterised, fought and despatched on screen, at long last.

Notes

1 Cherry Potter, *Screen Language: From Film Writing to Film-Making* (London: Methuen Drama, 2001), 231.
2 Quoted in Anthony Slide, *Selected Film Criticism, 1931–40* (Metuchen, NJ: Scarecrow Press, 1982), 78.
3 Gary D. Rhodes, '*Drakula halála* (1921): The Cinema's First Dracula', *Horror Studies* 1, no. 1 (2010), 25–48.
4 Robert Spadoni, *Uncanny Bodies: The Coming of the Sound Film and the Origins of the Horror Genre* (Berkeley, CA: University of California Press, 2007), 2.
5 Tom Brown, *Breaking the Fourth Wall: Direct Address in Cinema* (Edinburgh: Edinburgh University Press, 2012), 14.
6 Roy Huss, 'Vampire's Progress: *Dracula* from Novel to Film via Broadway', in Roy Huss and T. J. Ross, eds., *Focus on the Horror Film* (Englewood Cliffs, NJ: Prentice Hall, 1972), pp. 50–51.
7 Ken Gelder, *New Vampire Cinema* (London: BFI, 2012), vi.
8 David J. Skal, *Hollywood Gothic: The Tangled Web of Dracula From Novel to Stage to Screen* (New York: Faber, 2004), 179.
9 Peter Hutchings, *Dracula* (London: I. B. Tauris, 2003), 21.
10 John Yorke, *Into the Woods: A Five Act Journey into Story* (London: Penguin, 2013), 8.
11 Lajos Egri, *The Art of Dramatic Writing: Its Basis in the Creative Interpretation of Human Motives* (New York: Simon and Schuster, 1960), 106.
12 Gary D. Rhodes, *Tod Browning's Dracula* (Sheffield: Tomahawk Press, 2014), 269–70.
13 Kyle Edwards, '"House of Horrors": Corporate Strategy at Universal Pictures in the 1930s', in Richard Nowell, ed., *Merchants of Menace: The Business of Horror Cinema* (London: Bloomsbury, 2014), p. 16.
14 Potter, *Screen Language*, 233.

15 A. W., 'The Screen in Review', *New York Times* (6 November 1943), 16.

16 Frank S. Nugent, 'The Screen', *New York Times* (18 May 1936), 14.

17 Alison Peirse, *After Dracula: The 1930s Horror Film* (London: I. B. Tauris, 2013), 3.

18 Rick Worland, 'OWI Meets Monsters: Hollywood Horror Films and War Propaganda, 1942–1945', *Cinema Journal* 37, no. 1 (1997), 47.

19 Tim Snelson, *Phantom Ladies: Hollywood Horror and the Home Front* (New Brunswick, NJ: Rutgers University Press, 2015), 2.

20 Snelson, *Phantom Ladies*, pp. 67–68.

21 Tom Weaver, Michael Brunas and John Brunas, *Universal Horrors: The Studio's Classic Films, 1931–1946* 2nd edn. (Jefferson, NC: McFarland, 2007), 372.

22 Dain Goding, "Shadows and Nightmares: Lewton, Siodmak, and the Elusive Noirror Film", *Horror Studies* 2, no. 1 (2011), 21.

23 C. A. Lejeune, 'At the Films: A Taste of Blood', *Observer* (25 May 1958), 15.

24 Lejeune, 'At the Films', 15.

25 David Mamet, *On Directing Film* (New York: Penguin, 1991), 2.

26 Hutchings, *Dracula*, 47.

27 Barry Forshaw, *British Gothic Cinema* (Basingstoke: Palgrave, 2013), 44–45.

28 Egri, *The Art of Dramatic Writing*, 107, emphasis in original.

29 Egri, *The Art of Dramatic Writing*, 113.

30 Egri, *The Art of Dramatic Writing*, 33.

31 Marc Blake and Sara Bailey, *Writing the Horror Movie* (London: Bloomsbury, 2013), 181.

16

STACEY ABBOTT

Dracula on Film and TV from 1960 to the Present

'There is no such thing as "The Vampire"; there are only vampires', not just one Dracula but 'many Draculas', Nina Auerbach argues.[1] This is particularly the case with regard to Dracula's screen presence in the period from 1960 to the present. Following on from the success of the Universal *Dracula* films in the 1930s and early 1940s and subsequently its return to England within the British Hammer Studios in 1958, the vampire's presence on film from 1960 onward has grown exponentially, via official adaptations such as John Badham's *Dracula* (1979), as well as through parodies (*Dracula Dead and Loving It*, Brooks, 1995), spin-offs (*Van Helsing*, Sommers, 2004), rip-offs (*Blacula*, Crain, 1972), and transnational reimaginings (*Vampire Hunter D*, Ashida, 1985). This period has also seen the adoption of Dracula on television with the rise of Gothic horror TV, from the adaptation of Stoker's novel for the anthology series *Mystery and Imagination* ('Dracula' ITV 1968) to the Count's climatic appearance in the monster-mash series *Penny Dreadful* (Showtime 2014–16). He even has a lasting legacy within children's programming from Count von Count in *Sesame Street* (CTW 1969-) to the animated feature film *Hotel Transylvania* (Tartakovsky, 2012).

Like a palimpsest, Dracula's various screen appearances build upon each other, operating as much in dialogue with their cinematic and televisual predecessors as they do with Stoker's original text. Francis Ford Coppola named his 1992 adaptation *Bram Stoker's Dracula*, suggesting fidelity to Stoker's original book. The manner in which he integrated allusions to other cinematic adaptations within his telling of the story, however, including F. W. Murnau's *Nosferatu* (1922), Tod Browning's *Dracula* (1931), and Dan Curtis's *Dracula* (CBS 1974), highlighted how Stoker's novel is equally defined by the vampire's screen presence as Stoker's manuscript. Subsequently, the episode of *Buffy the Vampire Slayer* 'Buffy vs Dracula' (series 5, episode 1, WB 1997–2003) was influenced by Coppola's film in terms of its colour scheme, music and lush romantic visuals, while also containing intertextual nods to Browning's *Dracula* and the Count von Count, which is itself modelled on Bela Lugosi. In turn, Rudolph Martin, who played Dracula in *Buffy*, followed this performance in September 2000, with the television movie *Dark Prince: The True Story of Dracula* (Chapelle, 2000) which aired on Halloween of the same year, integrating allusion's to *Buffy* into the film's aesthetic bricolage of Dracula references.

Dracula on screen, however, is not only inward looking but has evolved in response to changes and developments within horror, as well as the increasing hybridisation of film and television. For the past fifty years, the Count has become a recurring figure across a multitude of genres and has transmogrified from an iconic arch villain to a diverse range of character types, including monster, hero, romantic lead, comic relief and children's educator. The aim of this chapter will be to examine how key developments within horror film and television have impacted upon Dracula, causing the figure to fragment from overarching nemesis into the multitude of Draculas that have come to define our twenty-first century conception of Stoker's work.

The Evolution of Horror from Secure to Paranoid

Many scholars identify 1968 as a pivotal moment in the horror genre as it shifted away from the security of classic horror, in which the threat of the monstrous is contained and 'normality' is restored. *Night of the Living Dead* (George Romero, 1968) and *Rosemary's Baby* (Roman Polanski, 1968) replace containment with an open-ended, paranoid horror.[2] This new approach to the genre wallowed in the monstrous, revelled in the visual depiction of blood and gore, provided no comforting resolutions, and 'flaunt[ed] its generic inheritance and its own identity as horror'.[3] By 1968, the Production Code was out of date and as Gregory Waller argues, it was the introduction of 'the MPAA R-rating [that] allowed for and perhaps even legitimised the presentation of explicit violence'.[4] In many ways, *Dracula* – traditionally associated with Gothic atmospheres, period drama and Victorian sensibilities surrounding gender and sexuality – came to embody the classic form of horror that was being overturned in this period with raw, brutal and contemporary-set films such as *The Crazies* (Romero, 1973), *The Hills Have Eyes* (Wes Craven, 1977) and *The Brood* (David Cronenberg, 1979), films that relocated the monstrous to the family and destabilised conventional notions of gender, family and patriarchy. This transition, however did not take place overnight and Dracula had a role to play in the 1960s re-imagining of horror that contributed to the genre's rebirth in the 1970s.

Between 1958 and 1974, Dracula had found a new cinematic home within British Hammer Studios, following their successful adaptation of the novel to the screen in 1958, the second in Hammer's horror revivals after *The Curse of Frankenstein* (1957). Hammer's *Dracula* (Fisher 1958) was followed by eight sequels. Through these and their other period horror films, Hammer Studios contributed to the revitalisation of the Gothic genre through their use of wide screen and Technicolor, alongside a youthful cast and a visceral aesthetic that modernised the Gothic for contemporary audiences. Hammer wallowed in graphic blood and gore, filmed in wide screen close-ups and garish colour, while its Dracula, as performed by Christopher Lee, was both monstrous and attractive, and seemed to offer a form of sexual liberation to women. Nina Auerbach – who recalls her own teenage fascination with vampires as offering 'promised protection against a destiny of girdles, spike heels, and approval' – argues that the vampire in Hammer's *Dracula* is 'an emanation of the anger, pride, and sexuality that lie dormant in the women themselves. Stoker's nightmare of violation becomes a dream of female self-possession'.[5] Dracula may not be sympathetic but he does seem to represent a more satisfying sexual partner for these new women. The film and its sequels, however, can also be seen to reinforce patriarchal authority through the dominating figures of Count Dracula and Professor Van Helsing. Initially, they seem to be a vigorous challenge to the conventional images of masculinity on display in the film, as well as their Universal predecessors in the form of Bela Lugosi and Edward Van Sloane. As the series progresses, however, Dracula is increasingly presented as monstrous and barbaric while Van Helsing is paternalistic and controlling, literally taking on the role of grandfather in *Dracula A.D. 1972* (Gibson, 1972), protecting his rebellious granddaughter from the monstrous Count who attempts to bring an end to the Van Helsing legacy by turning her into a vampire.

Therefore, while the women within Hammer's *Dracula* films demonstrate moments of liberation, they are fundamentally reduced to their place within the family or, in the manner of Stoker's Lucy, destroyed for daring to defy their position. This is best exemplified by Barbara Shelley as Helen in *Dracula: Prince of Darkness* (Fisher, 1966), presented as a sexually repressed and religiously fearful woman who is liberated from her repression and the shackles of her marriage when she is transformed into a vampire. She becomes strong, fearless and sexually confident, even going so far as to attempt to lure her sister-in-law Diana away from her husband Charles with the statement 'you don't need Charles' as she opens her arms to her in a 'loving' embrace. Here Helen embodies Barbara Creed's lesbian vampire – 'the female vampire who preys on other women' – who is 'doubly dangerous. As well as transforming her victims into blood-sucking creatures of the night ... she also threatens to seduce the daughters of patriarchy away from their proper gender roles'.[6] Helen's transformation offers liberation but it is short lived when she is brutally punished for daring to suggest that a woman does not need a man. In a scene that overtly references Lucy's demise in Stoker's novel, Helen is eventually captured within the monastery where Diana and Charles are recovering from their encounter with Dracula. The monks, an even more transparent symbol of patriarchal authority than Van Helsing, pin Helen down, writhing and screaming, as they brutally stake her through the chest. In contrast to Lucy's demise in Hammer's *Dracula*, which takes place off-screen, this staking is presented in close up with requisite blood spurting from the victim. Much like Stoker's original text, this film offers both progressive and conservative pleasures as it celebrates the liberated women through the excesses of Shelley's performance before punishing her and rescuing the wholesome woman who stands by her man, a tradition that continues throughout many of the studio's 1960s and 70s vampire output. Throughout the series, women are repeatedly transformed from 'self-possessed' to objects to be possessed by Dracula and his male opponents.

While the content of the films betray a conservative approach, stylistically Hammer's Dracula films contributed to the transition in the genre from classic to modern through the graphic representations of horror that exploited increasingly permissive attitudes to sex and violence on screen. Hammer repeatedly courted the UK's X-Certificate by pushing the boundaries of acceptability within the genre, causing the studio to come into conflict with both censors and critics who resisted the manner in which they were changing the cultural understanding of horror. As David Pirie explains, a closer examination of the British Board of Film Classification files demonstrates that the 'British censor's office was ... utterly disgusted by and enraged by the British horror films, constantly waging a frantic and hysterical campaign against them, with most of the examiners secretly trying to stop them being made at all'.[7] Colour was an issue for both censors and critics, particularly the studio's iconic use of red to revel in the genre's bloody content. Hammer's Dracula begins with splashes of red being dripped on the coffin, signalling the film's distinction from its Universal black and white predecessor by making clear that the central motif of the narrative, blood drinking, will no longer remain hidden. This transition to colour caused both censors and critics anxiety with the censors insisting on seeing colour prints in an attempt to ensure a 'tasteful' approach to horror while the critics bemoaned the studio for going too far in its graphic and realistic depiction of horror. One critic claimed 'from the moment that Dracula appears, eyes bloodshot, fangs dripping with blood, until his final disintegration into a crumbling, putrescent pile of human dust, this film disgusts the mind and repels the senses', while another complained that the film had 'so much blood in it you'd think all Wardour Street had split an artery'.[8] This use of colour was perceived as too realistic for horror cinema.

Hammer's place as the singular home of controversy surrounding gore and gruesome spectacle was, however, comparatively short lived when between 1959–1960 three films were released that took the depiction of screen violence on the body to new levels through the graphic depiction of deformity, decomposition, brutal bodily attack, and realistic facial surgery: *Les yeux sans visage* (Franju, 1959), *Psycho* (Hitchcock, 1960) and *Peeping Tom* (Powell, 1960). The impact of these films and the cultural backlash that surrounded their release was that Hammer's Gothic horror came under closer scrutiny by the British Board of Film Classification (BBFC).[9] As the decade progressed, however, their films began to seem tame and over familiar. In 1967 Roman Polanski's *Fearless Vampire Killers* parodied Hammer's Gothic vampire films, signalling the gradual demise of the classic cycle of Gothic vampire films while Romero's *Night of the Living Dead* offered a new vision for modern horror and the undead. So while the staking of Helen in *Dracula: Prince of Darkness* uses gushing red blood to enhance the brutality of her demise, by *Scars of Dracula* (Baker, 1970) the blood continues to flow but now evoking Gothic excess rather than the realism and brutality of Romero's film.

Hammer Studio's attempts to revitalise the genre in the 1970s by bringing the Count, as played once again by Christopher Lee, into a modern day setting in both *Dracula A.D. 1972* and *The Satanic Rites of Dracula* (Gibson, 1973) failed to tap into the spirit of modern horror. Dracula seems out of place in the modern world, although the recasting of Lee in *Satanic Rites* as a corporate property developer attempting to release an apocalyptic plague on humanity is an innovative reimagining of the genre and one that foreshadows the more apocalyptic plans of master vampires in the *Blade* (1997–2004) cinematic franchise and the television series *The Strain* (FX 2014–). Unfortunately as the film progresses, the narrative returns to familiar formulas surrounding the antagonistic relationship between Van Helsing and the Count. The attempt to revitalise the series concluded in the Hammer/Shaw Brothers transnational co-production *The Legend of the Seven Golden Vampires* (Baker, 1974), which marked Peter Cushing's final outing as Van Helsing but which featured John Forbes-Robertson take on the role of Count Dracula. This film operated as a hybrid Gothic horror/ Asian martial arts film in which Dracula uses his power to revive the Seven Golden Vampires in Szechuan China, an ironic twist given the reimagining of *Dracula* as a martial arts/heroic swordplay film was clearly designed to revive the Dracula films. If one considers that 1974 also saw the release of Tobe Hooper's *The Texas Chainsaw Massacre* (1974), a low-budget, independent and brutal horror film about unemployed slaughterhouse workers who practice their trade on unsuspecting teenagers – banned by the BBFC due to its 'atmosphere of threat and impending violence' – the studio-produced period dramas of Hammer spliced together with martial arts acrobatics seemed too cosy and comic to be frightening.[10]

At this point, the heyday of *Dracula* on film seemed to be at an end although this did not mean that he disappeared from cinema. Rather he was instead presented as anachronistic in the modern age, often an object of pastiche and comedy in films such as *Blood for Dracula* (Morrissey, 1974) and *Love at First Bite* (Dragoti, 1979) in which the world has become too modern to be terrified of a vampire. As Dracula explains in an exaggerated Lugosi-accent in *Love at First Bite*, 'in a city where taxi cab drivers sit in little cages, who's afraid of a bat anymore?' Alternatively, Dracula's decline as one of the great monsters is also presented as melancholic in Werner Herzog's *Nosferatu The Vampyre* (1979), in which the immortality of vampirism seems to weigh down on him like a curse. Rather than growing young and empowered as in Stoker's text, barbaric as in Hammer or anachronistic as in these other 1970s reworkings, Herzog's Dracula is wearied by continued existence and longs for release. This release eventually comes when, as in Murnau's *Nosferatu*, he is trapped in the light of dawn after feeding off Lucy. In contrast to Murnau's film, Dracula does not die a spectral death, fading quietly into the light, but is first frozen and then collapses into a series of seizures before curling up and dying in the corner of the room. He is subsequently staked off-screen by Van Helsing and virtually forgotten as Jonathan Harker, now a vampire, escapes into the daylight, a new vampire for a new age. As horror cinema retreated from traditional Gothic conventions, eschewing, as James Monaco argued, 'intelligence in favour of what Pauline Kael ... called the "visceral" response', Dracula seemed outmoded on film.[11] At the same time, however, Dracula found a new life on television.

The Golden Age of Gothic TV

While Dracula did not seem to fit in with the zombies, cannibals and slashers of 1970s horror cinema, Stoker's novel found a growing popularity on television, fast becoming the repository of Gothic horror on screen. In Gothic terms, it became the location for a return of the repressed: pushed out of cinema, it burst forth on television. This is, of course, an oversimplified explanation for the popularity of Dracula adaptations in the 1960s and 1970s. In fact, the growth of Gothic on television was due to a range of influences including the success of anthology series on radio such as

Appointment with Fear (BBC Home Service 1943–44; Light Programme 1945–55) and *Suspense* (CBS Radio 1942–62) and the desire to legitimise television through the adaptation of literary classics. As Helen Wheatley argues, the 'development of Gothic anthology series in the 1960s and 1970s ... fulfilled a dual remit for popular, entertainment television ... and for respectable, culturally valued television drama, often adapted from the Gothic "classics"'.[12]

Gothic TV in this period was part of a broader development of TV horror, utilising the restrictions inherent within the medium as a means of experimenting with narrative and form.[13] While cinema was becoming increasingly graphic, television was still heavily regulated and therefore became an ideal space to explore approaches to horror that often favoured suggestion. This televisual approach, in many ways, had more in common with the earlier Universal black and white horror films than with Hammer's more explicit films. In fact, the 1950s and early 1960s saw a growing affinity between Universal horror and television. In the late 1950s, Universal Studios sold its back catalogue of horror films to television, under the package title *Shock!* or Shock Theatre and these titles became commonplace on TV. Similarly the 1950s saw numerous stars of classic horror movies such as Boris Karloff, Lon Chaney Junior and Peter Lorre performing as their most famous horror monsters in the episode 'Lizard's Leg and Owlet's Wing' of *Route 66* (26 October 1962). Bela Lugosi also appeared on television in his Dracula cape, comically reprising his iconic role on such variety programmes as the *Texaco Star Theatre* with Milton Berle (27 September 1949), *The Spiedel Show* (2 October 1950) and *You Asked for It* (27 July 1953). TV seemed to offer a secure space in which to embrace the perceived cosiness of Gothic horror in the light of developments within big screen horror. Yet the presence of Dracula on television often challenged the perception that Dracula was outmoded or that horror was unsuited to TV, instead reimagining the King-vampire for a new age. In fact, Dracula on TV often shared indie horror's preoccupation with the dysfunctional nature of family, while also destabilising traditional understandings of gender and patriarchy.

From the early 1960s through to the late 1970s, a diverse range of Dracula-inspired texts began to emerge on television, each offering a new and significant re-imaging of Stoker's Count. From 1964–1966, Dracula appeared in the form of the ageing, comic and loveable Grandpa Munster, as performed by Al Lewis, in the 'MagiCom' *The Munsters*, contributing to the series' subversion of suburban life by presenting classic screen monsters as a family who believe themselves to be 'normal' and in so doing questioning our understanding of normality. While the show fundamentally reinforces traditional family values, it also, in a period of conformity, celebrates physical and social difference in a televisual landscape dominated by the white, middle class family. In 1966 the first long running horror television series *Dark Shadows* (ABC 1966–72) was launched, which also focused on family, this time the upper-class Collins family. In 1967, the show introduced the newest, or oldest, member of the family in the form of the Dracula-like vampire, Barnabus Collins. Not an actual adaptation of Dracula, the series drew liberally from literary Gothic storylines such as *Dracula, Frankenstein, Wuthering Heights* and *The Turn of the Screw*, which provided a wealth of material to sustain the show's daily broadcast. As creator-producer Dan Curtis explained, the staff writers would provide their own interpretation and re-imagine these familiar Gothic narratives.[14] In so doing, Collins offers a modern re-working of the classic vampire that would influence later adaptations of Dracula. *Dark Shadows* initially presented Collins in the Dracula-mould, drawing upon both Stoker's text and Browning's film. Collins haunts the night-time landscape of the town of Collinsport Maine, stalking and murdering its young women, while also concealing himself in plain sight by presenting himself confidently within the drawing rooms of the community's social elite. In keeping with the contemporary preoccupation with family in modern horror, Barnabus poses as a cousin from England and charms the contemporary members of his family into a complacency that facilitates his infiltration into the town. As the series developed and Collins's popularity grew, however, the show introduced the notion of the sympathetic vampire, self-loathing of his condition and struggling to find a cure. This served the series' long running narrative as this enabled audiences to sympathise and identify with Barnabus as well as providing material to stretch out his narrative over months and even years, providing a notable blueprint for vampire television shows to come.

The Munsters and *Dark Shadows* featured the intrusion of a Dracula-type vampire within the established conventions of the sit-com and the soap opera, which served to destabilise the genres' more conservative traditions. These texts were subsequently followed by three Gothic horror adaptations of Dracula, 'Dracula' (*Mystery and Imagination*), *Dracula* (Dan Curtis CBS 1974) and *Count Dracula* (BBC 1977), demonstrating that rather than being outmoded *Dracula* still embodied transgression, made more apparent by their presence on television. In contrast to *Dark Shadows'* emphasis upon Gothic romance and Collins's Victorian past, *Mystery and Imagination* offered a version of Dracula, played by Denholm Elliot, who seemed to be in touch with late-1960s modernity, despite the adaptation's Victorian setting. Sporting a beatnik-styled goatee and rectangular sunglasses made popular in the 1960s by rock stars such as George Harrison and Roger McGuinn (and later worn by Gary Oldman in Francis Ford Coppola's adaptation), Elliot plays Dracula as suave, commanding, and, fundamentally, cool. The adaptation begins with Dracula is already ensconced in Britain, a visitor in Whitby and a guest of Dr John Seward, along with Lucy Weston and her mother. Lucy, engaged to Seward, performed as a rather patrician, almost fatherly, medical professional, seems indifferent to her fiancé from the start. Instead she is fascinated by the Count and breaks with decorum to seek out personal meetings with him. He speaks to her rebelliousness and incites her sexual attraction. His 'attack' of Lucy is overtly presented as sexual, depicting the penetration of her neck with his *Nosferatu*-styled fangs. Although withholding the close up of his fangs entering the skin, the scene highlights the image of him withdrawing from her neck with a mouth filled with blood before biting into her neck once more, the glimpse of blood in this sequence startlingly graphic even in monochrome.[15] Lucy writhes and moans in ecstasy throughout the scene, which ends on a close up of her smiling face. Furthermore, long before either Lucy or Mina are turned both display anger and contempt for their marital status. Lucy's indifference toward Seward turns to disdain when Mina chastises her for improperly pursuing the Count, reminding her to think of her fiancé to which Lucy responds by mocking him before recovering her decorum and decrying his over-commitment to his work as the root of their problem. Later, when the now-vampiric Lucy attempts to seduce Mina, Mina seems quite enthusiastic and responds with disdain when questioned about her willingness to join Lucy. Dracula's offer of vampirism seems to tap into a more fully realised desire for liberation by the women in keeping with the rise of feminism within the late 1960s as well as the era's overall spirit of rebellion. The conclusion to this TV adaptation prefigures the often-praised end of Badham's *Dracula*, in which Lucy smiles as she watches Dracula's cape blowing away in the daylight, suggesting that he has once again escaped death. In the 1968 version, Mina similarly offers a transgressive smile, implying her continued vampiric state and undermining the belief that she could reconcile with her husband. There is, however, no suggestion of Dracula's survival and so this conclusion seems all the more self-possessed as if now liberated, Mina chooses not to return to her demure, wifely self.

While Elliot's Dracula incites rebellion, Jack Palance's Dracula (1974), and Louis Jourdan's Dracula (1977) embody strength, offering a vision of the Count as empowered military leader, brutal and, in the case of Jourdan, Machiavellian in his machinations. Palance plays the Count as physically strong and formidable; an imposing and ferocious figure. In contrast, Jourdan's performance is defined by stillness and quiet that conceals hidden power. He is the most 'othered' of the vampires, presented as largely unknowable and spectral through his repeated transformation into dust

200

and wolves, harking back to the spectral qualities of Orlok's *Nosferatu* and looking forward to the digital effects that have been used to represent the uncanny qualities of the vampire in films such as *Van Helsing* and *Dracula Untold*.[16]

Palance, on the other hand, is the most human of the screen Draculas from this period in film or TV, provided a backstory to ground the vampire within his human history. This story takes two forms. First, this is the first screen Dracula to be associated with the historical figure Vlad Tepes, following the publication of Raymond T. McNally and Radu Florescu *In Search of Dracula* in 1972, in which they make the compelling and popular case for the notion that Tepes was the inspiration for Stoker's Count Dracula. While this association has been challenged by some scholars, Tepes has become indelibly linked with *Dracula* in numerous films including the docu-drama *In Search of Dracula* (1975), *Bram Stoker's Dracula, Dark Prince: The True Story of Dracula* (2000), *Dracula: The Dark Prince* (2013) and *Dracula Untold* maintaining this association. In Curtis's film, Dracula possesses an ancient painting in his castle which depicts him as a warrior observed by his loving wife, with the label Vlad Tepes 1474 printed on the frame. The presence of this painting within the narrative overtly links Stoker's vampire with the real historical figure of Tepes, locating his monstrosity within human history. It also presents him as a figure bound by a personal history, embodied in the tragic love story in which the vampire seeks reunion with the reincarnation of his departed wife, in this film reborn into Lucy Westenra. This reincarnation narrative which recurs in many subsequent adaptations was influenced by Curtis's television show *Dark Shadows* which underpinned much of Collins's popularity within the romance narrative surrounding his belief that waitress Maggie Evans was the reincarnation of his true love. It was also a feature of the Blaxploitation vampire film *Blacula* in which the vampire similarly seeks reunion with his lost love, reincarnated in 1970s America. Arguably this narrative dates back to Universal Studios' *The Mummy* (Freund, 1932), in which the immortal Imhotep similarly attempts to reunite with the reincarnation of his departed lover. It is, however, via Curtis's *Dracula* that this narrative becomes indelibly linked to Stoker's Count and it serves to humanise the vampire, if not overtly making him sympathetic. While he is often presented as brutal and ferocious in his attacks on humanity, his first glimpse of a photograph of Lucy, yields a softer side, accompanied by a love theme, which recurs repeatedly through the film to remind us of the inherent humanity at the core of his monstrosity. In fact, it is his human love that fuels his ferocity when Van Helsing and Harker stake Lucy after she has been transformed into a vampire but before Dracula has been able to reunite with her. This leads him to pursue Mina out of revenge, much like Christopher Lee often sought women to punish the men who hunted him, but here his motivation is personal.

While 1970s TV horror seemed to mark a retreat into the Gothic that stood in contrast to the transition to a more brutal approach to horror within contemporary cinema, these adaptations of Dracula demonstrate that television was equally preoccupied with destabilising the status quo by undermining traditional notions of family, gender and patriarchal authority. Furthermore, as Helen Wheatley argues, viewing Gothic horror on television 'draw[s] parallels between the domestic spaces on screen and those homes in which the dramas are being viewed'.[17] As a result, the broadcast of these adaptations on TV in the domestic space, with all of its associations with women, children and family, renders them all the more transgressive. Furthermore, while the increasingly humanised vampire in Dan Curtis's *Dark Shadows* and *Dracula*, may seem to render the monster de-fanged, in keeping with Waller's argument about Dracula on film, it also takes the first step toward the construction of the vampire point-of-view which serves to invite the audience to identify with the King-vampire and in so doing, implicate them within his monstrosity.[18] This shift in his representation would play a significant role with the development of Dracula on screen in the decades to follow.

Rise of the Sympathetic *Dracula*

The humanity on display in Jack Palance's portrayal of Dracula is increasingly transformed into sympathy in many of the *Dracula* adaptations that followed, particularly post-Anne Rice's *Interview with the Vampire* (1976). From *Love at First Bite* and *Dracula* to *Bram Stoker's Dracula* and *Dracula Untold*, the Count has been reimagined as a romantic and, in the later films, tragic figure, cursed to walk the earth, feeding off the blood of humanity, but defined by a romantic longing. This is in part the result of the shift within the vampire genre more broadly away from recounting the stories from the perspective of the living, where the vampire is the antagonist, to the perspective of the vampire. This is a significant alteration to Stoker's story, in which the vampire is the one voice that is not heard throughout the narrative, except through other people's descriptions of their encounters with him. Stoker's narrative structure renders the vampire as fundamentally unknowable, virtually abstract as it is entirely subject to interpretation. Providing the Count with a voice and a point- of-view renders him as knowable, transforming him, as Lindsey Scott argues, 'from [an] object of anxiety into [an] object of desire' but also to a subject of identification.[19] As Margaret L. Carter argues where the vampire's otherness posed a terrifying threat for the original readers of *Dracula*, however, today that same alien quality is often perceived as an attraction. As rebellious outsider, as persecuted minority, as endangered species, and as a member of a different 'race' that legend portrays as sexually omnicompetent, the vampire makes a fitting hero for late twentieth-century popular fiction.[20]

This transition in perspective contributed to the cinematic repositioning of Dracula from niche genre to high concept cinema, as evidenced in *Bram Stoker's Dracula*. Coppola's film was self-consciously designed as a prestige blockbuster horror film, bringing together the conventions of the Gothic with horror, romance and period drama. The target audience included late teenagers and young adults and with an emphasis upon women, not traditionally seen to be the primary viewership for horror. This was part of a bigger trend toward the mainstreaming of the horror genre that took place in the 1990s and early 2000s.[21] The shift in point-of-view to the now tragic Dracula was a key contributing factor in the expansion of the film's audience. While the film purports to adopt the novel's epistolary structure, featuring scenes in which many of the characters, including Jonathan, Mina, Seward, and Van Helsing are shown to be writing in their diaries as well as narrating through the use of voice-overs, it is Dracula's perspective that overwhelms the film through its lush and sumptuous aesthetics. The rich colours, layering of imagery through superimpositions and Gothic orchestral score that are used throughout the film convey his emotional register, including anger and betrayal, passionate blood lust, and romantic longing. In particular the film's use of costume and make-up as Dracula adopts different personas, not only suggests the otherness of his vampiric state but significantly his self-loathing. These costumes convey his view of himself, appearing as the wolf-man consumed by animal-lust when he ravishes Lucy; as the Romanian Prince overwhelmed with love for Mina as well as possessing a melancholic yearning for his past life; as the exotic androgynous old man for the modern business man Jonathan; and finally as the man-bat when he confronts Van Helsing with the hypocrisy of his religion by decrying 'look what your God has done to me'. It is through Dracula's point-of-view that he is able to embody not simply the monster but also a composite of villain, victim and romantic hero. Lindsey Scott argues that the film 'challenges its audiences to feel horror and compassion in equal measure: to be repulsed by a monster that we must also empathise with; to desire its destruction as much as we desire its redemption; to find something beautiful in the "waste of desolation" that Stoker's novel presents'.[22] This shift toward rendering Dracula sympathetic within film and TV therefore does not necessarily defang Stoker's monster but rather highlights the tension between monstrosity and humanity as he embodies the liminal space between the two. The composite nature of Dracula within this film also served the genre hybridity of the film that led to it being a blockbuster success, earning a box office gross of $81.4 million.

Since Coppola's film, the presence of the sympathetic vampire at the heart of a romance narrative grew exponentially, particularly in response to the global popularity of *Twilight*. Increasingly, therefore Dracula continued to be reimagined within high concept terms, merging Stoker's monster and its horror legacy with the conventions of romance and action cinema. The Dracula origin story, *Dracula Untold*, presents the Romanian Prince as a martyr who accepts the curse of vampirism to protect his country and save his family. Once a vampire he leads a CGI-fuelled war, staged as an action spectacular, with Dracula changing from a lone man on the battlefield into a flock of bats in fluid transformation before swooping in and decimating the enemy army. In the blockbuster animated family feature, *Hotel Transylvania*, Dracula has once again been presented as the central protagonist but this time in a world in which normality has been inverted so that humanity is perceived by the monsters as threatening and dangerous. Rather than seeking to infiltrate the human world, Drac retreats into his castle that he has transformed into a hotel for monsters only. That is until Drac and his companions are forced to go out into the world and in so doing, they not only realise that humanity no longer fears them but that they are the object of adoration and fandom. This high concept family film presents its narrative from Drac's point-of-view in order to break down cultural opposition and the desire to retreat behind borders and re-inscribe the vampire narrative with a celebration of global inclusivity.

While mainstream cinema continues to use hybridity to galvanise the largest audiences, twenty-first century television has generally shifted toward narrow casting, targeting niche but loyal audiences with disposable income rather than the largest audiences. This, along with a relaxation of the regulations on the depiction of sex and violence, has led to an upsurge in TV horror. Despite this trend, the British-American television series *Dracula* broadcast on network television in America and produced by Carnival films, the company behind *Downton Abbey*, was designed along the hybrid terms of Coppola's film, presenting itself as a period drama with a touch of the Gothic and horror. Combining a mixture of action, sex and horror set against a backdrop of Victorian London and spectacular period costumes and sets, the series was aimed at a broad audience to include vampire and horror fans alongside those drawn to its tale of romance, history and period exoticism. As such, Dracula is once again presented as the self-loathing romantic vampire as well as a visionary modern man at the turn of the century. He is romantic lover to Mina Murray, a hero working to undermine a patriarchal secret society that controls governments, armies and industries form the shadows, and a loathsome monster hunted by vampire slayers who, because he is the hero of the story, are presented as bloodthirsty and cruel. Dracula is fundamentally hybrid in order to appeal to fans of *Downton Abbey* and *True Blood* (HBO 2008–14).

Conclusion

In contrast to NBC's *Dracula* series, *Penny Dreadful* – a series on the subscription channel Showtime – signals yet another transformation of the text by overtly celebrating its place as horror within mainstream media by bringing together a conglomeration of classic monsters presented with Gothic stylistic excess, body horror and lashings of blood. Like the NBC series, it sets its Gothic trappings against a period backdrop, beautifully conveyed through extravagant costumes and set design but never at the expense of horror. This is a prestige approach to the genre but TV horror nonetheless. Here, Dracula, like the vampire in Stoker's book, haunts the periphery of the narrative for the first two seasons. He is no longer the series' hero but its antagonist, an invisible threat to be feared. When he does appear in season three, he is reimagined as a harbinger of the apocalypse, once again seductive and alluring but surrounded by his monstrous vampiric children that eventually overrun Victorian London. His Dracula is less influenced by *Interview with the Vampire* and *Twilight*, and more by contemporaneous TV horror like *The Strain* and *The Walking Dead* (AMC 2010-), the success of which are marking a transition in TV horror toward the apocalyptic. Dracula here is once again presented as a monster, signalling a broader move with the vampire across film and TV away from romance; a transition reaffirmed by the emergence of a new series, *Van Helsing* (Syfy 2016–), in which the daughter of Abraham Van Helsing must fight the vampires that plague a future post-apocalyptic landscape. These series remind us that the Dracula cycle continues to shift and change in response to developments within contemporary media and culture. Yet the co-existence of *Penny Dreadful* and *Van Helsing* with *Dracula Untold* and *Hotel Transylvania* reaffirms the continued splintering of Dracula into multiple forms and identities, embodying not simply a Dracula for every age but for every audience.

Notes

1 Nina Auerbach, *Our Vampires, Ourselves* (Chicago and London: University of Chicago Press, 1995), 51.
2 Gregory A. Waller, 'Introduction', in Gregory A. Waller, ed., *American Horrors: Essays on the Modern American Horror Film* (Urbana and Chicago: University of Illinois Press, 1987), p. 2.
3 Waller, 'Introduction', 2.
4 Waller, 'Introduction', 5.
5 Auerbach, *Our Vampires*, 4, 124.
6 Barbara Creed, *The Monstrous-Feminine: Film, Feminism, Psychoanalysis* (London and New York: Routledge, 1993), 61.
7 David Pirie, *A New Heritage of Horror: The English Gothic Cinema* (London and New York: I. B. Tauris, 2009), 37.
8 Nina Hilbin, 'Dracula's Macabre Decline', *Daily Worker* (24 May 1958) and Donald Zec, 'DRACULA-A-GH!', *Daily Mirror* (23 May 1958).
9 Pirie, *New Heritage*, 128.
10 Stevie Simkin, 'Wake of the Flood: Key Issues in UK Censorship, 1970–5', in Edward Lamberti, ed., *Behind the Scenes at the BBFC: Film Classification form the Silver Screen to the Digital Age* (London: BFI/Palgrave, 2012), p. 80.
11 James Monaco, "AAAAEEEAARGGH!" *Sight and Sound* 49, no. 2 (1980), 80.
12 Helen Wheatley, *Gothic Television* (Manchester and New York: Manchester University Press, 2006), 27.
13 Lorna Jowett and Stacey Abbott, *TV Horror: The Dark Side of the Small Screen* (London and New York: I. B. Tauris, 2013), 3–5.
14 Jeff Thompson, *The Television Horrors of Dan Curtis: Dark Shadows, The Night Stalker and Other Productions, 1966–2006* (Jefferson, NC: McFarland, 2009), 62–63.
15 See Stacey Abbott, *Angel* (Detroit: Wayne State University Press, 2009), 53–54 for a discussion of the use of the 'glimpse' as a strategy within TV horror.
16 See Stacey Abbott, *Celluloid Vampires: Life after Death in the Modern World* (Austin: University of Texas Press, 2007), 204–14.
17 Wheatley, *Gothic Television*, 18.
18 Gregory A. Waller, *The Living and the Undead: Slaying Vampires, Exterminating Zombies* (Urbana: University of Illinois Press, 2010), 233.
19 Lindsey Scott, 'Crossing Oceans of Time: Stoker, Coppola and the "New Vampire" Film', in Sam George and Bill Hughes, eds., *Open Graves, Open Minds: Representations of Vampires and the Undead from the Enlightenment to the Present Day* (Manchester: Manchester University Press, 2013), 114.
20 Margaret L. Carter, 'The Vampire as Alien in Contemporary Fiction', in Joan Gordon and Veronica Hollinger, eds., *Blood Read: The Vampire as Metaphor in Contemporary Culture* (Philadelphia: University of Pennsylvania Press, 1997), p. 29.
21 Stacey Abbott, 'High Concept Thrills and Chills: The Horror Blockbuster', in Ian Conrich, ed., *Horror Zone*, (London and New York: I. B. Tauris, 2010), pp. 29–37.
22 Scott, 'Crossing Oceans of Time', 121.

GUIDE TO FURTHER READING

Stoker

Belford, Barbara. *Bram Stoker: A Biography of the Author of Dracula*. London: Weidenfeld and Nicolson, 1996.

Byron, Glennis (ed.). *Dracula: New Casebook*. New York: Saint Martin's Press, 1999.

Dijkstra, Bram. *Idols of Perversity: Fantasies of Feminine Evil in Fin-de-Siècle Culture*. Oxford: Oxford University Press, 1986.

Farson, Daniel. *The Man Who Wrote* Dracula: *A Biography of Bram* Stoker. London: Michael Joseph, 1975.

Gibson, Matthew. *Dracula and the Eastern Question: British and French Vampire Narratives of the Nineteenth-Century Near East*. Basingstoke: Palgrave, 2006.

Glover, David. *Vampires, Mummies and Liberals: Bram Stoker and the Politics of Popular Fiction*. Durham: Duke University Press, 1996.

Greenway, John. 'Seward's Folly: *Dracula* as a Critique of "Normal Science"', *Stanford Literature Review* 3 (1986), 213–30.

Hughes, William. *Bram Stoker's* Dracula: *A Reader's Guide*. London: Continuum, 2009.

Hutchings, Peter. *Dracula*. London: I. B. Tauris, 2003.

Kittler, Friedrich. 'Dracula's Legacy', *Stanford Humanities Review* 1 (1989), 143–73.

Leatherdale, Clive (ed.). *The Origins of* Dracula. London: William Kimber, 1975.

Ludlam, Harry. *A Biography of Dracula: The Life Story of Bram* Stoker. London: Foulsham, 1962.

Miller, Elizabeth (ed.). *Bram Stoker's Dracula: A Documentary Volume*. Detroit, MI: Thomson Gale, 2005.

Miller, Elizabeth and Robert Eighteen-Bisang. *Bram Stoker's Notes for Dracula: A Facsimile Edition*. Jefferson, NC: McFarland, 2013.

Murray, Paul. *From the Shadow of* Dracula: *A Life of Bram Stoker*. Rev. ed. Dublin: Fitzpress, 2016.

Roth, Phyllis A. *Bram Stoker*. Boston: Twayne, 1982.

Senf, Carol. Dracula: *Between Tradition and Modernism*. New York: Twayne, 1998.

Smith, Andrew and William Hughes (eds.), *Bram Stoker: History, Psychoanalysis and the Gothic*. Basingstoke: Palgrave, 1998.

Stiles, Anne. 'Bram Stoker's Brother, the Brain Surgeon', *Progress in Brain Research* 205 (2013), 197–218.

Gothic Traditions

Beresford, Matthew. *From Demons to* Dracula*: The Creation of the Modern Vampire Myth*. London: Reaktion, 2008.

Botting, Fred. '*Dracula*, Romance and Radcliffean Gothic', *Women's Writing* 1, no. 2 (1994), 181–201.

Frayling, Christopher. *Vampyres: Lord Byron to Count Dracula*. London: Faber, 1991.

Gelder, Ken (ed.). *The Horror Reader*. London: Routledge, 2000.

Groom, Nick. *Gothic: A Very Short Introduction*. Oxford: Oxford University Press, 2012.

Halberstam, Judith. *Skin Shows: Gothic Horror and the Technology of Monsters*. London and Durham: Duke University Press, 1995.

Penzler, Otto (ed.). *The Vampire Archives: The Most Complete Volume of Vampire Tales Ever Published*. New York: Vintage, 2009.

Punter, David. *The Literature of Terror: A History of Gothic Fictions from 1765 to the Present Day*. London: Longmans, 1980.

(ed.). *A Companion to the Gothic*. Oxford: Blackwell, 2001.

Williamson, Milly. *The Lure of the Vampire: Gender, Fiction and Fandom from Bram Stoker to Buffy*. London: Wallflower, 2005.

Contextual Readings

Arata, Stephen D. 'The Occidental Tourist: Dracula and the Anxiety of Reverse Colonization', *Victorian Studies* 33, no. 4 (1990), 621–45.

Backus, Gayle. *The Gothic Family Romance: Heterosexuality, Child Sacrifice, and the Anglo-Irish Colonial Order*. Durham: Duke University Press, 1999.

Barber, Paul. *Vampires, Burial and Death: Folklore and Reality*. New Haven: Yale University Press, 1988.

Bentley, C. F. 'The Monster in the Bedroom: Sexual Symbolism in Bram Stoker's *Dracula*', *Literature and Psychology* 22, no. 1 (1972), 27–34.

Bräunlein, Peter J. 'The Frightening Borderlands of Enlightenment: The Vampire Problem', *Studies in History and Philosophy of Biological and Biomedical Sciences* 43, no. 3 (2012), 710–19.

Case, Alison. 'Tasting the Original Apple: Gender and the Struggle for Narrative Authority in *Dracula*', *Narrative* 1 (1993), 223–43.

Chez, Keridiana. '"You Can't Trust Wolves No More Nor Women": Canines, Women, and Deceptive Docility in Bram Stoker's *Dracula*', *Victorian Review: An Interdisciplinary Journal of Victorian Studies* 38 (2012), 77–92.

Dijkstra, Bram. *Idols of Perversity: Fantasies of Feminine Evil in Fin-de-Siècle Culture*. Oxford: Oxford University Press, 1986.

Funke, Jana. '"We Cannot Be Greek Now": Age Difference, Corruption of Youth and the Making of *Sexual Inversion*', *English Studies* 94, no. 2 (2013), 139–53.

Galvan, Jill. 'Occult Networks and the Legacy of the Indian Rebellion in Bram Stoker's *Dracula*', *History of Religions* 54, no. 4 (2015), 434–58.

Gelder, Ken. *Reading the Vampire*. London: Routledge, 1994.

New Vampire Cinema. London: Palgrave/British Film Institute, 2012.

George, Sam and Bill Hughes (eds.). *Open Graves: Open Minds: Representations of Vampires and the Undead from the Enlightenment to the Present Day.* Manchester: Manchester University Press, 2013.

Gibson, Matthew. Dracula *and the Eastern Question: British and French Vampire Narratives of the Nineteenth Century Near East.* Basingstoke: Palgrave, 2006.

Glover, David. *Literature, Immigration, and Diaspora in Fin-de-Siècle England: A Cultural History of the 1905 Aliens Act.* Cambridge: Cambridge University Press, 2012.

Haggerty, George E. *Queer Gothic.* Urbana: University of Illinois Press, 2006.

Herbert, Christopher. 'Vampire Religion', *Representations* 79 (2002), 100–27.

Kreuter, P. M. 'The Name of the Vampire: Some Reflections on Current Linguistic Theories on the Etymology of the Word *Vampire*', in P. Day (ed.), *Vampires: Myths and Metaphors of Enduring Evil* (Amsterdam: Rodopi, 2006), pp. 57–64.

Ledger, Sally. *The New Woman: Fiction and Feminism at the Fin de Siècle.* Manchester: Manchester University Press, 1997.

Linneman, Laura. 'The Fear of Castration and Male Dread of Female Sexuality: The Theme of the "Vagina Dentata" in *Dracula*', *Journal of Dracula Studies* 12 (2010), 11–28.

Luckhurst, Roger. *The Invention of Telepathy, 1870–1901.* Oxford: Oxford University Press, 2002.

McDonald, Peter. *British Literary Culture and Publishing Practice, 1880–1914.* Cambridge, Cambridge University Press, 1997.

Moretti, Franco. 'The Dialectic of Fear', in *Signs Taken for Wonders: Essays on the Sociology of Literary Forms.* London: Verso, 1983.

Olmstead, John Charles. *The Victorian Art of Fiction: Essays on the Novel in British Periodicals 1870–1900.* New York and London: Garland, 1979.

Palmer, Paulina. *Lesbian Gothic: Transgressive Fictions.* New York: Continuum, 1999.

Piatti-Farnell, Lorna. *The Vampire in Contemporary Popular Literature.* London: Routledge, 2013.

Pick, Daniel. *Faces of Degeneration: A European Disorder c.1848–c.1918.* Cambridge: Cambridge University Press, 1989.

Reyes, Xavier Aldana, '"Who Ordered the Hamburger with AIDS?" Haematophilic Semiotics in *Tru(e) Blood*', *Gothic Studies* 15, no. 1 (2013), 55–65.

Schaffer, Talia. '"A Wilde Desire Took Me": The Homoerotic History of *Dracula*', *ELH* 61, no. 2 (1994), 381–425.

Senf, Carol, 'Stoker's Response to the New Woman', *Victorian Studies* 26 (1982), 33–49.

Showalter, Elaine. *Sexual Anarchy: Gender and Culture at the Fin de Siècle.* London: Bloomsbury, 1991.

Simmons, Clare A. 'Fables of continuity: Bram Stoker and Medievalism', in *Bram Stoker: History, Psychoanalysis and the Gothic*, ed. Andrew Smith and William Hughes. Basingstoke: Palgrave, 1998, pp. 29–46.

Sparks, Tabitha. 'Medical Gothic and the Return of the Contagious Diseases Acts in Stoker and Machen', *Nineteenth-Century Feminisms* 6 (2002), 87–102.

Stevenson, John Allen. 'A Vampire in the Mirror: The Sexuality of *Dracula*', *PMLA* 103, no. 2 (1988), 139–49.

Summers, Montague. *The Vampire* (1928; London: Studio Editions, 1995).

Twitchell, James. *The Living Dead: A Study of the Vampire in Romantic Literature*. Durham: Duke University Press, 1986.
Wicke, Jennifer. 'Vampiric Typewriting: *Dracula* and its Media', *ELH* 59, no. 2 (1992), 467–93.
Zanger, Jules. 'A Sympathetic Vibration: Dracula and the Jews', *English Literature in Transition* 34, no. 1 (1991), 33–44.

III New Directions

Byron, Glennis (ed.). *Globalgothic*. Manchester: Manchester University Press, 2013.
Case, Sue-Ellen. 'Tracking the Vampire', *Differences* 3 (1991), 1–20.
Craft, Christopher, '"Kiss Me with Those Red Lips": Gender and Inversion in Bram Stoker's *Dracula*', *Representations* 8 (1984), 107–33.
Fisher, Mark. *The Weird and the Eerie*. London: Repeater Books, 2016.
Glover, David. *Literature, Immigration and Diaspora in Fin-de-Siècle England: A Cultural History of the 1905 Aliens Act*. Cambridge: Cambridge University Press, 2012).
Hughes, William and Andrew Smith (eds.). *Ecogothic*. Manchester: Manchester University Press, 2016.
Morton, Timothy. *Dark Ecology: For a Logic of Coexistence*. New York: Columbia University Press, 2016.
Palmer, Paulina. *The Queer Uncanny: New Perspectives on the Gothic*. Cardiff: University of Wales Press, 2012.
Schopp, Andrew. 'Cruising the Alternatives: Homoeroticism and the Contemporary Vampire', *The Journal of Popular Culture* 30, no. 4 (1997), 231–43.
Thacker, Eugene. *In the Dust of This Planet: Horror of Philosophy I*. Winchester: Zero Books, 2011).
Viragh, Attila. 'Can the Vampire Speak? Dracula as Discourse on Cultural Extinction', *English Literature in Transition* 56, no. 2 (2013), 231–45.

IV Adaptations

Abbott, Stacey. *Celluloid Vampires: Life After Death in the Modern World*. Austin: University of Texas Press, 2007).
Deane, Hamilton and John Balderston. *Dracula: The Ultimate Illustrated Edition of the World-Famous Vampire Play*, ed. David J. Skal. New York: St. Martin's Press, 1993.
Forshaw, Barry. *British Gothic Cinema*. Basingstoke: Palgrave, 2013.
Gelder, Ken. *New Vampire Cinema*. London: BFI, 2012.
Hutchings, Peter. *The Horror Film*. Harlow: Longman, 2004.
Jowett, Lorna and Stacey Abbott. *TV Horror: The Dark Side of the Small Screen*. London and New York: I. B. Tauris, 2013.
Pirie, David. *A New Heritage of Horror: The English Gothic Cinema*. London and New York: I. B. Tauris, 2009.
Rhodes, Gary D. *Tod Browning's* Dracula. Sheffield: Tomahawk, 2014.
Rigby, Jonathan. *English Gothic: Classic Horror Cinema, 1897–2015*. Cambridge: Signum, 2015).

Skal, David J. *Hollywood Gothic: The Tangled Web of Dracula From Novel to Stage to Screen*. New York: Faber & Faber, 2004.

Tudor, Andrew. *Monsters and Mad Scientists: A Cultural History of the Horror Movie*. London: Routledge, 1989.

Waller, Gregory A. *The Living and the Undead: Slaying Vampires, Exterminating Zombies*. Urbana, Chicago and Springfield: University of Illinois Press, 2010.

Weaver, Tom, Michael Brunas, and John Brunas. *Universal Horrors: The Studio's Classic Films, 1931–1946*. 2nd edn. Jefferson, NC: McFarland, 2007.

Wheatley, Helen. *Gothic Television*. Manchester and New York: Manchester University Press, 2006.

Wynne, Catherine. *Bram Stoker, Dracula and the Victorian Gothic Stage*. Basingstoke: Palgrave, 2013.

(ed.). *Bram Stoker and the Stage: Reviews, Reminiscences, Essays and Fiction*. 2 vols. London: Pickering and Chatto, 2012.

INDEX

Cambridge Companions to ...

AUTHORS

Edward Albee edited by Stephen J. Bottoms

Margaret Atwood edited by Coral Ann Howells

W. H. Auden edited by Stan Smith

Jane Austen edited by Edward Copeland and Juliet McMaster (second edition)

Balzac edited by Owen Heathcote and Andrew Watts

Beckett edited by John Pilling

Bede edited by Scott DeGregorio

Aphra Behn edited by Derek Hughes and Janet Todd

Walter Benjamin edited by David S. Ferris

William Blake edited by Morris Eaves

Boccaccio edited by Guyda Armstrong, Rhiannon Daniels, and Stephen J. Milner

Jorge Luis Borges edited by Edwin Williamson

Brecht edited by Peter Thomson and Glendyr Sacks (second edition)

The Brontës edited by Heather Glen

Bunyan edited by Anne Dunan-Page

Frances Burney edited by Peter Sabor

Byron edited by Drummond Bone

Albert Camus edited by Edward J. Hughes

Willa Cather edited by Marilee Lindemann

Cervantes edited by Anthony J. Cascardi

Chaucer edited by Piero Boitani and Jill Mann (second edition)

Chekhov edited by Vera Gottlieb and Paul Allain

Kate Chopin edited by Janet Beer

Caryl Churchill edited by Elaine Aston and Elin Diamond

Cicero edited by Catherine Steel

Coleridge edited by Lucy Newlyn

Wilkie Collins edited by Jenny Bourne Taylor

Joseph Conrad edited by J. H. Stape

H. D. edited by Nephie J. Christodoulides and Polina Mackay

Dante edited by Rachel Jacoff (second edition)

Daniel Defoe edited by John Richetti

Don DeLillo edited by John N. Duvall

Charles Dickens edited by John O. Jordan

Emily Dickinson edited by Wendy Martin

John Donne edited by Achsah Guibbory

Dostoevskii edited by W. J. Leatherbarrow

Theodore Dreiser edited by Leonard Cassuto and Claire Virginia Eby

John Dryden edited by Steven N. Zwicker

W. E. B. Du Bois edited by Shamoon Zamir

George Eliot edited by George Levine

T. S. Eliot edited by A. David Moody

Ralph Ellison edited by Ross Posnock

Ralph Waldo Emerson edited by Joel Porte and Saundra Morris

William Faulkner edited by Philip M. Weinstein

Henry Fielding edited by Claude Rawson

F. Scott Fitzgerald edited by Ruth Prigozy

Flaubert edited by Timothy Unwin

E. M. Forster edited by David Bradshaw

Benjamin Franklin edited by Carla Mulford

Brian Friel edited by Anthony Roche

Robert Frost edited by Robert Faggen

Gabriel García Márquez edited by Philip Swanson

Elizabeth Gaskell edited by Jill L. Matus

Goethe edited by Lesley Sharpe

Günter Grass edited by Stuart Taberner

Thomas Hardy edited by Dale Kramer

David Hare edited by Richard Boon

Nathaniel Hawthorne edited by Richard Millington

Seamus Heaney edited by Bernard O'Donoghue

Ernest Hemingway edited by Scott Donaldson

Homer edited by Robert Fowler

Horace edited by Stephen Harrison

Ted Hughes edited by Terry Gifford

Ibsen edited by James McFarlane

Henry James edited by Jonathan Freedman

Samuel Johnson edited by Greg Clingham

Ben Jonson edited by Richard Harp and Stanley Stewart

James Joyce edited by Derek Attridge (second edition)

Kafka edited by Julian Preece

Keats edited by Susan J. Wolfson

Rudyard Kipling edited by Howard J. Booth

Lacan edited by Jean-Michel Rabaté

D. H. Lawrence edited by Anne Fernihough

Primo Levi edited by Robert Gordon

TOPICS